In Remembrance

AN UNBROKEN BOND

AN
UNBROKEN
BOND

The Untold Story of How the 658 Cantor Fitzgerald Families
Faced the Tragedy of 9/11 and Beyond

Edie Lutnick 11/4/11

EDIE LUTNICK
Co-Founder and Executive Director,
The Cantor Fitzgerald Relief Fund

EMERGENCE
PRESS

EMERGENCE PRESS

Emergence Press, LLC.
P.O. Box 1566
New York, NY 10150

An Unbroken Bond may be purchased for
educational, business, charitable, or sales promotional use.
For information, please write:
The Cantor Fitzgerald Relief Fund
199 Water Street, 19ᵗʰ Fl, New York, NY 10038

For information about bringing the author to your live event for a speaking
engagement please visit our website at www.AnUnbrokenBond.com
or call Emergence Press at 212-203-3258

Grateful acknowledgment is made for permission to reprint:

Rick DeTorie, *One Big Happy,* on page 262.

Cox and Forkum cartoon on page 240.

"It's My Life"
Copyright 2000 Sony/ATV Music Publishing LLC, Aggressive Music,
Universal Polygram, Publisher(s) Unknown.
All rights on behalf of Sony/ATV Music Publishing LLC,
Aggressive Music administered by Sony/ATV
Music Publishing LLC,
8 Music Square West, Nashville, TN 37203.
All rights reserved. Used by permission.

All photographs courtesy of Edie Lutnick unless otherwise noted.

FIRST EDITION
Designed by Maris Bellack

ISBN 978-0-9839266-0-3

www.AnUnbrokenBond.com
10 9 8 7 6 5 4 3 2

This book is dedicated to the 9/11 families, without whose courage and love I would not have survived, and by whose resilience and strength I am awed. Your loved ones were outstanding human beings; I have learned this more every day. With their absence, the world has been robbed, but by living each day with dignity and honor, you are a testament to them, and to us all.

You are not alone.

Though we're far apart, you're always in my heart.

-performed by Michael Jackson

CONTENTS

Foreword by Clarence B. Jones x
Prologue xii

PART I

2001
The Three of Us 1
Good-Bye 3
Cantor Fitzgerald 7
Lost Days 10
Cantor Reopens 13
The Fund 19
Lost Records 24
A Promise 31
The United Way, The Red Cross and Others 38
Small Battles 43
Bears 49
Survivors 51
Together 53
The Facts 58
Hierarchies 66
The Victim Compensation Fund 74

2002
Moving On 81
Heroes 84
Politics 86
Answers 91
Remains 94
Sacred Ground 100

Families in the Way 103
Support 106
A Dream 111
Fresh Kills 114
A New Beginning 117
The Children 120

PART II

No Escape 137
Bloomberg 139
A New Phase 143
Charity Day 146
Flashbacks 150
Change 158
Love 161

2003

Giuliani 163
The Families vs. Ken Feinberg and the VCF 166
Memorial 169
The Hamptons 174
Rules 178
United 180

2004

Plans for Revival 182
Echoes 189
Names 195

2005

Random Meaning 197
Hangar 199
Zero Ground 204

2006

911 213
Hope 220
The Proposal 222
Legacy? 226

2007

Who They Were 237

2008

A Record 241

2009

Terror Trials 249

2010

The Layout 251
An Unbroken Bond 255
Controversy and Peace 263
Nerves Of Steel 267

2011

Those Who Fought 271
9/11 Never Closes 276
Osama bin Laden Is Dead 279

Epilogue 287
Acknowledgments 295
Notes 298

FOREWORD

Earlier this year, through a mutual friend, Jake Loveless, an executive at Cantor Fitzgerald, I met Edie Lutnick for the first time. Edie is the sister of Howard Lutnick, chairman and CEO of Cantor Fitzgerald. Their younger brother Gary was killed at the World Trade Center on 9/11. She is also the co-founder and executive director of the Cantor Fitzgerald Relief Fund.

Jake had shared with me that Edie was in the process of writing a book about her experience caring for the families of Cantor Fitzgerald, whose loved ones were murdered on that day. I told Jake I'd like to meet her.

When the meeting happened and she began to share those experiences, it was clear she had a story to tell that few people know. There have been untold devastating effects and consequences of that historic day. As I listened closely and saw the anguish in her eyes and face, born from all the pain she has witnessed over the past decade, Edie seemed to have some hesitancy about laying bare the intimate details of loss and survival. "Not publishing your book is not an option," I told her.

There are some events past and present that challenge our ability to comprehend the magnitude of human pain, suffering and the destruction associated with them. The Holocaust, slavery in the United States, Hiroshima, genocide atrocities in Rwanda and Serbia, and terrorist killings in Mumbai—it is difficult for us to wrap our minds around the enormity of pain and destruction associated with such events.

The terrorists' airplane attacks against the World Trade Center, the Pentagon and the White House on September 11, 2001 challenge our ability to grasp and comprehend the enormity of the horror and loss experienced by fellow Americans. On that day, almost 3,000 people were murdered.

There are lots of television shows and documentaries about 9/11. There are also numerous books and articles that have been written about that event. But none like Edie Lutnick's *An Unbroken Bond.*

If you read nothing else about 9/11 on its 10ᵗʰ anniversary, you must read this book. Poignantly and painstakingly, Edie lets the reader sit like a 24/7 video camera on her shoulder as she narrates a first-person account, beginning with being awakened by a phone call on September 11, 2001 that would change her life, and continuing through this anniversary. Edie poses challenging questions about personal responsibility and justice. She asks, "Have we truly honored the victims who were murdered on what should have been an ordinary day in their lives?" *An Unbroken Bond* reminds us that the single greatest sacrilege we could perpetrate concerning the events of 9/11 is forgetfulness.

The author, through the experience of all her pain and disappointment with the integrity of our political system and leaders, nevertheless remains optimistic and hopeful. She muses that "out of something broken will emerge something new and resilient." Speaking about the Cantor Fitzgerald families she says, "We are broken. We will never be the same. But we have persevered through unfathomable obstacles, and we are still here with our shared humanity intact."

The most challenging issue the book poses is not expressly stated. It is the same haunting question raised by Simon Wiesenthal in his book, *The Sunflower: On the Possibilities and Limits of Forgiveness.* Writing about his experiences as a prisoner in a Nazi concentration camp, he describes a dying Nazi soldier who has asked for forgiveness. Wiesenthal asks the reader, "What would you do?"

After reading Edie Lutnick's book we must all ask ourselves, what should WE do, now, after 9/11?

-CLARENCE B. JONES

Former counsel, draft speech writer, Martin Luther King, Jr.; Scholar Writer in Residence, Martin Luther King, Jr. Research & Education Institute, Stanford University; co-author of *BEHIND THE DREAM: The Making of the Speech that Transformed a Nation.*

PROLOGUE

It has been a decade since September 11th, when my family, countless other families and the world along with us changed forever. On that fateful morning, I lost my brother Gary Lutnick, a senior executive at Cantor Fitzgerald who died beside 657 friends and colleagues. With offices above where the first plane struck, Cantor was hit the hardest, suffering the greatest percentage of lost lives of any company, as well as of the total nearly 3,000 killed in the acts of terrorism that day. It was only by fortune that my other brother, Howard Lutnick, chairman and CEO of the company, survived. But it was by will and determination that on September 13th Cantor Fitzgerald reopened and began the long process of corporate recovery.

Days after the tragic events, when he was reeling from the pain of losing so many, Howard asked me to start and run a fund to help our victims' families. I agreed, but I didn't know at the time exactly what I was taking on. When people ask me what I do now, I tell them that I fight battles that should never even be conversations. A decade later, I continue to be the voice of the 9/11 families when they have none. I've become the continuity and consistency in a community once made up of strangers who are now family, bonded by one unified and tragic history. I suffered an immeasurable loss on that terrible day but it was also the day that I became part of this much larger family, made up of 1,011 Cantor Fitzgerald Relief Fund families and their 932 children, and includes victims from Cantor Fitzgerald, eSpeed, TradeSpark and 14 other companies.[1] From the beginning, I've seen it as my job to protect the ones left behind.

I wanted to write this book because there's more to be said than readers have already heard or think they might know. Ten years later, there are not just more stories of what happened on September 11th to hear, and the ongoing needs of struggling families to look after, but also important questions to ask ourselves. Has justice yet made order out of the chaos following those days, and have we all lived up to the responsibility the events of 9/11 heaped upon us? Amidst all the disagreements about the memorial to be built on the site, have we truly honored the victims who were murdered on what should have been an ordinary day in their lives? What is the legacy of these lost lives that their children will carry with them? How do our governments and societies treat those in need and how should they when the next tragedy strikes?

On this milestone anniversary, I think it important for us to examine these questions and also hear those stories not yet told, many of which show the depth of humanity and individual strength that was borne of that historic event. These are the stories of the victims themselves but also of the survivors, and the people who rallied to fight for them, from the couple who drove across the country collecting teddy bears for the children, to the many volunteers who worked long hours to gather lost information on the dead, to the family members who took on shocking government bureaucracy and politicians. Only through these stories can we understand the full breadth of what happened on that devastating day.

PART I

Edie's photo of the WTC, where she and her two brothers worked on the 101ˢᵗ–105ᵗʰ Floors, December 18, 1998

2001

THE THREE OF US

"Hi, Edie-Pie. This is your brother, Gary…" He was calling me with details for the evening. "I'm going to come pick you up. Howard and Allison will meet us at the restaurant." Gary had arranged to take our brother, his wife and me to dinner at his newest favorite Japanese restaurant, and managed to get us all tickets to the Michael Jackson concert in Madison Square Garden. Almost every spectacular event I have gone to has been on the arm of one of my brothers. Several days before, Gary took me to the President's Box at the U.S. Open, with tickets he bought at a charity auction. There he announced, "My date this evening is my sister Edie. I hope someday that I am lucky enough to meet someone just like her." That was my brother—he had an uncanny ability to make you feel like the most special person in the world.

Thwak. Thwak. That's what it sounded like. Michael Jackson just finished singing a song. Gary was clapping so loudly that it was actually hurting my ears. I was about to tell him to cut it out when I turned from the stage and beheld his profile. I will never forget the unabashed delight on his face. "Yeah!" he screamed along with almost everyone else in the audience. His good time was so infectious. I thought, "Aw, let him clap." Gary told us how lucky we were. He went to the same concert on Friday night with a group of friends and there were countless technical problems. The concert didn't end until after 1 am. But on Monday, September 10, 2001 everything was different and went perfectly. We were out of there by 11 pm. Howard and Allison had a big next day.

They were taking my nephew Kyle, the oldest of their three children, to his first day of kindergarten.

We all got into the car and drove uptown together as we lived within blocks of each other. Howard and Allison got out first. There were kisses all around. Then Gary got out. "Goodnight, Edie-Pie. I love you." "I love you too, Gary."

This is the way it was. We worked together. We loved each other as siblings should, but too often don't. We may not have had parents—we had lost them many years earlier—but we had each other. We were, in fact, the luckiest unlucky people we knew.

GOOD-BYE

I am asleep. As a labor lawyer with my own firm housed in the World Trade Center, I make my own hours. Unless there is a specific reason for me to be in the office early, I'm usually not—11 am to 7 pm (minimum) are my regular hours. I have an 8:30 am meeting with my lead plaintiff, to discuss the multi-plaintiff suit we have brought against a hotel for failing to pay its banquet waiters their gratuities. He has called to cancel until tomorrow, so I have gone back to sleep. I am not a morning person in even the best of circumstances. My phone starts ringing. "Who the hell is calling me so early in the morning?" I ignore it. Then it rings again. I still ignore it. But then my cell phone rings. Through my haze, I think, "That's odd." Then the house phone rings again. "Oh, all right. This is ridiculous." I plod to the kitchen and answer. It is my friend Suzy. She tells me to turn on the television. A plane has just hit the World Trade Center. I hang up and walk the six steps from my Upper East Side galley kitchen to the television set in my living room.

I can't believe what I am seeing. Smoke is pouring out of the office building where my two brothers and I work. I don't know how long I am standing there or how many calls I answer while staring at the television, before my cell phone rings again. I put a call on hold and answer. It is my brother Gary. I hear his voice and I know that, just like with the bombing in 1993, I have been spared.

"Gary, thank G-d you aren't there," and he says, "But, Edie, I am here." I softly scream, "Gary, Noooooo…" as something deep down inside me breaks. He tells me he is in a corner office with the door closed. I think he says on the 103rd floor. I can picture the windows as he speaks. He works on the 104th floor of One World Trade Center—the North Tower. He has made it down one floor. He is calm. I am not calm. He's my baby brother. He's only 36. I raised him after our parents died so he's not only my brother; he's also like my child. He says black smoke is pouring in and he's having trouble breathing. I tell him to conserve his strength, his voice. I try to talk about rescue. He doesn't talk about escape routes. He is calling to say good-bye. I cannot accept this. He tells me he loves me. His breathing is becoming labored. I am listening carefully to his breath. I keep thinking, "Not my Gary... Please G-d, not my Gary." He stops talking. I say, "Gary... Gary... Gary." There is no more of his voice and I hang up.

Later I learned that Gary called Howard's cell phone several times trying to reach him. He also called 911 four times to calmly report on the mayhem that surrounded him. He never told me he was seeing people jump to their deaths from the windows. He also called his ex-girlfriend Ann, with whom he had a bad breakup, to say good-bye and allow her to live the remainder of her life without guilt. Many years later, Shiya Ribowsky of the NYC medical examiner's office told me that sometimes they could tell where someone had died (if they knew where the person worked), by where the remains were recovered and the state they were in. Shiya wasn't telling me anything I didn't already know. My brother Gary was trapped inside the burning building and he ran out of air while I was talking to him.

Later, my boyfriend, Lewis Ameri, recalled trying to reach me. He was walking to midtown down Fifth Avenue, listening to his Walkman when a newscaster broke into his music and said that a plane had hit the towers. He told me he thought it was a prank and changed the station. But then a second report told him that another plane hit the World Trade Center. He was not that far from my brother Howard's apartment so he raced there. Howard's doorman tried to stop Lewis from going in. Lewis said, "A plane just hit the World Trade Center. I am going to the Lutnick's apartment. You can't stop me." The doorman stopped trying. A staff member let him in. Howard and Allison were with Kyle on his first day of kindergarten. Lewis called me from Howard's but didn't reach me, so became frantic. He thought I'd gone to my meeting. I worked on the 101st floor. He tried again and again and finally got me. I yelled into the phone, "Gary is trapped. Gary is trapped."

My phone keeps ringing and ringing and I must be answering, but the words coming through the wire are meaningless and aren't registering. The next phone call I remember receiving is from Howard. "What did he say, Eed, what did he say?" Through my tears I tell him. "He told me he loves us." Lewis comes in and shortly thereafter we are joined by my friend who is visiting from Barbados and staying nearby. She hasn't picked a very good time to visit.

I can't breathe and I can't stay in my apartment. I have to get out of there. I go downstairs to the backyard of our building, needing air. I am already sobbing uncontrollably when Lewis comes downstairs to get me. He says, "I am so sorry, Edie." I look at him questioningly. "The building collapsed." And I say, "No...No." I look searchingly into his tear-filled eyes and scream, "Nooooooooo..." and then I collapse. The next thing I remember is the doorman pulling my clothes back over my exposed body and adamantly and officiously telling Lewis that I cannot remain on the lobby floor.

I know Gary is dead. I know they are all dead. Despite the fact that others make missing persons posters and hang them in various locations around the city, I never make a missing flyer. I never call a hospital. Later, friends will make the rounds of the hospitals looking for Gary because they feel powerless, but I know they won't find him.

Lewis is upstairs manning the phones, which never stop ringing, while I sit out front with my friend. The streets are eerily quiet uptown. There is only shock, disbelief and sorrow. I go back upstairs. I am like a caged lion. There is no place that I am comfortable. I want to get out of my own skin. An old friend, Barbara Lamb, comes to my apartment. We were close, but had a bad falling out a few months before and hadn't been speaking. Barbara is visibly relieved to see my face. She realizes just how easily I could've been in the towers. Her relief is short lived when I tell her Gary is there. We hug each other tightly and cry. All is forgiven and so unimportant.

My best friend Angela's husband, Glenn Zagoren, is a businessman, but also a volunteer fire chief. He tells Angela that he feels compelled to go down to the WTC site. She tells him two things: first, "Be careful," and, second, "Take me to Edie's." This is no small thing, because Angela gave birth to her daughter Genna two weeks earlier. Angela comes over with her and tries to console me. She is looking at the back of my head. I turn around and she sees the grief on my face and the pain that has immediately aged me. "Angela, Gary's gone." Angela had hope before that moment, but my vehemence tells her I'm sure. She asks about Howard. I tell her that I spoke to him and that he is alive. I then turn to Lewis and I say, "I love you, but if I had lost both of my brothers, you would not have been able to get to me fast enough." They all know how close the three of us are. They know that there is no melodrama to my words. It's merely a statement of fact. Genna begins to cry inconsolably. At two weeks old, she has captured my emotions perfectly.

I turn to my assembled friends and tell them I'm sorry but that I need to go to Howard's. I need to run my hands over his face. I know he's alive because I have spoken to him, but I have to see him with my own eyes. With the death of my parents, and now my brother Gary, Howard is the only immediate family that I have left. It will be days before I learn that he left Kyle's school when he heard the news and raced down to the World Trade Center. It will be weeks before I realize that he almost died there as well. If I knew this at the time, my brain was incapable of processing it. If the plane had hit at 2 pm, all three of us would be dead. As it is, it hit at 8:46 am and the wrong one of us is dead. Gary was not even supposed to be at work. He'd planned to take the week off.

CANTOR FITZGERALD

Howard and Allison's apartment immediately becomes the hub and Allison's closet, a room that previously housed elegant clothing on metal racks, becomes the command center. Our friends make their way there. I have no recollection of any of us ever being idle. Howard makes his home phone number public. Rollover lines are installed. At Allison's suggestion, he sets up crisis centers, first in the Pierre Hotel and then in the Plaza. As the news of who the terrorists were and how they trained is disseminated to the public, we aren't focused on it. Howard's goal is to communicate with the Cantor Fitzgerald families, and try to figure out the extent of our losses.

I am no help. I'm a mess. Gary is dead. Gary is dead. How is it possible that he is *dead*? Someone hands me a valium and urges me to take it, and I do.

Howard is in the center of operations in the den. He listlessly sits on the couch with vacant, red-rimmed, teary eyes, shaking his head. I sit with him, in no better shape. For him, this is a tragedy of epic proportion. While I'm having trouble grasping the loss of Gary, I can't even comprehend the hell that he's in. I don't even know what it is. He and Allison go to the crisis centers. They talk to grieving and confused families. They are also trying, in the midst of all of this, to be parents to their three children. Allison's family, her brother Gary and her father Joel, also work for Cantor Fitzgerald. Thankfully, they are both alive. She is "lucky," but it is impossible to feel that way. While profoundly grateful for this, her brother-in-law is "missing," her best friend's husband is "missing," her other best friend's brother is "missing," and her husband's company is in rubble. Like Lewis, her job as the emotional backbone for her spouse is infinite.

The days surrounding September 11ᵗʰ blurred together, and through the years I have only had flashes of recollection. I am in the bathroom outside Howard's den. Howard is with me. He says, "Can you smell it? It smells like death." We realize it is September 12th, the anniversary of our father's death. After being diagnosed with lung cancer, my father began chemotherapy. The nurse accidentally injected him with 100 times the prescribed dose and he died.

Lewis and I must go back to my apartment. Friends must come see me. I obviously talk on the phone and go back and forth between Howard's apartment and mine. But I remember none of it. My sole function and the function of those around me is to help me keep a hold on my sanity. It's a very tall order. Sleep doesn't come. Only the horrible realization remains that without Gary, any life I've known is gone. Lewis tries to comfort me but there's nothing he can do or say. I'm inconsolable.

Those working in the closet have started cataloguing the Cantor Fitzgerald employees who are still alive. They've found only 127. Cantor Fitzgerald had 960 people employed on September 11th, many of them Howard's close friends. Days later, fewer than 15 percent are confirmed alive. The list of survivors is published for the families. Our hope is that by seeing the list, families and employees will be able to add more survivor names. It is staggering to think that our losses could top 800. Cantor Fitzgerald was on the 101st through 105th floors of One World Trade Center—the North Tower. These floors were above the impact of the plane strike and beyond the scope and possibility of any rescue effort launched. Everyone who was on Cantor's floors when the plane hit had died. Being the company with the largest loss of life is a badge we will wear unhappily and permanently.

On September 13th, Lewis and I go to Cantor's crisis center at the Pierre Hotel. Donna Dudek, a friend, is among the grief counselors and other volunteers galvanized by New York Congresswoman Carolyn Maloney. They are on computers recording information from anyone who will give it. Donna is the type of person who anticipates what is needed in crises and does more. Because we were so close, my brothers and I knew each other's friends well. There was a special bond between Donna and Gary. She is tall and large-boned. To her constant delight,

Gary always addressed her as "little one." Donna represses her own grief and compassionately handles the stream of devastated people coming to her. "My friend is missing." (Still not dead.) "His name is (blank)." Donna then asks, "Do you have his phone number?" "Is he married?" (Still no past tense.) "Does he have children?" "Do you know his parents' names, where they live, their contact information," and so on. At this point they are still sons, daughters, husbands, wives, brothers, sisters, friends and colleagues. Soon they will all fall under the universal term *loved ones*. It's less emotional to hear and easier to digest.

The walls of the hotel ballroom are plastered with missing flyers. The faces, young and full of life, burst forth from the papers, along with ages, company names, work locations and family contact information. The hope when these flyers were made was that the people in the photos are walking around dazed and confused, or in a hospital somewhere. Devastated family and friends are everywhere. Howard is speaking to them and telling them what he knows. He was down at the site when the buildings collapsed. He does not believe they are "missing." It is a tough message to deliver and an even tougher one to receive.

Lewis, along with Gary's friends, help me out of the Pierre. That is when I remember. "Oh my G-d, the cat." Gary has a cat named Bocchi that must be locked in his apartment. In an odd coincidence, a few days before 9/11 during dinner with Gary and some of his friends, we ended up having a conversation about spare keys. Gary reminded his friend that he had his key. Now the recollection is somewhat bizarre but also very important because it means they can get into his apartment and get the cat. Ultimately, we will give Bocchi to Gary's ex-girlfriend, Ann.

LOST DAYS

Several days after September 11th, while President George W. Bush is telling the nation that catching Osama bin Laden is our top priority, I am only a bit stronger. Lewis and I join those hard at work in Allison's closet helping on the phones. Howard has a six-month-old list of all of the employees of Cantor Fitzgerald, eSpeed and TradeSpark at home. Copies are made and it becomes indispensible. We are calling people trying to find out who is alive.

Eight people were laid off the day before the 11th due to downsizing. It is cause for celebration because we might be able to find those people. When we discover that one of those valued employees went back in early to clean out his desk, it is a new and horrifying blow that visibly crushes Howard. We find ourselves praying that people have been late, called in sick or been on vacation. Like other leading investment banking houses, most Cantor employees begin work at 7:30 in the morning, so we know our numbers will be staggering.

One of Allison's friends, bossy under the best of circumstances, has taken control of the closet. Her leadership is welcomed. We are coordinating our information with the facts being gathered at the crisis center. We are also taking calls from people searching for answers and needing help. One woman frantically screams that her impossible-to-get tickets for *The Producers* are in the building. I know she isn't being shallow. She just can't wrap her mind around the bigger loss that awaits her. She still thinks the person who is supposed to sit next to her in that theatre seat is coming home.

Names are being read off of the employee list. We announce "missing" or "alive" after each name. Howard's oldest friend and Cantor employee Dave Kravette is working in the closet when we get to his name. In a monotone, the reader of names says, "Alive" and moves on. "That's it?" Dave says. "That's all I get?"

Dave was in the lobby when the planes hit, having gone down to get some visitors who had forgotten their IDs, to spare his eight-months pregnant assistant the task. A fireball nearly killed him, but he is among the lucky to be alive. We are so grateful that he survived, and he is absolutely right, but everyone is emotionally drained as it is becoming apparent how few survivors there are.

Allison puts up big color photographs mounted on children's construction paper from Howard's 40th birthday party eight weeks earlier, of all the guests who are now unaccounted for. It was a costume party—Georgian—and all the guests are young, handsome, happy and elegant in their finery. Howard's best friend, Doug Gardner, his college buddy Calvin Gooding and Gary, among others, are in the shots. Calvin's wife LaChanze couldn't attend because she was too far along in her second pregnancy. Now her husband is among the "missing," and her soon-to-be-born child is fatherless.

˅   ˅   ˅

The Jewish high holy days creep up on us. I am too numb to revere G-d, but I go to the 92nd Street Y to say Kaddish (the prayer for the dead) for my father and mother and, now, my brother. I try to adhere to my father's words after my mother died, "What? You only believe in G-d when he is on your side? When G-d does what you want?" It isn't easy. Faith is a hard commodity for me to find these days. Gary and I used to play this game in temple and I find myself focused on that. He would grab hold of my hand and he would gently squeeze one time. Then I would squeeze his back. One, two. Then he would try to trip me up. One, two, three…fourfivesixseveneight…nine, ten. I would frantically try to mimic his squeezes without laughing, then do the same back to him. We were just kids, three lone children, when we moved to Manhattan and started going to the Y to pray for the souls of our parents 18 years earlier.

Back in Allison's closet, the calls start coming in with information about funerals and memorial services. Really, they are all memorial services no matter what you call them, because there are very few bodies. The Office of the Chief Medical Examiner started making identifications within 36 hours, but none are from Cantor Fitzgerald.

Ten years later, in May 2011, when they identified a 32-year-old man, 1,119 victims still remained unidentified.[2] Even those considered fortunate enough to receive remains rarely received full bodies back to bury.

Downstairs in Howard's apartment, Gary's ex-girlfriend Ann plays Twister with my five-year-old nephew Kyle. He does not know that he is the hero of this story because going to his first day of school saved his father's life. In every story of survival or death, there is always one fact or detail that can alter the course of events. One of our employees is alive because his new pair of shoes hurt him, so he went home to change back into his old ones. Finding a reason to go on without those we have lost is near impossible.

In Howard's family, like so many others, the children provide the reason. People have told me that during this time they spoke to me on the phone often but I was clearly not processing what was going on. One friend told me I called him three times to report Gary's death. Another friend was on the third of five ferries that managed to leave the World Financial Center to New Jersey. He got home safely, but at the time I had no ability to process that he was ever in danger. He reminded me that when I spoke to him I said, "We have to find them. We have to find them." He thought I was referring to hospitals. I was referring to the bodies of the dead.

CANTOR REOPENS

Cantor Fitzgerald has been regrouping in a large conference room on loan from a law firm since September 12th. Surviving employees have returned to work, keeping up a grueling pace. Cantor's competitors are using September 11th as a way to rid the market of the leader. Howard, the senior staff and the survivors are determined to keep the firm afloat in honor of their friends and colleagues, and stave off the company's demise. The Swiss global investment bank and Cantor client, UBS, offer Cantor a temporary, but more permanent home, and traders and salesman set up in a small area at the end of a hall on the 29th floor. With a handwritten Cantor Fitzgerald sign taped to the door, and additional loaned space in New Jersey to set up accounting, operations and the processing of stock and bond purchases and sales, Cantor Fitzgerald begins again.

The normally high-tech firm is now restarting with pens and paper. They have to open for business when their competitors open the bond markets on Thursday, September 13th or the firm will be lost. The stock market wouldn't open until Monday the 17th, and football would be cancelled that weekend, but that didn't slow Cantor's competitor Brokertec, which insisted the bond market reopen two days after September 11th. When so much of Wall Street is affected by the tragedy, there is no reason that the bond market couldn't have opened with the stock market on Monday to give the firm a few extra days to regroup. But Howard's phone call to the Bond Market Association doesn't even yield an "I'm sorry, Howard" or a "What can we do to help?"

The Cantor Fitzgerald survivors open the first part of their business within 47 hours. It is nothing short of miraculous.

Howard calls me at my apartment late the night of the 13th. He says, "Edie, we need to do everything we possibly can to help these families. I want to start a charity and I need you to run it." I think, "He has lost his mind." In my head, I start ticking off the names of all the people I consider to be far more suitable for this task than I and in better shape than I presently am. And then it hits me. They are all gone. I say, "Howie, I'm barely functioning." He responds, "Edie, I need you to do this," and I say, "Why?" Howard has figured out how to add another 24 hours of personalized "Lutnick" time for the families to each day. He says, "Because you *are* me." Then he tells me that with the firm destroyed he has lost almost all of his money, but that he's giving $1 million to get us started. It never occurs to me to question why he is doing this.

❤ ❤ ❤

I never thought to try to hold onto my pre-9/11 professional life as an attorney. I tied up the loose ends and turned my legal cases over to my partners. When I consider my life choices, they always seem dictated by circumstances. By my third year of college, both of my parents had died. Before President Ronald Reagan changed the law, if you were an orphan and remained a full-time student you could receive social security until you were 21. So I graduated from college in three years instead of four, went to graduate school for a joint degree program on the advice of a professor and then went to work as a labor lawyer. It wasn't about passion. It was about survival. Once again after 9/11, death changed my path. This time however, it is driven by passion. My before-9/11 life, like Gary, is gone.

On September 14, 2001, Cantor applies for and, on an emergency basis, receives 501(c)(3) not-for-profit status. The Cantor Fitzgerald Relief Fund is formed and I am its executive director and co-founder. The following day Lewis and I go to see Rosanna Scotto, a local newscaster for Fox Channel 5 who lives in my building. She doesn't know me and has only seen me in passing, yet she lets us into her apartment. I explain to her who I am and plead with her to put our donation information on the air. She agrees. It's a kindness for which I will always be grateful.

Howard tells the families at the crisis center that he has set up a charity and that his sister Edie is going to run it. Now I can start fielding more of the phone calls. "Hi, this is Edie Lutnick." "Oooh, Edie." My last name is all the introduction they need. There are however, some things that I just cannot do or say, because the next thing they ask me is, "Did you know my son/daughter, husband/wife," and I have to say no because I only knew a handful of them. But I can listen as they teach me about their son or daughter, husband or wife, and I start to feel like I knew them, just as I am getting to know each family.

On September 14th, Howard calls the chairman of Cantor's insurance company, CNA. He asks him to come to the crisis center and hand deliver the corporate life insurance payment of $100,000 per person. The chairman responds by saying that they can't, they need death certificates, and that there is a process. Howard says, "This is your chance to be a human being. These families need support now, not later. I guarantee that if you come to the crisis center and give checks to a family when someone has not died, I will make sure that we pay it back to you." He said that he would think about it and call back. Howard said, "You don't have to call back. Either you'll be there will checks for every name we've sent you on the list, or we'll know you aren't coming. But if you come, we will always speak highly of you."

The next morning CNA came to the crisis center at the Pierre. The next of kin filled out a form and CNA gave out $100,000 checks. The Cantor Fitzgerald families were the first families to receive insurance payments, and Howard knew that, at least for the short term, they had financial assistance.

On September 15th, the medical examiner published the first list of 39 identified bodies. A handful are Cantor families. The first memorials are scheduled for September 16th and the choice to have a service has no relationship to whether there are remains, because most are proceeding without them. The first three services are for Douglas Gardner, Howard's best friend, Karen Klitzman, a 38-year-old twin, and Greg Richards, the cousin of Cantor's general counsel, Stephen Merkel. Cantor embraced rather than frowned on nepotism. People who worked at Cantor wanted their friends and family to work with them. If they were qualified, Cantor hired them. The family relationships between the dead as well as the survivors are readily apparent.

The scheduling of services signals the loss of hope. Once the scheduling starts, it is like a deluge, with a dozen memorials every day. That it is not humanly possible for Howard, or any of the Cantor survivors, for that matter, to attend every funeral becomes immediately evident. I, along with others in the closet, start keeping track of all the memorials and services as they are being called in, and we quickly send the information back out to the families, friends and surviving colleagues and post it on the CantorUSA website. Survivors will have to choose which and how many funerals to attend every day, oftentimes divvied up by geographic location.

˅   ˅   ˅

Lewis is an artist. Like mine, his life was changed entirely by 9/11. Instead of spending his time creating in his studio or home on Long Island, Lewis spends all of his time with me. Every night Lewis and I come back to my apartment as morning approaches, bone weary and exhausted. Sleep is not a comfort with the possibility of dreaming too terrifying.

I saved Gary's message to me from September 10th, and I play it repeatedly. "Hi, Edie-Pie. This is your brother, Gary…" Just like seeing Howard's face, hearing Gary's voice is a lifeline for me. One night, as I lie in bed, Gary's picture comes crashing down off the wall in another room. Despite being frightened by the loud noise, I hoped it meant that he was still here with me. Other families have similar experiences. No one wants to believe they might actually be gone.

A few weeks after 9/11 the desks and phones are removed, the lists put away and the people dispersed. Allison's closet returns to a place that houses clothing, but the calls to Howard's house and offices, his and mine, are still coming in relentlessly. All the families want to talk to him. They want to hear stories and capture memories that only Howard can tell. They all want him to attend the memorial services or funerals of their loved ones, but the numbers are just too great. There aren't enough hours in the day to field all of the calls or attend all the services. But he tries.

Cantor Fitzgerald, among all its businesses, is the hub for everything that does not trade on the stock exchange. They are the exchange for the U.S. bond market, the corporate bond market, foreign exchange options, to name just a few examples. eSpeed was its public electronic trading company. Monday, September 10th was one of the busiest days of the year. All business transactions made on Friday and Monday must routinely be paid for on Tuesday. Payment was due on $75 billion worth of stocks and bonds that had been bought on the days leading up to September 11th just as the computers were destroyed and the staff killed. Not only would the emotional toll be immeasurably high, Cantor Fitzgerald would be in a fight for its corporate life.

Howard needs the banks to loan him $75 billion, and he needs to convince them that even with the limited number of survivors, Cantor can recover and should be allowed to do more trades. It seems impossible that the banks would ever let him take this kind of risk.

To make matters worse, it was almost a certainty that when the stock market reopened on September 17th it would suffer a major crash. The $75 billion in securities would be worth significantly less. With the firm's business at a standstill and economic turmoil likely around the world, combined with the cost of the current payroll, the firm was losing $1 million a day.

The only way to convince the banks to lend the money was for Howard and the survivors to get the backup records restored and running. Cantor had to be able to deliver its purchased securities and prove who it had resold them to. Cantor had a password system in place in case anything ever happened to an individual. You shared your password with the five people around you. There was a password repository in the building. There was also a second backup repository under Two World Trade Center, a 15-minute walk away. But the once-logical system had been destroyed.

To help solve this massive problem, Microsoft flies in 50 people and Howard and the survivors work around the clock for days breaking into the Cantor computer systems.

Between trying to get the company up and running, which he must do if we are to take care of the families, and speaking to them in every free moment for as long as they need, my brother Howard is, out of necessity and understandably, lost to me.

THE FUND

Howard has gone on television to talk about what has happened to his families and to his firm. He shows up for one interview and discovers he has been booked for three, back to back. He announces that Cantor has reopened for business and thanks all those employees who made it possible. He commits to helping the families of the employees he lost. As he starts to talk about those losses, it is impossible to keep his emotions from showing. Since 9/11 I haven't been able to turn on the TV because I don't want to see the images, so I don't actually see his appearances. But the world has seen him and understands that Cantor Fitzgerald is not a soulless investment banking house but a company made up of human beings, and the families of those human beings are suffering. As a result, Americans and people from all over the world want to help. Piles and piles of mail come to the Fund, which Lewis and I have set up in a small office outside the conference room Cantor is regrouping in. Offers to volunteer, cards, letters, condolences, prayers, and, yes, checks and cash are being mailed in. In the face of all this pain and suffering, the generosity is astounding.

Howard has assigned a Cantor executive to assist me with the administrative needs of getting started because I am learning how to start a charitable nonprofit on the job. My first order of business is obvious: we need basic things like a bank account, and checks to pay the families. We also begin to collect the names of all the donors to ensure that we thank them in the future.

Though we still don't have a final list of the dead, with each day we get a little closer. The Relief Fund is offered a larger home at Fish & Neave. They are Cantor Fitzgerald's patent attorneys and they cannot be more accommodating. After all the trauma, I find it hard to let Howard out of my sight, but he is moving over to UBS and I have to move elsewhere to accommodate all the people willing to volunteer.

For the banks to loan Cantor the money to keep it afloat, Howard had to sign over control of the company. The conditions the bank imposed were very clear. Cantor could make no errors or mistakes. It had to reduce the $75 billion in loans and Howard could not make any decision that would cost the firm money. Howard told the families that September 15th would be the last paycheck. There was no other option. The continuation of salaries to families of the dead, with no revenue coming into the firm and the bank's conditions, would result in the bank's foreclosing. His reasons were unimportant to many of the families, who still wanted to believe that their loved ones were alive and owed a salary. Howard knew at the time that he would find other ways to help the families, but until he regained control of the company, something that was a long shot, there was nothing else he could say. The media and even some families didn't allow him any time to put a plan in place. They descended on him. The same media that had turned him into a hero a few days before, now recast him as a villain. This new negative media onslaught in the face of all we had already suffered was untenable.

I knew my brother was doing everything he could think of for the families despite having no obligation to do so. Many were looking for someone more accessible and tangible than an Islamic extremist named Osama bin Laden to blame. At the same time, his competitors were looking at this as an opportunity to force Cantor Fitzgerald to close its doors. At Fish & Neave we get to work in a large conference room. I try to get laptops donated from a major company that shares the building with us but I am unsuccessful. My friend Barbara (the one I am no longer fighting with) is completing a divorce. Her soon-to-be ex-husband agrees, as his contribution to our relief effort, to help support her while she works for me. In addition to being an artist, Barbara has a computer software background and great managerial skills. In the days following the tragedy, I will be amazed with how many friends come forward to help.

A hotline has been set up in another location to collect and give information. The people manning it are volunteers Sharon Lefkowitz, who is an author, and her 19-year-old daughter Juliet McIntyre. Juliet and Sharon are Scientologists. I've never met a Scientologist in my life prior to this. I can't articulate what they believe in and I don't really care. They are loaded with compassion, they are offering to help and I need them. In fact, I need tons of help and they have a help ministry. They come in droves. More friends come, too, along with others who are drawn to help after having suffered through traumas of their own. We start calling the people who wrote in after seeing Howard on television or heard about our need through other sources. In the end, we have a team of hundreds. First we open mail. There are postal bags of it. Then we photocopy checks and correspondence before depositing the checks. When a phone rings, we answer it, "The Cantor Fitzgerald Relief Fund." It doesn't take me very long to realize that we can't handle all of the phone calls coming in, even though we have ten rollover lines. I get a call service to start answering the calls and take credit card donations and messages.

It takes one shift to discover that I have to feed all these volunteers, and there are a lot of them. At one point we have about 100 volunteers at a time. We work two shifts, so I need lunch and dinner. Lewis, Barbara and I are working at least 20 hours a day. I assign one of our volunteers, Pat Rodgers, to food detail. Pat is a breast cancer survivor and a tough-as-nails Irishwoman. She saw Howard on television and wrote us a letter. Pat feels comfortable calling the Irish pubs, first in our neighborhood, then all over the city. She is very good at getting them to donate. Soon food starts arriving. We get used to receiving Irish pub fare and we are grateful. We get shepherd's pie—a lot. Then one day the elevator doors open and brawny pub workers in white shirts and black-and-white checked pants walk out carrying four huge trays covered in aluminum foil. I am thinking, "This does not look like shepherd's pie." The guys put the trays down on the table. Pat pulls back the aluminum foil and, with a big smile, reveals her crowning achievement, a tray full of pigs. Whole pigs, head and all, which frankly look like they are grinning right back at Pat. Roasted pigs. And cabbage. Lots of cabbage. I tell Pat maybe she should try for sandwiches. Lewis and some volunteers start begging food from the Cosi downstairs. Pat starts concentrating on Chinese.

While we were trying to get food donated for our volunteers uptown, restaurant owners and chefs were working alongside rescue workers who were tirelessly looking for their brethren and ours down at the World Trade Center site. They set up tents and cooked and fed the recovery workers for months on end at their own expense.

The donations room has moments of liveliness. When someone writes a particularly inspirational note, it is read aloud. When a child sends pennies in a letter, we are touched. One young boy sent out birthday party invitations telling his eight-year-old friends to give money to the Relief Fund instead of giving him birthday presents. The outpouring of love and support is tremendous. Once, when I hear cheering and clapping coming from the room, we all stop what we are doing and make our way there. Carolyn has opened a check that looks like any other. An Indian immigrant who lives in California, and asks to remain anonymous, tells us that America has been very good to him and that he wants to give something back. He has sent us a check for $1 million. We are amazed. The volunteers are overjoyed. They don't really believe it will clear. It does. We respect his wishes for anonymity, but I track him down and call him personally to thank him anyway. We receive about 20,000 donations in a matter of days. The volunteers are always busy.

At this point I was unaware of any other financial aid coming to the victims or any government programs being put into place. I also wasn't aware that in a short amount of time, donations from the general public would become only a very small fraction of our distributions, the vast majority of funding coming from Cantor Fitzgerald and the public successor to eSpeed, BGC Partners.

A strong camaraderie has developed in the room. When someone has a birthday, a cake is brought in. One day, a Scientologist from Los Angeles who has come to work for us sends an enormous care package of ice cream. It comes with cups, little wooden spoons and more flavors than you can imagine. This really excites the volunteers. Fish & Neave doesn't, however, have the freezer space to accommodate it, so volunteers consume ice cream all day long, until they are eating multicolored ice cream soup. They don't care. It makes them happy.

I still can't keep food down. Lewis tries to put grapes in front of me, or bread. I rarely eat, but sometimes I pick and bread is the easiest thing to go down. I arrive home after work late one night and there is a basket of bread waiting for me sent by one of Lewis's best friends and his wife. Small unsolicited acts of kindness will always be remembered.

LOST RECORDS

When the terrorists used planes as missiles and leveled the World Trade Center and Cantor Fitzgerald along with it, they took an incredible number of lives and an unfathomable toll. They also destroyed all the computers and all the employee records. Insurance policies no longer had beneficiaries attached to them. Victim addresses were unknown. Next of kin, also unknown.

Unfortunately, while today disaster preparedness is a high priority for the government, the devastation we experienced in the aftermath of Hurricane Katrina showed us that we haven't yet taken the lessons from 9/11 regarding coordinated information gathering and dissemination very far. The inadequate communication system for recovery workers remains as prominent and as unresolved as it did in the wake of 9/11. At Cantor Fitzgerald and many other companies, the lessons learned have resulted in backup systems and databases both for front and back offices existing in multiple locations.

▾   ▾   ▾

For the task of finding information, not money, we need another room for another team. In that room, we have loose-leaf binders with all the information collected on the hotline, at the crisis centers and from Allison's closet. I also get a list of insured employees from Cantor's insurance agents. This gives me the names of family members who were covered under their spouses' health insurance. This is a huge leap forward in trying to formalize the list of the dead and figure out who the next of kin are. At least this tells me the names of the spouses and children of most of our married victims, and so far it looks like it is going to be about half of the total.

As of September 20th, we think that we have more than 700 dead. We call every person we have information from. We ask them whether they have heard from the person they reported missing. If they say no, we ask them for any next-of-kin information.

Oftentimes we are calling family members. When I tell them who I am, the phone calls get long and emotional. I talk to them for as long as they need. I listen to them cry. Sometimes I cry with them. They teach me about their dead family member. I no longer refer to them as "the" families. I start referring to them as "my" or "our" families.

Every once in a while, someone tells us that, yes, they have heard from the person we are calling about. That person's name is crossed off the list with a sigh of relief. Every person that doesn't end up on that list is a small miracle. It is the only light we have. When I see the name of a person I know to be alive, the number drops by one and brings me into the 600s. While whittling down the number, we are also confirming the dead, and it's an emotionally grueling task. Each interview is painstakingly hand recorded and our binders are getting larger and fuller. We're learning how many children have lost a parent. We're seeing how many families have lost more than one member. Working around the clock, we are not just creating our master list of our dead but also seeing how far the losses have spread.

One day over the Jewish holidays, Howard takes me with him to visit three of our four burn victims in New York Presbyterian's burn unit: Lauren Manning, a vice president of global market data, Harry Waizer, assistant general counsel and Renée Barrett-Arjune, an integral member of accounting. The fourth, Virginia DiChiara, a vice president of internal audit in risk management, is in a hospital in New Jersey. Lauren was in the ground floor lobby when a fireball raced toward her. Renée and Harry were in elevators that dropped back down to the 78th floor.

Lauren's husband Greg called Howard after he found her. Greg's first words to Howard were, "I'm sorry about Gary." Howard had to try to focus on what was being said and couldn't if the conversation shifted to Gary. "Forget about that...what's going on?" As Greg talked, they decided that Howard would be presented as his brother so that he could visit Lauren. Howard's voice was raspy and he could barely speak from all the inhaled soot and debris, but he said to Greg, "We love you, we're here for you. We love you."

Greg doesn't know how he found himself in this situation. He and Lauren were both running late on September 11th, she by 15 minutes, he significantly more, as he had agreed to take a neighbor recovering from surgery on an errand. He was supposed to be at the Risk Waters conference at Windows on the World on the 107th floor that morning. With the change of plans, he gave his badge to a colleague who was also late. Normally, when Greg and Lauren entered the WTC elevator lobby, she would go to the left to catch elevators to Cantor's offices, he to the right. No one who went to the left survived. The fireball caught Lauren from behind as it swept through the lobby and only the explosion of the glass on the lobby's west side prevented the blast from sweeping over Dave Kravette, who was standing at the security desk in the lobby. He felt the heat, but it broke like a wave in front of him and imploded. Greg, from the safety of their Greenwich Village apartment, looked at what was happening on the television set and had a brief vision that Lauren survived, but no one else. He then looked in horror at what was happening, counting the windows that made up Cantor's offices and thought, "How will anyone survive?" Helplessly, he held their young son, trying to figure out what he could do, knowing that there was nothing.

Greg received a phone call from the companion of the man who helped Lauren, saying, "We got her on an ambulance." Then the phone went dead. Greg screamed, "Where did she go? Where did you take her?" He started making calls, found her at St. Vincent's, and was by her side before the second tower fell. Doctors and nurses were suited up to care for thousands of critical victims who never came. By mid-afternoon Greg had succeeded in getting Lauren transferred to the burn center at New York Presbyterian. Only 16 critically injured patients ever made it to the burn center.

Dressed in what looks like a yellow hazmat suit, with sterile surgical cap, gown, mask and gloves, Howard is allowed to go in and visit. I am sitting out in the waiting room with the families. It is difficult to keep an optimistic outlook when your loved ones are badly burned—in Lauren's case, over 82 percent of her body—but they are trying. All three have partners. All three have at least one child.

Unlike all of the other families, however, these have guarded hope. We talk about how strong and resilient they are. The spouses tell me the things that they are going to do when they recover. I hug them. Whatever strength I still possess I want to send to them. Howard comes out from the double doors that don't allow people or germs inside. This is not the first time he has visited. He is a familiar face. Howard runs into Gilbert Scharf. Like Howard, Gil is chairman of the board and CEO of his company Euro Brokers, a firm that was located in Two World Trade Center. Unlike Cantor, Euro Brokers had survivors among those in their offices. He is there visiting his one burn victim, and to see Greg, who works for him. Howard and I are both touched that he is there. It is one thing to give money. It is quite another to walk inside a burn unit and personally offer solace to critically burned and disfigured people. Howard immediately decides that the Cantor Fitzgerald Relief Fund will now help out the Euro Brokers families until they can establish a relief fund of their own. I go back to Fish & Neave and contact Euro Brokers to get a verifiable list of the missing and their next of kin. Their 61 victims and families are now in my fold.

❧ ❧ ❧

No matter what I am engaged in, Gary never leaves my thoughts. Lewis comes with me to Gary's apartment. It is only 24 blocks from my own. I don't know what I am looking for or what this will do for me. Where are his clothes? I want things that have his smell, anything to hold onto. It is, however, the end of summer and Gary has had a long rental in the Hamptons so his clothing isn't at home. He sent most of it out to be cleaned. I find a laundry basket and take out a pair of his jeans. The thought would have disgusted Gary, but I just want to feel him near me and know I'm grasping at straws. My brother was crazy about sunglasses and had an extensive collection, so I open a drawer and take a pair.

His answering machine is blinking furiously. The tape is filled up. I try to retrieve the messages but can't. The machine is way too complex. Gary loved gadgets and the latest technological advancements. Fittingly, his answering machine is no exception. It keeps barking orders at me. Gary always called me his Amish sister. I have no head for technology. He once excitedly bought me the newest flat screen computer monitor only to discover that I didn't own a desktop computer. He shook his head, took back the monitor and bought me a computer. Lewis tackles Gary's answering machine as I walk around the apartment. This was a temporary home for him and it feels that way. Gary had bought an apartment downtown in Greenwich Village from floor plans a few years ago. The building finally closed and he was able to start construction on the apartment three weeks before September 11th. Gary has a very important-looking safe in his closet. I don't know his passwords or combinations and, by the look of it, it will be a major ordeal for the locksmith. When he comes, it takes him only a few seconds with a diamond cutter to open it. The safe is empty except for Gary's divorce decree.

In the meantime, Lewis finally gets the answering machine to spit out messages without Gary's verbal command, which seems to be the issue. The answering machine, like me, needs to hear his voice in order to function. I grab a pad and start writing down messages. "Gary, please call me," from Gloria. Who is Gloria? "Gary, if you are there, pick up the phone," says a girl with a Texas accent. "I'm worried, Gary. Call me." There are messages from girls whose names I recognize, girls whose names I don't and from male voices. The calls get more frantic as the tape plays on. And always Gloria—five, six times. I will have to call all of these people back. I will have to confirm all of their worst fears. I call back this Gloria. Through her hysteria she explains to me who she is.

Gary met Gloria when he was trying to hail a cab one day on the way home from work. An old model town car pulled up with Gloria at the wheel, and he got in. On the ride home from the World Trade Center, she explained her situation. Gloria was down and out. She lost her job and her daughter was sick, which depleted all of her finances. She was in a bad way and she looked it. Gary believed that if you gave people an opportunity, you would find that they were fundamentally good and could turn their lives around. He backed his words with his money. He hired Gloria to drive him to and from work every day. Once she proved herself trustworthy by showing up on time and on a regular basis, he started paying her extra to work for him, cleaning his apartment and running errands. When he had paid her enough to get her self-esteem and confidence back, he helped her get her livery license. No one was more distraught on the answering machine than Gloria. Like so many, Gloria has also now lost the person providing for her financial well-being.

I find some of Gary's sweaters and take these, too. I won't fully grasp what has happened for some time to come. Gary was so young. My mother died when she was 42. My father at 51. Gary was only 36. How is it possible that Gary didn't even outlive my mother? We close the door and walk back to Fish & Neave. I have the crosstown walk to collect myself. At the office, I pull on Gary's sweater. It is a black cable knit Donna Karan that I bought him for Chanukah.

Allison, immediately after the closing of the crisis centers, begins working with Cigna, Cantor's employee assistance health care provider, to set up support groups for the families in the tristate area. Once I get the Relief Fund up and running, I concentrate on setting up counseling sessions for the families, as well as procuring coverage for individual therapy sessions. Cantor has already tapped Cigna to assist its surviving employees, but this is different. Technically, since the loved ones who are now deceased were the policy holders, our married families will no longer have insurance for themselves and their children. They may not be able to afford counseling. No health insurance is a huge and wildly expensive ball that I drop in Howard's lap. We also need to get therapy for our families that never had insurance with Cantor (parents, siblings and friends), if they need or want it. I start calling all the therapists who contacted us through letters or by phone, and get them to agree to assist our families on an individual or group basis as well. I task my volunteers to get churches and synagogues donated as locations for these sessions. We begin posting the locations of support groups on our makeshift website. I contact Yahoo and get an email account set up for the Relief Fund so the families can get in touch with me directly.

A PROMISE

Howard and his fellow Cantor survivors have met the demand of the banks. They have lowered their debt from $75 billion to $58 billion by successfully settling many of the trades. Howard is now certain that he will be getting the company back. The same day, September 19th, he announces that he's figured out a plan to take care of the families for the long term. Cantor Fitzgerald will give the families 25 percent of the firm's profits for five years, and 10 years of health care for any victims' families who are eligible. He does this to assist those families who now have the added burden of being a single parent or single-family unit. He pledges that each family will receive a check on a quarterly basis, and that over the next five years, each family will receive a minimum of $100,000—totaling almost $66 million. September 11th was only eight days earlier, the firm is barely on its feet, the death toll is still unknown and Cantor has just pledged over $130 million to our families. Cantor Fitzgerald is a privately held partnership. Every dollar of firm profit will come from the surviving partners, including Howard, who holds the largest share.

The Cantor Fitzgerald Relief Fund victims' families are not only in the tristate area. They are located across the United States. They are also in England, France, Brazil, Russia, India, Australia, Japan, among other countries. Visas become a big issue. Some Cantor employees were in the United States on work visas. With their death, will their family members, who have established lives and homes here be deported? Other family members are out of the country and now need visas in order to come here. In a few cases, the guardianship issues of our 9/11 children now cross international lines. Information that supported visa applications and records of same were, in many cases, in the World Trade

Center. One of our newly widowed wives, who recently emigrated from another country, found herself with no documents. Her new husband had brought their passports, visa applications and marriage license to the office. She was now in a new country with no husband, no papers and no friends. She camped out at the WTC site, always looking for her young husband, never believing that he would not return to her. One of our volunteers made it her personal mission to get this young woman's papers sorted out so that she could stay in the country. Ultimately, I believe she decided to return to her native land. The issues confronting the families, and by extension me, become more complicated and far reaching daily. I start engaging with Cantor's legal team, finding pro bono immigration attorneys and learning all that I can about visas. We are successful in resolving most of the issues.

Jennifer Gardner is walking into the Reebok Gym on the Upper West Side, taking her son Michael to his karate lesson. She hears her own voice, looks up at a television set and sees herself. She is talking about the death of her husband and Cantor's COO, Doug Gardner, on *Oprah*. Connie Chung's producers on ABC had told Jennifer that if she gave them an interview, they would play it only once and it would never be replayed. They have, however, spliced her interview and unbeknownst to Jennifer it is now on *Oprah*. Jennifer is blindsided by the words and the images as she tugs five-year-old Michael away. When Jennifer tells me this, I become acutely aware that families need to be prepared in advance for what they hear and see to avoid being emotionally punched. We all have buttons we are unaware of, but I see it as my job to protect the families from the ones I can identify.

I receive a phone call that Nile Rodgers, who produced "We are Family" with Sister Sledge in 1978, has decided to remix the song using the voices of many famous singers and actors, including Roberta Flack, Dionne Warwick and Patti LaBelle. The theory is that the song will be released and the proceeds will go to different 9/11 organizations. I am invited to participate as the Cantor Fitzgerald Relief Fund will be a recipient. I don't feel that I can refuse. On September 22nd, I go to a studio in Manhattan for the recording. I am in a row near the back. We are handed the words that Nile has changed slightly. "We are family. My brothers and sisters with me." But I do not have my brother with me. I will never have him with me again. This is excruciating. Against a backdrop of clapping, singing and dancing celebrities, the tears are coursing down my face. I cannot leave. I am trapped between faces anyone would recognize and be delighted to be with. But I can't be excited about being there. It's way too early for me to be around a joyous experience, even for a good cause. They take our picture. I try to smile. All the participants are then lined up to give an interview. I jump the line ahead of Rosie Perez and explain to the producer that I have to leave to attend a funeral. Rosie complains to me and the producer but I don't care. It is still September and there are multiple funerals every day. I am only here because I want the world to know about the Cantor Fitzgerald Relief Fund. I want people to donate to us so that we can help our families. I don't know the status of this fundraising effort. We never receive any money from their project, although I am fond of Nile for trying.

Throughout my years with the fund, one of the most disheartening things was to hear stories of funds that allegedly raised money for the benefit of the 9/11 families and then didn't follow through on their marketing claims. The problems surrounding the distribution of funds from the Red Cross, the United Way and Families of Freedom (Scholarship America) were heavily reported in the press. But charities such as ours were always being asked to consider ideas (and schemes) that would supposedly enrich the charity, but more often than not would really enrich the creator. We employed the "pure of heart" standard when considering any ideas in which we were asked to partner.

The effort to recover victims from the World Trade Center is ongoing, but I am not paying attention. The news carries continuous 9/11 coverage, but I am not watching. We are working. Fish & Neave's operation's officer has secured me an office. I need one because the conversations I have with family members are very personal and don't belong in a bustling conference room. The calls from family members keep coming in and I keep talking. Word has gotten out that I spoke to Gary on September 11th. Families are desperately trying to piece together what happened that day. Information is power and control. If only they can figure out exactly what happened to their loved ones, then maybe they can find a way to deal with it. They are trying to gain control of a situation for which there isn't any by trying to connect dots and put puzzle pieces together. The conversations go something like this, "You talked to Gary, right?" I say, "Yes." "He worked on 104?" Again, "Yes." "My son/husband/wife worked on 104. Did Gary see him/her?" "Were they together?" "Where did Gary go?" I feel so inadequate, but I have few answers. "Did you know my son/daughter/husband/wife? I am having such nightmares." I get used to telling the story of my brother's death. I will tell it only if it will help one of my families. I know that I am considered lucky because I got to speak to him. I got to hear his voice one last time. I know where he was. I try to be the dispeller of nightmares. None of us can close our eyes. It isn't that our loved ones are dead. It is how they died that torments us. It is the unthinkable unknown. I spoke to Gary. Howard was down at the site.

To many, I hold the key. I tell them that their loved ones died peacefully. I tell them that Gary's voice stopped while we were on the phone. I believe that he passed out. I say that his voice was calm—that he was not screaming. I tell them that Howard was down at the site and when the smoke came toward and overwhelmed him, he also was calm. Both of my brothers had very matter-of-factly thought, "Hmmm… I am going to die."

One by one, all day every day, I convince our families that their loved ones were asphyxiated from the smoke and had passed out when the buildings fell and burned. The alternative is an image that cannot be accepted. They are willing to be led. I am selling tranquility for all I am worth. But, like faith in G-d, it is just that … faith. Deep down in my heart, with every ounce of strength I possess, I pray what I am saying is the truth. In my own case, I work until I am numb. I have to keep moving. If I stop, I will think and I cannot allow that. Gary died of asphyxiation. They all died that way. That is what I believe.

That is what I have to believe. But families call with their horror story nightmares. They hear their loved one screaming in their head. And they communicate this to me, over and over again. "Were they crushed?" "Did they jump?" "Did they die in pain and terror?" "Were they burned to death?" Methodically, I weave my story. Slowly, I lay their loved one to rest peacefully. Patiently, I convince our families to adopt my version. If a different reality surfaces later, we'll deal with it, but for now, they need to rest.

I am contacted by the Office of the Chief Medical Examiner. We have to notify the families that DNA evidence of the victims is being collected at the Park Avenue Armory and on Pier 94 on the West Side of Manhattan. Family members (including ours) are being asked to bring items that contain DNA of their "lost"—we still can't say dead—loved one. These are mostly hairbrushes and toothbrushes. Eventually a lot of the DNA evidence will be comingled and contaminated, but for now this is extremely important. This is the evidence that might result in your family getting "remains" (not a person) back to bury. The other location is Pier 94, where relief organizations and governmental agencies have set up an assistance center. The theory is that all organizations offering goods and services to the 9/11 families will be housed in one place.

It is an unnavigable labyrinth on a day when you have all your wits about you, and instantly depressing if you do not. The bureaucracy facing families is daunting at best. I decide that we need Cantor Fitzgerald Relief volunteers at the pier to walk our families through this maze. We send over teams of our most sympathetic and compassionate volunteers every day. The Victims of Crime application one must fill out to get funeral (or in our case, memorial) expenses reimbursed is complicated. If I am a lawyer and I can't fight my way through this application, what the heck are the others going to do? Unfortunately, this form is just one of many, many applications. A volunteer tells me about a Buddhist organization that is giving each family $1,500—no questions asked. I think, "They have the right idea." These widows and widowers and parents are being subjected to an indignity they don't deserve. In addition to all the pain, they shouldn't have to be begging, bills in hand for assistance.

The offerings at the pier, albeit positive in so many ways, double and triple the number of family phone calls, because they need information in order to fill out these forms. They need to prove who they are, who they lost and who their loved one worked for. I'm the one who can do that for them. And they need death certificates without having a body. This is not an easy thing.

Normally, if you do not have a body, you need to wait seven years to have a person declared dead. I need Howard to get the rules changed here also. All 9/11 victims' next of kin need death certificates in order to set up estates or collect on insurance policies, if they have any. Howard has already arranged for Cantor's life insurance company, CNA, to pay out the corporate life insurance claims without the normal proof of death. Since most of the families do not have remains and death certificates still need to be obtained, this is way out of the ordinary.

Howard gets the law firm of Skadden, Arps, Slate, Meagher & Flom LLP & Affiliates to start working on the death certificate problem, and we start investigating how to help families set up estates without one. Ultimately, they work with the medical examiner and Surrogate's Court for a direct streamlined process. Family members, along with Cantor, fill out an affidavit and after a review by the Surrogate's Court, the medical examiner issues a temporary death certificate dated September 11, 2001.

Newscasters are calling constantly. They want a story, either from me or from one of our families. "How are you handling your grief?" "Has a baby been born?" "How are you paying for things?" "Has a loved one been buried?" "Can we have a picture? An interview? An emotional crying moment? Do you have any orphans we can speak with?" The media is absolutely transfixed by the concept of 9/11 orphans. I become extremely possessive of the confidentiality of our list and family information. Our families have the right to grieve privately. If they want to share their grief or their story publically, that is their decision, but access to them will not be through me without their consent.

My protection of the confidentiality of family information extends beyond the media. We actively engage in partnering with other organizations to assist our families, but we keep our families information confidential.

Some of the organizations help in small but immensely meaningful ways. For example, 18-year-old Pamela Spitz's father William worked in government bonds and didn't survive 9/11. He and his daughter Pamela never missed a Mets opening day game—it was their father/daughter ritual going back as long as she could remember. Opening day usually fell on her birthday. Her father always got them Cantor's seats on the field level on the first base line. Opening day for the 2002 Mets game was sold out. Pamela called me in a panic. Could I please help her get tickets? I called Tuesday's Children, an organization that five brothers who lost their siblings at Cantor had established to help children by providing adults to take them to sporting events, and they secured tickets for her. She took her mother. Years later, I called Pamela to refresh my recollection. Without realizing, I got through to her 10 years later on her birthday, April 12th. Her mother froze when she saw "Cantor Fitzgerald" come up on the caller ID. Pamela, recounting a story she had forgotten because the first four years after 9/11 were a blur, says, "If I had any remains I would scatter them in the old Shea stadium."

We have culled our list of victims and are now identifying their next of kin. We are 657 victims until we lose Renée Barrett-Arjune, one of our four burn victims. Then we are 658. That number becomes etched into my mind and becomes part of who I am.

THE UNITED WAY,
THE RED CROSS AND OTHERS

At 658, Cantor Fitzgerald victims make up more than one-quarter of the New York casualties. The Relief Fund victims make up more than one-quarter of the total 9/11 deaths from all three locations. As hard as we are working and as fast as we are racing, we are still not set up to make monetary distributions on such a massive scale. Even Howard's initial million-dollar donation would have only amounted to $1,500 per Cantor family if we had a complete list of victims and their next of kin as well as the systems in place to begin making distributions. We need to get our families substantial assistance immediately until we are able to assist them on our own. Howard and I pow-wow in the middle of the night. We don't talk about Gary. There is no time. Howard sends his senior executives to Washington to meet with the Red Cross and the United Way. We are going to ask them to give our families money. This is an emergency. This is a necessity.

The United Way with NY Community Trust holds a star-studded concert telethon to raise money for the families of the September 11th victims. *America: A Tribute to Heroes* airs September 21st. That telethon alone raises over $200 million.[3] Combined with other high-profile fundraising events including the Verizon Music Festival in LA, the United Way, calling itself the September 11th Fund, is the recipient of approximately half a billion dollars.[4] When senior representatives from Cantor Fitzgerald, the company with the largest loss of life, request a meeting with the United Way in order to get help for its families, the United Way says no. They refuse assistance to the largest block of 9/11 families after raising $500 million from a generous public that wants to assist them. We are here, begging for help and, with hundreds of millions of dollars at the ready, they refuse to answer the door. We never received an explanation, but I believe they didn't assist us because though they raised money using the pathos of 9/11 victims' families, they spent the money as they would ordinary United Way funds.

The Red Cross, on the other hand, takes the meeting and agrees to help. We will create a one-page application for every victim for whom we have an identifiable next of kin, which will provide the Red Cross with all the information they need to make a distribution. No receipts or showing of special need will be required. It is understood that all of our families, no matter their economic strata, are in need. I, along with my volunteer Sharon Lefkowitz, will fill out the forms for each victim for whom we can verify the next of kin. We make the Red Cross sign a confidentiality agreement, promising they will not share the contact information of our families with anyone.

The Red Cross and the United Way are amazing marketers. When a tragedy strikes, they are the first presence asking for donations, under their own name, or a name created especially for the particular tragedy (in this case, the Liberty Fund and the September 11th Fund, respectively). At least with respect to 9/11 victim's families, they are not the charities that do the most good.

The Red Cross eventually came under severe criticism and scrutiny for not distributing funds donated for the 9/11 families,[5] but at least initially they did distribute $30,000 per Cantor Fitzgerald Relief Fund family for whom we provided an application. In June 2002, they also gave a one-time disbursement of $45,000 to the estate of each victim.[6] But, unlike the United Way, which chose not to assist the families, at least when the representative from the largest group of victims asked the Red Cross for emergency assistance, they gave it.

❧   ❧   ❧

"Victims" fraud, while surprising, is an issue that can't be ignored, and we work diligently to make sure that no one claims to be a victim or a recipient who isn't one. It isn't easy. We seek out the companies that were Cantor contractors and readily agree to assist them, but they must provide me with a verifiable list of their deceased and their next of kin. They do. Individual claims that someone is a contractor, but hasn't been identified with a particular company, are harder to gauge. I add them to my list, but put them in a separate category, awaiting verification. We get a call that someone on our list has been spotted. We are elated. We investigate and find that it isn't true. We are deflated. We have one victim who had three wives. None of them are lying, but neither do any of them know of the existence of the others. It's an issue I have to delicately confront with all involved. Some survivors who knew this victim claim that he never came in early. They do not believe that he is actually a victim, but rather got caught in a web of his own deceit and fled. I find myself hoping that they are right. Unfortunately, we never receive any evidence that he is alive.

We get a call from the police. They say that a woman by the name of Sandra Miranda has stolen the credit cards of and has been impersonating one of our victims, a beautiful young woman named Laura Gilly. I am outraged. Laura's parents deserve so much better than this. We cooperate fully with the police.[7] We do the same when a man named Brian Lynch goes to the Red Cross claiming to be a Cantor Fitzgerald employee and receives $800 from them.[8] Lynch is a very common last name among Cantor victims. We have four, two of whom are brothers, but none of them is a contractor named Brian.

ˇ ˇ ˇ

On September 28th, I am invited to a meeting hosted by the NY Carnegie Foundation of approximately 50 charity leaders to discuss what the charitable response to September 11th should be. I am sure of the date because I have to miss the funeral for Fred Varacchi, the president of eSpeed (Cantor's public company), in order to attend. All of the major charities are there: the Red Cross, the United Way, NY Times Neediest Foundation, FEMA, among others. These are the respected players in a world I am just learning about.

The upshot of the meeting is this: the definition of poverty in the United States is income of $16,000 a year or less. Since the vast majority (if not all) of 9/11 victims made more than $16,000 a year, any contribution made to a 9/11 family would not be to someone who is indigent. They raise concerns about whether a distribution to this class of people is appropriate. The collective wisdom is that they should "wait" and do nothing.

Excuse me? I am fit to be tied. I missed Fred's funeral for this? I cannot be cowed. I raise my hand and I say, "In this situation, I hold a position very different from the rest of you. My brother Gary was killed on 9/11 so I am a family member. My law firm was on the 101st floor of Tower One so I am a survivor as well as a small business owner. I also run a charity that represents more than a quarter of the World Trade Center victims, and I am quite sure that I am the only person at this table who is missing the funeral of a 9/11 victim to be here. And you are telling me that you are going to do *nothing* to help these people, because you are worried that they aren't below the poverty line?"

No one says a word. Later, I am privately thanked by the Red Cross representative for bringing a much needed dose of reality into the proceedings. Needless to say, I am never invited to another meeting.

After Howard comes back from Fred's funeral, I recount the meeting for him, in less than polite terms. I am shaking and furious. Howard calmly tells me not to worry. "It doesn't matter. Any requirement they are trying to come up with to say they can't distribute money to the 9/11 victims is absurd. We will try to get them to give the families money." We are not waiting, and we are not doing "nothing."

This has become a familiar dynamic between my brother Howard and me. When I come in raging about an injustice being done to our families, he will calmly go about fixing it. Howard understands that as long as it isn't life or death, it's a little thing.

Our charity is going to give money directly to the victims' families. Unlike the other charities, we never considered how we would "look." We considered only the daily growing need. In almost all circumstances, the major breadwinner in the household has died and the family needs immediate assistance.

SMALL BATTLES

"You have one message whose retention time is about to expire." "Hi, Edie-Pie. This is your brother, Gary…."

Oh my G-d. I'm about to lose his message. "Lewis, do we have a tape recorder? I need to record Gary's message. I am going to lose Gary's voice." We try to record the message on a small dictaphone. It is scratchy and barely recognizable. A friend calls and I am on the verge of hysteria. I play her Gary's message over the phone and she tries to record it. Same result. Barely audible. She calls Gary's home phone and tries to record his outgoing message on her tape recorder. Nothing works. I call Howard's designated "get it done" guy Kent in a panic. "Kent, when is Gary's phone being turned off? I'm going to lose Gary's voice, I can't lose him again." If I'm about to lose Gary's message on my cell phone, what about the outgoing message on his telephone? What about the "Hi, this is so and so, leave a message" on every victim's phone? These phones are all going to be shut off if they haven't been already. Kent starts calling the phone companies. He gets Verizon to agree that they will record the messages left by the 9/11 victims and send each family member a tape recording of their loved one's message. This may seem like a little thing, but for the affected families it is a huge win at a time when not much feels like a win. "Hi, Edie-Pie. This is your brother, Gary…" Ahhhhhhhhh.

Physically, the long hours and emotionally charged days are taking a huge toll on me, but there is so much to be done and I can't stop. The vomiting that started almost immediately after 9/11 hasn't stopped. My body is on automatic pilot. Everyone who works for me is used to my bolting for the bathroom without explanation. I live in Gary's sweaters. They are oversized and I am dwarfed within them, but I will not wear anything else. It is the only way that I can try to feel him around me. I have dropped more than 20 pounds. The last time I was this thin was after a car accident in 1986. I am not the only one. The 9/11 families are getting thinner and gaunter by the moment, and we are not wearing it well. It is what is expected of grief, which runs on its own time.

Everyone is looking for that "something" that will ease the pain. It isn't food and it isn't sleep. Family members start showing up at my office to work for me. They want to help. They think it will be cathartic. It's the opposite. We are working with lists of the dead that include the name of the person they love. I try to dissuade them from helping because they will be facing reminders of their loss. Most don't last even an hour. Usually, family members who come end up sitting and talking to me for the majority of their time in the office.

A distraught mother comes in. Her son wasn't married for very long before 9/11 and now she is being completely shut out of the funeral arrangements. She wants to know whether I can get her notification of when her son's wife receives remains. She pleads with me. I listen helplessly. Legally, she is not the next of kin. There isn't much I can do except to call the daughter-in-law and try to broker a peace.

In families where the mothers and wives didn't get along very well when the son was alive, communication is very difficult at times. Now that the peacemaker is gone, the reasons to be civil are gone as well. Some are rising above their complaints. Some are vanquishing with an iron fist. Regardless of whether they are next of kin, every family member is important and every issue one that needs to be resolved.

Only three family members of victims can handle working at the Relief Fund, and all of them are siblings. Cindy Morgenstern is a slight, freckled, absolutely adorable young design student. She offered her assistance at one of Howard's town hall meetings and he sent her to me. Cindy can handle it. Her sister Nancy worked for Cantor's travel agent before coming to the firm. Nancy was so beloved by all the brokers she worked for, that one of them finally convinced her to leave her job and come and work for him instead. It's tough to watch Cindy, because I knew Nancy and it's easy to see her personality in her sister. But she fights through her tears and is determined. Day after day she shows up. Alongside Lewis, she helps organize the charitable bulk mail system.

The first time they bring letters to the post office, the postal inspector wants to reject them. We don't realize that there is an incredibly labor intensive and arcane set of rules applied to bulk mail. Lewis says, "Forget it. I'll take care of it." His work will save us money in postage but the man hours involved are onerous.

I tell Howard that we really need computers and I have not been successful at getting any donated. Cantor comes through again, and we get about 30 laptops. Now we can really start working. I get a fourth room from Fish & Neave. This is the computer programming room. We get volunteers from Anderson and from Microsoft and expertise from Cisco. They, along with Debbie Click from Fish & Neave, start building us computer systems. This is incredibly important, not least because this is something I do not have the expertise to accomplish myself. Barbara Lamb has a computer software background so she is also instrumental in making sure the programs do exactly what I need done. Basically, I tell Barbara what I need and she articulates it in computerese to Debbie. These amazing people start designing us five systems simultaneously.

First, Debbie leads the team to design us a website to harness all the information we have about the families. We call it the Family Database. We need to record the name of the victim, the next of kin, their address (remember, unless they are married, the address of the victim is now irrelevant), whether there are children and if so how old they are, the name and address of the parents, and then a place for notes and comments. I am discovering with horror just how many sets of multiple victims from a single family Cantor has—22. And how many children lost parents—805. We also need to record which company the victim worked for, as we are assisting Cantor Fitzgerald, eSpeed, TradeSpark (all Cantor companies), Euro Brokers, and all of Cantor's contractors and visitors. The health insurance list becomes invaluable in creating our master list. When I look on the health care list and see that there are insured children at different addresses, I realize that quite a few of our victims have ex-wives with children, as well as children from their current marriage. It doesn't take long for the ex-wives to start calling because, in many cases, the deceased was the major financial support in that family as well. I talk to Howard and tell him that we have victims with multiple families who need to be covered. We decide that we will not divide the payments between the families. We will support both families even though they are from the same victim.

This is an expensive decision. Howard has committed 25 percent of profits for five years with a minimum of $100,000 per family. By deciding that the ex-wife's children and the current wife and children are to be covered, that victim's "family" will receive at least $200,000 in cash and both families will receive health insurance for 10 years. We will be covering way more than 658 Cantor families.

Carol Parks, the sister of Robert Parks, has an accounting background and is my second sibling volunteer. Carol is one of four Parks siblings, all of whom are extremely accomplished. The oldest, David, was a bond trader and gave Cantor a lot of business and had relationships with many of its employees. When his brother Robert wanted a new job, David sent him to interview at Cantor, where Robert was hired in 2000. Devout Irish Catholics, the Parks family learned the value of education and philanthropy from their parents. When they realized how far-reaching the devastation at Cantor went, Carol pushed her personal grief into the background and said, "We have to help them." Betsy, the youngest sibling, took over coordinating the bureaucracy surrounding the death of their brother. Carol's husband went down to the WTC to hand out water and food. Carol, a recently retired VP for Chase, comes to us. She helps me learn what information I will need to keep track of.

The second database is to record donations. We have to be able to keep track of every donation we receive, whether cash, check or credit card, and send everyone a thank-you note. If someone makes a donation in a deceased person's name, we want to notify the family and apprise them of this kindness. To this point we have just been copying checks and correspondence. This database will also have to generate my as-yet-unwritten thank-you letters. I will also have to figure out how to coordinate with our call centers to generate thank-you notes for their donors as well. Normally a charity would be concentrating on harvesting the information about their donors so that they could ask for additional funds. I'm not thinking that far ahead. At this point I am still reacting to things as they come up.

The third team designs a bulk mail system for us that will make that process easier. When you are a charity and 100 percent of all you receive in donations goes directly to the recipients (in addition to profit sharing with the families, Howard decided that Cantor will cover our expenses so every dollar donated goes to the families without any deductions), the cost of anything is an issue. Mail can get very expensive when you have to send out tens of thousands of letters.

Next, we need an inventory system for the donations of material goods. There are different rules for the donation of "things." Thank-you letters matter to me and I want to send one to everyone, regardless of the size of the donation.

The last system is a password-driven website for our families. We use it to communicate any goods, services, support groups or financial resources available to them through us and others.

Additionally, the Cantor IT team has set up a Family Tribute site. Howard has a college friend whose younger brother Andy wanted to go into investment banking and Howard therefore hired him. At Andy Kates's memorial service, his wife asked attendees to write a memory of Andy on a card that she could keep for their children when they grew up. That experience was the impetus behind this site. The family tribute site allows people who want to write something to or about a Cantor victim, or send a note to the family, to do so. I become the arbiter of questionable material that people want to post. Like the television images, however, this hits too close to home for me, and I can't look at the site.

When the donation system is finished, I march into the big conference room and announce, "Everybody stop what you are doing. We are all doing data entry." Twenty thousand files must be created before we can even think about thank-you letters. The volunteers galvanize and we sit at every available laptop and do data entry around the clock for a week.

This is when I get my third sibling volunteer, George Stergiopolous. George's brother Andrew worked for Cantor, and George looks a bit like him. George's hair dips down almost over one eye; he has a swagger to his walk and an embracing personality. He comes to me because he feels a need to be around people who understand what he is going through. Two days a week he is mine, and he instantly bonds with my core volunteers. Everyone tackles data entry, and when we get bleary eyed, someone relieves us, but we don't stop. We have to catch up to at least make the process manageable.

By the end of September, Debbie Click and the computer room have almost finished designing our Family Database. And we have manually finished our master list of victims and have identified and located their next of kin.

BEARS

In addition to receiving letters, cards and donations, we receive pins and quilts, books and CDs, flags, clothing new and used. People are incredibly generous and they send us whatever they can think of. Mostly, however, we receive teddy bears. The teddy bear has become an unofficial symbol of 9/11.

The country saw the ticker running along the bottom of the TV screen in the days following 9/11 identifying victims as being from Cantor Fitzgerald. The average person may not have known that 658 people died at Cantor, but they knew there were a lot. So people sent a lot of teddy bears. They came in all different shapes and sizes, from Beanie Babies on up to difficult-to-carry. Ultimately, every usable bear and donated item went to a family member. If they couldn't be used by the Cantor families, we donated the items to other charities that needed them.

One day, Fish & Neave's receptionist and our lifeline to the outside world tells me that there is a truck delivery for us and the drivers are coming up. I have absolutely no idea what she is talking about. I am expecting no one. A husband and a wife have driven a truck across their home state of Michigan collecting teddy bears—for us—and they are now here with thousands of them. I send every volunteer I have down to the loading dock to bring up teddy bears. It is then that my focus shifts from mail, which we pretty much have in hand, to warehouses. I am hugging and thanking these wonderful people, and all I am thinking is that I need to find a home for these teddy bears until I can figure out how to get them to our families, and before this respectable law firm throws us out on our butts.

Several friends join the fund, including one who defers the start date on her new job, as do people we bring on who sent us letters. Lewis is in charge of operations and interfaces constantly with Fish & Neave's director of operations to get us whatever we need. My volunteers, including me, are—after all—unpaid and we work nonstop.

To house the bears, I delegate the task of getting warehouse space donated to one of the volunteers—there is just no room in our cramped Fish & Neave quarters for all of these bears. Along with warehouse space we find a truck company willing to donate transportation.

Alongside the generosity comes the reality of working with a volunteer force. Fish & Neave's receptionist brings to my attention that one of our volunteers has been stealing food and the condiments from the kitchen. When we confront the volunteer and she justifies the thefts with the logic of her donation of time, it alarms me. This is only the fourth volunteer of 300 that we have had to let go, but it sets off a red flag about our potential financial vulnerability.

We are dealing with a lot of money and, with the exception of my friends, the vast majority of our help is transient.

I call Howard and I tell him I need a bonded and known Cantor employee to be in charge of our books, accounting and money. He sends us Ari Schonbrun. I didn't know Ari before 9/11, but he worked for Cantor as an accountant.

SURVIVORS

Of the 960 people employed by Cantor at 8:46 am on September 11th, Ari Schonbrun is one of only 302 survivors. He was on the 78th floor of the North Tower, on his way up to his office on the 101st floor, the same floor I worked on, when the plane hit. The 78th floor was the elevator exchange. You took one elevator from the lobby to 78 and then changed to a different elevator to ride to the upper floors. Ari was running late, so he took a slightly shorter route by taking the elevators all the way on the right side of the lobby. This bank was farther from the connecting elevators that took you to the floors in the 100s that he needed to take up to Cantor's offices. As he walked straight ahead, everyone else entered the elevators they needed for floors in the 80s or 90s. He was alone in the hallway. When he was about eight feet from his connecting elevator, the building shook, the lights went out, smoke came pouring toward him and he was thrown to the floor.

At the same time, Virginia DiChiara, Renée Barrett-Arjune and a non-Cantor employee, Roy Bell, were in an elevator. The doors started to close but remained open about a foot. The cable snapped, the elevator walls and ceiling collapsed. Jet fuel came down the shaft and ignited off the sparking cable. The three passengers jumped through a wall of fire onto the 78th floor lobby. Renée Barrett-Arjune was the last one out. Ari saw Virginia DiChiara walking toward him. Her arms, hair and clothing were badly burned. Her face was not. She managed to put her hands over her face as she squeezed through fire and "dropped and rolled" out of the elevator. The fire warden on the floor directed them to a stairwell on the left. Virginia, our fourth burn victim, fighting through excruciating pain, walked very, very slowly, with Ari's constant coaching, down 78 flights of stairs. Virginia refused to let her ambulance leave unless Ari was with her. Virginia saved Ari's life, because had he not gone with her, he would have been crushed when the building collapsed.

Now, Ari takes us in hand and sets up books, checks and balances, reviews our computer program and makes us compliant. I breathe a sigh of relief.

˅   ˅   ˅

Howard and I go and see the apartment Gary bought downtown. As we walk through the loft, which Gary had already started deconstructing, Howard looks out the north windows of the apartment toward the Empire State Building and says, "You know, Edie, the only person that this apartment is more perfect for than Gary is you." I'm not sure I agree with him, but I know that Gary loved this place and even though he never got a chance to live in it, I can't give it up. This is where his dreams reside. We go up onto the roof. The apartment has east, west and north views. The wrap-around view is interrupted by a high fence on the southward side. When Gary bought the loft this fence wasn't there. He commented that he could see the World Trade Center from his apartment. That view is now blocked. Howard and I are both glad. If the apartment had a south-facing view, I don't think I could live here.

TOGETHER

Howard decides that we should have a memorial service for all of the Cantor victims, now that we know who they all are. He charges Kent Karosen to pull it all together. He plans the entire memorial from his apartment as a labor of love. He has worked for Cantor before; in fact, Kent's father and Bernie Cantor, the firm's deceased founder, were friends. You could say that Cantor Fitzgerald is in Kent's blood. He started working for Howard as an intern in the summer of 1987 and is now a partner. Kent, like Howard, knows many, many people who died on 9/11. He was a friend of Gary, among countless others.

The memorial service will be held on October 1, 2001 at Summer Stage in Central Park. If I am involved in any of the planning, I don't remember. Like many others, I am still operating on autopilot. I do know that I get all of the volunteers to "work" the memorial. We bring truckloads of teddy bears and quilts to Central Park. We help set up the chairs and we place a donated quilt on the back of each and a bear on every seat. It warms up the main tent, which faces the stage and now contains thousands of teddy-bear-laden chairs. People who are grieving need something to grasp and I think the teddy bears will help. Kent has rented two additional tents. We are expecting a lot of people but none of us is sure just how many. The two secondary tents contain boards with the names of all of our loved ones on them. Grief counselors are in attendance and clearly visible for anyone in need. Tissues and water are everywhere. There are small sandwiches and beautiful flowers. The volunteers will also be working registration and greeting our families. We all go home to change.

October 1st is a Monday and the weather isn't bad. Our service is a closed one. Only family, friends and colleagues are invited. We do not invite the press or cameras.

I stoically walk into the service with Lewis and Gary's best friend Pat Troy, a long-time Cantor employee. Everyone is dressed in black. I meet up with my brother and kiss him. We start greeting the families. There are a lot of people here. I introduce myself to those I don't know and greet the ones I do. I hug each and every one of them.

And then, as I am walking into the main tent, I see them—Cantor employees Anthony Larocco and Gene Arbeeny. Our victim list has so many names on it. I knew Anthony and Gene only by their first names, and we have victims with those first names. I thought they were dead. I take in their faces, burst into tears and run into Gene's arms. If he is taken aback, he has the good grace to hide it. I move my hand first down his and then down Anthony's face, much like I patted Howard's on September 11th, and every time I see him.

My office was on the 101st floor of the North Tower. My small labor firm focused on the rights of hotel employees denied their gratuities. Howard had given me office space within Cantor's offices. Everyone knew me because I was the boss's sister, but I didn't know many people. Gene, however, is a security guard and Anthony works in operations. I saw them all the time so I knew them both.

It never occurred to me before actually seeing their faces that they had a later work shift. Gene and Anthony were both scheduled to work the 3 to 11 pm shift on September 11th, so they are alive. Their faces are a small miracle. They tell me that they both still work for Cantor. I know that every time I see them, I will consider their lives a gift and I will hug them.[9]

Howard is up on the stage. I sit between Lewis and Pat. The NYPD Honor Guard posts the colors. The Boys Choir of Harlem sings "We Shall Overcome" and I lock eyes with my brother. We will get through this. We have to.

Family members Nancy Shea, Maura Coughlin (children in tow), Joan Kirwin and Eileen Varacchi tell us about their husbands—what good men they were, what good fathers. Sam Ellis tells us about his beautiful and accomplished wife Valerie Silver-Ellis.

Mayor Giuliani is there to speak. As he is sitting up on the stage, he turns to my brother with an incredulous face and says, "Look at all these people." Six hundred and fifty-eight deaths translate to more than 5,000 suffering people. And those are just the ones who are here.

Howard speaks. It is the most emotional I have ever heard my brother. He tells the crowd that in the past three weeks we have felt more pain than we ever thought we could bear. He talks about how we miss our friends and family and that they are a part of us. He says that he has experienced more love from friends and from the families than he ever thought possible, and that he has received hundreds, or even thousands of calls from family members. He says that the calls were so extraordinary because the family members, despite their losses, were trying to make him feel better. A wife in her 30s called to tell him how much her husband loved working at Cantor and how they have to carry on. He says that now we are superhuman, walking a foot above the ground. He thanks everyone for their hugs and kisses, because "without those hugs there is no chance I could go on." He shares the strong commitment of the survivors who, with one voice, came together with a unified message that they loved their friends and family. So they "bound together as one person and they came up with the view that we would go on for all of those we lost." He thanks the volunteers and clients, too many to name.

He tells a story about one client who, when Cantor opened its equities business on Monday, and limited trading to one trade per account because they were unaware of the degree of their fragility said, "We're giving you every order we have or I'm going to lose my job." Cantor was almost killed with kindness.

Then he tells the families about what I had seen, over and over again, the outpouring of love and support from America. Howard shares how the entire eighth grade class in a Boise, Idaho school wrote letters of love and encouragement to us. He goes on to say that each division within Cantor, eSpeed and TradeSpark were extremely close. That is why we lost over 20 sets of relatives, because "you brought your friends and relatives to work with you so that we could all succeed together."

Howard is apologetic about his failings, and commits to stay connected to us for the rest of his life. He says, his voice choking on his emotion, that he could not be more proud to be associated with the families of those we lost and that it is an honor to speak for the survivors. He means every word. We are going to build a Cantor community out of a sea of strangers whose only thing in common is that their loved ones perished while working together at the same company. The Cantor employees and survivors read the names of our dead, their friends.

I see Stephen Merkel and wonder where he finds the strength to recite the names of his cousin, friends and colleagues. He is Cantor's general counsel, and he survived because he was in the elevator. He heard a loud crashing noise, and the elevator dropped to the lobby level. When the doors opened automatically, a ball of fire raced by him. He is lucky to have escaped with his life and he never forgets it. Neither do his wife and children. When Howard made it to Stephen's apartment on September 11th, Stephen's shirt was covered in blood that didn't belong to him. His strength humbles me. I look around and people are frantically clutching at teddy bears. The sounds of crying abound, but we are all listening intently. There are just so many names. Some of the names are easy to pronounce: Cahill, Smith, Lynch. Some of them are extremely difficult: Boryczewski, Varadhan, Katsimatides. I have spoken to some families and know that some of the pronunciations aren't exactly correct. The names are being read from a place of love and no one minds, but I make a silent note to try to figure out how to do it better next time.

Kent has done a great job. The service is reverent and beautiful and strikes just the right tone. But we are miserable and, even surrounded by people, we still feel alone and lonely. There is just no getting around that. Survival is an uphill battle.

Years later a family member told me that the bear on her seat at the memorial, like so many of them, had a note attached to it. Hers was from a nine-year-old girl. Our family member contacted the little girl to say thank you and they remain in touch to this day.

ᵛ　ᵛ　ᵛ

Back at the Relief Fund, I am ready. We have a defined list of the dead. We know who the next of kin are, and where they are located. I have opened a bank account and have a new large corporate checkbook that says "The Cantor Fitzgerald Relief Fund" on the checks. We have created a temporary logo for stationary. It is our name in front of the stars on the American flag, and in large letters it says, "For Families of the Victims of the World Trade Center Disaster."

Cantor's equity business is back up and running, headed by Phil Marber and driven by branch offices across the county. Howard and Phil have been hiring dozens of equity traders and salespeople, trying to rebuild Cantor's New York presence. It will be the equity business of Cantor and the U.S. government bond business of eSpeed along with Cantor's London office that start to provide the profits that will be dispersed by the Relief Fund to the families.

Howard and I decide that we will stick to our original goal to give our families money directly—distributing to each family without question. Things have never been done this way before, but Howard has changed the way things are done. My admiration for my brother is profound. I agree with him and take our analysis a step further. I am not Solomon. I don't believe that our victims' next of kin ceased knowing their family's needs because their spouse was murdered. I won't supplant them in their decision making. We will distribute all the money as it comes in. If families need money for college (which in theory they don't because Howard has gotten the tristate governors to agree to make college tuition free for 9/11 victims' children), then they will save the money. The monetary decisions were their job before 9/11 and it is their job now. We decide that the first distribution of checks will be for $5,000, and they will go to families with a child under the age of one. I write every check by hand. I use a green highlighter and run it through the name of every family that gets a check on my master list.

It is October 4, 2001 and we have sent out our first round of checks. Three weeks ago we didn't exist. Three weeks ago we didn't need to.

THE FACTS

She is the wife of Paul Fiori. Before this moment, I only know her as his next of kin. Her name is familiar to me because I have just sent her a check as part of our first check run. It is October 5th and very angry phone calls are coming in because of what we have done to, or not done for, Lynda Fiori. Neither I, nor any of the volunteers have any idea what is going on. Lewis and I didn't leave the office last night until after 2 am. I call over to Howard's offices to ask whether anyone there knows.

Apparently, when Bill O'Reilly failed to get Howard to come onto his show, his producers found a Cantor widow. In a nutshell, she said that she had called Howard's house, that no one ever called her back, that she gave notice of her husband's funeral service and no one from the firm attended and that she never received any information or money from the firm. O'Reilly then disgustedly painted my brother as a huckster and a fraud. I listen to this recitation in disbelief and sadness. Howard has promised to give 25 percent of the profits of the company to the families for five years and pay for health insurance for her and her children for 10. Did she call the Relief Fund and somehow we missed the call? Didn't we post her husband's funeral along with all the other Cantor funerals on our site? The firm paid full payroll on September 15th. Even if Cantor had been able to continue paychecks, families would not have received another one until October 1st. How could she not have received the $5,000 check from us? What about the $30,000 we assisted in getting distributed from the Red Cross and the $100,000 life insurance checks that Howard guaranteed which had been distributed at the crisis center?

Phil Marber ran equities. His department lost 114 people on 9/11. Phil spoke to Lynda. "Okay," I think, "This is all a misunderstanding." "O'Reilly is a jerk for unfoundedly attacking my brother, but this is all nonsense." Everybody back to work.

Unfortunately, we can't. Angry phone calls, emails and faxes are coming in, and they are getting more vitriolic by the minute. They grind the Relief Fund to a halt as one volunteer after another fields unkind and sometimes obscene calls. One particularly irate fax was addressed to me: "You dirty Jew. When was the last time you let a cop or fireman into your highfalutin country club. I hope you die." I stop everyone from answering phones and I call a meeting to discuss what to do about this. The calls are becoming more and more threatening and I'm now worried about the safety of both myself and Howard. I'd like to say that I'm particularly calm through this, but I'm not.

I'm quite sure I call Howard crying hysterically. Juliet says, "Edie, they are calling and asking for their money back. What am I supposed to tell them?" I snap back at her to "ask them which 9/11 widow with a child under one year of age they would like me to take the money back from?" We field pounding call after pounding call.

There are families in intense pain and this is what I have to deal with? While O'Reilly is lambasting my brother, everything Lynda Fiori is complaining about falls within my purview. I am overwhelmed, frustrated, angry, sleep deprived and hurt. I miss Gary soooo much and I have failed to protect Howard. *What the hell am I doing here? How is this my life?* I tell Howard that I don't want to do this. I have not helped him. I want to stop. I want to quit.

Once again, Howard is rational. He understands that people need someone to be angry at, and he's become that person. Howard will not go on *O'Reilly* (which is really all they want) to defend himself, even though O'Reilly will continue to adjudicate him "questionable" for choosing not to appear. O'Reilly wants someone to be angry at. Instead of choosing Osama bin Laden, he chooses my brother and goes after him relentlessly. When Phil Marber, who knew Lynda's husband well and had hired him, calls O'Reilly to tell him that of course he and other Cantor employees had attended Paul's funeral, and that he personally had offered to pay her bills, O'Reilly neither responds nor changes his tune. When it becomes clear that we are sending out money, O'Reilly continues to make it seem as if $5,000 is an insignificant sum, without ever acknowledging that 658 victims means we have sent out a total of $3.2 million.

Howard will continue to communicate his positions through his actions. I do the only thing I can do. I get back on the phones. One family at a time, one enraged donor at a time, I'm going to fix this media-manufactured problem.

Subsequently, I learned that many of the widows moved in with their parents after their husbands died. We were calling and sending letters to the only name and address we had from our insurance records, but they weren't there. Lynda Fiori didn't know there was $135,000 and the promise of $100,000 more sitting in her mailbox at home.

Then Rosie O'Donnell jumps on the *O'Reilly* bandwagon and vilifies Howard and Cantor in her magazine *Rosie*. The worst televised pillory, however, comes from Connie Chung on *20/20* on October 10, 2001.

After *O'Reilly*, it became clear that all of our families had not received word of Cantor's commitment despite our best efforts to communicate the plan. Howard went on *20/20* to lay out the coverage that would result in a minimum of $130 million being distributed to the Cantor families.

Connie Chung had other ideas. Instead of highlighting all the economic support Cantor would be providing, she spun a tale of Howard as a hardnosed business man who "cut off" paychecks and feigned emotion. He had cried more than once on television and she didn't believe he was sincere.

Howard thought he had gone on television to tell the families that they need not worry financially. Instead, *20/20* edited and twisted his story into a "bad news" story. Our family and friends all watch the show together and we are flabbergasted. The show's first 12 minutes are unmercifully brutal. Connie Chung, it turns out, had gone to seek out widows who did not know about Cantor's plan. When she found family members who knew what Cantor was doing, she dismissed them. She wanted only women who weren't living at home. At the very end of the segment, Ms. Chung tells the families of the plan, and one woman, Anne Wodenshek, starts crying and apologizes. I am furious, but when I speak to Howard he is okay. He says, "Did you see that? Did you see the bounce? They like the plan."

The world that turned topsy-turvy on 9/11 refuses to right itself. Howard and I continue to do what we have been doing but I have developed a healthy distrust of the media. I tell my brother that he should stay away from reporters.

Out in the world, life is returning to normal, but there is no normalcy for me. Gary's best friend Patrick Troy, Lewis and I have gone to a restaurant to discuss Gary's memorial service. The boisterousness is disconcerting to me and I have a difficult time handling it. Pat says that there are two people at the bar who would like to say hello. They are long-standing Cantor clients in from Chicago to attend the Cantor Memorial service. Pat brings me over to meet them and they tell me that they are sorry for my loss and that they too have lost friends who were their individual brokers. They then hand me checks they have written to the Relief Fund for over $5,000. I am genuinely touched.

On October 7th, the war in Afghanistan begins. Osama bin Laden in a pre-recorded interview said, "I say these events have split the whole world into two camps: the camp of the faithful and the camp of the infidels. Every Muslim should support his religion."[10]

We hold a memorial service for Gary at the 92nd Street Y in Manhattan on October 8th. About 800 people are there. The service is closed to the press, but, unbeknownst to Howard and me as we exit the car to enter the service, we are being filmed. Howard's driver has an enlarged posterboard-size photo of Gary that will be displayed on the stage at the front of the auditorium. As the driver is holding the photograph, an uncharacteristically strong wind kicks up and blows Gary's likeness down Lexington Avenue. Howard's driver is chasing Gary down the block. Howard and I look at each other in disbelief. It is abundantly clear that Gary is not ready to go. His picture is finally caught and placed on the front of the stage.

The memorial service begins. Gary's two best friends, Pat Troy and Peter Farmer, speak, as does Howard. I then talk about how with the death of our parents so young and so close together, and the trials Gary faced, that he had every excuse to not become an extraordinary human being. But at some point Gary decided that he would not allow the bad things that had happened in his life define him. He rose above them, made his own choices and took responsibility for his actions.

After my mother died of cancer in 1978, and my father a year and a half later, Gary was only 14. I took over raising him. He lived with me and went to high school while I went to law school. He was like a son to me as well as a brother. And, just like with Howard, the older and more successful he became, the younger I got in his eyes. At some point, all roles reversed and I had two older brothers instead of two younger ones. I looked out at the crowd and saw Elise Fraser, a close friend of Howard and Allison, who also lost her brother at Cantor on 9/11. I locked eyes with her, because to me, she looked like she was drowning. I charged her, and everyone in that room, to rise above this and become extraordinary. I walked right off the stage, straight into the bathroom and threw up.

Lewis, who has a beautiful voice, sings the Michael Jackson song "You Are Not Alone" (with lyrics that I altered slightly), accompanied by a friend on the sax. At the end of the song, Lewis raises his hand, as if he has a glass and says, "To Gary." The memorial service ends and Gary is "officially dead."

We are blindsided when friends start calling about a *Larry King Live* trailer for October 9th with Gary's ex-girlfriend Ann slated to be on the show. She is discussing their doomed love affair because of the collapse of the towers. This is inaccurate because Gary had broken up with Ann several weeks before. It is being billed as a dramatic "love and loss" story. When we learn that Ann will be playing a tape recording of Gary's call to her from the World Trade Center, Allison and I become very upset. We implore the producers to not play the tape. They proceed anyway. And we are horrified. Because anyone who listens to Gary's tape will substitute their loved one into his place, or try to figure out if their loved one is one of the voices you can hear around him. While Gary may be calm, the activity around him is frenetic. Smoke is pouring in. People are screaming and trying to close vents and doors.

> *GARY LUTNICK, VICTIM OF WTC: Hey, baby. It's me. I'm in the World Trade Center and—a plane hit this building and I'm on the 104th floor and it's filling up with smoke. I love you very much, and I'm sorry that we had to go through what it is that we went through. Oh, my God. My life is probably going to end very, very shortly. I love you, baby. Bye-bye.*

> *UNIDENTIFIED MALE: Let's go. Hold the vents. Is there any vents in here?*

> *UNIDENTIFIED MALE: No. Close the door.*

> *LUTNICK: Bye, baby. Bye.* [11]

As Larry King congratulates Ann on coming forward, and she is telling people to "live each day with passion," I know with a certainty that chills my bones that no one who loved someone in the towers and hears that tape is going to be sleeping tonight. I wonder how I am going to undo the damage she has done.

Even though Gary was home in bed at the time, in her interview Ann claimed to have called his office phone in the early morning hours of September 11th and left him a message agreeing to marry him. I now know from firsthand experience how easily a person can manufacture themselves as a fiancé. Throughout this process I noticed that people aggrandized their relationships with the deceased. It seemed to make it more about the person left behind than the departed. It was almost as if "I knew him slightly," or "She was a nice person" would not be enough to garner the speaker sympathy.

Howard and I have previously discussed the issue of fiancés, domestic partners and same sex couples and we have decided to cover them. This is not a small thing. We have 49 fiancés. The direct cash commitment to them will top $6 million, and then Cantor will pay for health care for each of them for 10 years.

Howard's pledge to assist the families of 658 victims covers significantly more than 658 families. In a situation where there is a fiancé, we are also financially assisting the parents, because the victim was still technically single. That means covering two families. The same holds true for families whose victim was divorced with children and became engaged to someone else. We cover the children from the first marriage, the parents and the fiancé, so this victim created three distinct family units. We try to be inclusive rather than exclusive.

Fiancés are a thorny issue. We decide that if the parents of the deceased are willing to acknowledge the existence of the fiancé, it is sufficient. This is the case with most, but where there is an issue, we require the fiancé to provide proof of one of the following things: insurance for an engagement ring, a contract from the hall or wedding ceremony location, or bills from the residence of the deceased in the name of the domestic partner. This works well for us in all circumstances except one.

We have one fiancé who actually becomes very vocal for fiancé rights and has fairly regular contact with us. I get press calls asking for fiancés and I ask her if she would like to do any media interviews. She readily agrees. Shortly thereafter, I get a call from the victim's mother, who says to me, "X was my son's girlfriend. She is not my son's fiancé. I have checked with all of his closest friends and none of them knows anything about his being engaged to her. I didn't mind her making her relationship with my son more important than it was at the beginning, but there are so many families who need money and it just isn't right for her to be taking money that belongs to them." Uh oh. The mother is recanting. I call the young woman in, and explain that I am going to need proof of her engagement. The mother is adamant and angry. She calls repeatedly. I tell the victim's girlfriend that I'm sorry, but unless she can deliver satisfactory proof, which she has been unable to do, I won't be able to continue to honor her claim as a fiancé.

HIERARCHIES

Howard has been holding town hall meetings to keep the families informed about what we are doing on their behalf. I go with him. My role is to comfort, but also to fix whatever problems they are having, to fill every unfilled hole. If one person is having a problem, it is almost assured that others are as well. We go to locations in Manhattan, Staten Island, Westchester, Long Island, New Jersey and Connecticut. Howard always gives my name and the Relief Fund phone number. He tells the families that he is committed to expediting bonuses and commissions that the families are expecting, despite the fact that the firm has lost all of its profits. Cantor will begin paying them by October 22nd. He tells them about the 25 percent of profits and 10 years of health care, which will be in addition to bonuses. Some of the families tell me that they have enough money right now and that I should remove their names from my distribution list so that there is more money available for others. I am deeply moved by this. I run a pink highlighter through those names and mark them ineligible. I do the same through Gary's name.

I am asked to help families with the plethora of paperwork and requirements that are coming at them from all directions. Setting up support groups in outlying areas and making them more specific to individual groups and needs becomes one of my tasks. I am asked to keep family members who are not next of kin in the loop, and to resolve issues between them and the next of kin. I am informed that some of our grandparents are going to sue in order to be able to see children, or try to stop daughters-in-law from moving. I am asked whether parents of married victims will receive any support, because they are not the next of kin and not legally dependent, but their child took care of them. We decide we will try to figure out a way to assist them as well. I take contact information everywhere we go.

I am asked to help with death certificates, estates and remains. I am told about wedding rings, watches, pictures, and asked to help with the location and/or return of personal effects that the loved one had in the World Trade Center. I am asked about checks, and helping establish charities in loved ones' names. I am asked to help with a child who needs to live with neighbors now that her custodial parent is gone.

Each conversation brings forward a heretofore unaddressed issue or concern. Over and over again, Howard tells the families to call his sister, and that she will take care of it. I will be the consistent voice on the other end of the phone if a family member calls. In an unstable time, I represent stability. My list grows and my involvement in the daily lives of the victims' families increases. And always, I hug them. I absorb their tears. We are building a community of Cantor families, one family at a time. We can't worry about the naysayers. There is just too much to be done.

On October 12th, NBC anchorman Tom Brokaw's assistant tests positive for anthrax, and it is believed it was transmitted through the U.S. mail.[12] The amount has decreased, but we are still getting significant deliveries of unsolicited mail every day. Barbara Lamb is with another volunteer when she opens a suspicious letter. It comes in a plain white envelope with no return address. Inside there is nothing but gibberish letters and numbers. It doesn't contain visible powder, but she and the other volunteer are afraid. I decide that lots of people opening mail in a conference room is no longer a good idea. We get masks and gloves, and I require anyone that is going to open mail to wear them. I won't allow my volunteers to assume a risk I do not assume myself, so I move them into my office.

We don't receive anything else suspicious at work, but I get something at home. I receive a bulky letter in handwriting I don't recognize and a stamp I've never seen before. I open it without thinking and when I see what it is, I get concerned. It has multiple pages that have obviously been copied. Most of it is in Arabic, but the parts that are in English are hateful. There is white powder in the envelope. I call the police. Two officers from the hate crimes unit come to my apartment. They tell me that they have seen this letter before and it has been sent out to "prominent" people. I wonder how I have managed to fall into that category. They tell me that I have gotten lucky, because some of the letters have powder in them (which is harmless), but others have feces. They take the letter and tell me that they will analyze it, but that they don't think I should worry about it. But clearly, I don't like that I have now received hate mail at my home address. I never hear anything further from the officers and I don't receive anything else.

On October 20th, the Robin Hood Foundation puts on the star-studded "Concert for New York City" to benefit all September 11th victims' families. It is a joint event of VH1, Cablevision and Miramax, and is spearheaded by Paul McCartney. More than 60 performers play for four hours. Six thousand prime tickets are given to the police, firefighters and EMTs free of charge.[13] The same courtesy is not extended to our families. They raise almost $36 million. I recognize and respect the sacrifice of the police and firefighters, but I find myself getting worried. Mayor Giuliani has raised $500 million for the uniformed service victims through his Twin Towers Fund, and the Widows and Orphans Fund, which also only benefits uniformed service workers, is not far behind. This Robin Hood concert, which is said to benefit all victims of 9/11, is being geared toward the uniformed services. On November 16th, Jimmy Buffet will also hold a concert to benefit the 9/11 police and firefighter families. When a uniformed service worker dies in the line of duty, the family continues to receive his or her pension. There is no break in financial support. I wonder whether any charitable organizations will assist the civilians in a comparable way so that their financial needs and surrounding insecurities will be addressed. So far, with the exception of the minor commitment from the Red Cross, I feel like I'm out here on my own, and, with loss numbers larger than theirs, parity seems impossible.

My fears would be justified. The three largest uniformed services workers charities, (Twin Towers, IAFF, Widows and Orphans) distributed more than $900,000 to each police and firefighter family and more than $700,000 to each court officer's family. FEMA and numerous other smaller charities also made distributions only to these 436 families.[14] These distributions were in addition to the disbursements they received from charities that distributed to all victim's families, such as the Red Cross.

❦ ❦ ❦

Gary's landlord wants his apartment back. We need to figure out what to do with everything inside. Howard and I decide that we will have movers pack up the contents and put it in storage. We know from experience that if you decide what you want to keep and give away too soon after a death, you will almost always make the wrong choices. Time is the greatest gift you can give yourself before making these decisions and the best way to avoid regrets. Howard and I go to Gary's apartment and tag the things that we want brought to our homes instead of storage. Howard takes most of the electronics. I take the contents of Gary's kitchen. I know this sounds like a very strange choice, especially since, other than grilling tuna steaks, my hardworking bachelor brother didn't really cook. But, when Gary found something that he thought was "great," he would buy a lot of it, so that he could share it with us. This penchant ran the gamut, from CDs to jackets, to a gadget to smash a car window in case of an accident. His recent purchase was butter. Gary had found what he considered to be the "greatest butter." I want it. And the popcorn that he would only buy if it was on the ear of corn, and the can of Budweiser, which he didn't drink, but that he always kept in the refrigerator for Pat. We pack it in boxes and have it brought to my Upper East Side apartment.

❦ ❦ ❦

They have trained. They are ready, and they are running. Tens of thousands of people have taken to the streets to run the New York

City Marathon. Thousands more are cheering them on. It is November 4, 2001, the day after Gary's birthday. Lewis has taken our Maltese, Norma, downstairs for a walk and to look out for friends of ours who are running. I am on the 32nd floor, sitting on the ledge of my window looking out over First Avenue, and just for a moment I think, "Wow, just like that, all of this pain can be over."

Looking down I see that Lewis has Norma in his arms and he is staring up at me from beside a lamppost. His eyes are intense, and they refuse to break the connection. And I hear him silently imploring, "Don't you do it. Don't you do it." I know I can't be that selfish. After what seems like forever, I sigh, come back in off the ledge and sob with every ounce of my broken heart. That night I put on Gary's Theta Chi sweatshirt from college, where in another life he and Howard played ping-pong for the family title of "master of the universe." Lewis and I meet Howard and Allison and a large group of Gary's friends at a restaurant. I bring another poster-sized picture of Gary and place it at the head of the table. If this is his 37th birthday party, at least his likeness should be there. I ask a waiter to snap a picture.

When American Airlines flight 587 crashed into Bellport Queens, NY all of our fears resurfaced. Was this another terrorist attack? The plane barely missed the homes of some of our families. Our hearts broke for the Dominican community that was about to experience a shattering loss we knew only too well. Several years later, I was a "Principal for a Day" at a school in the neighborhood where many of the victims resided. I will forever be touched by the strength and community I witnessed.

Patrick Troy is getting married. He loves Sheila (which is perfectly understandable, because she is fabulous) and wants to marry her. Gary was supposed to be Pat's best man and he is having a difficult time with this. Pat wants to leave an empty chair next to him during the ceremony where Gary would stand. What should be one of the happiest days of Pat's life is marred by sadness. The last thing Gary would want would be for Pat to make his wedding about Gary and not about him and Sheila.

I know that I'm doing that annoying thing that I hate when people do it to me. "Gary would want…" "Gary would think…"—but I can't help it. It's the only leverage I have. Like so many of Gary's inner circle, Pat has become a very real part of my life, but I can't be Gary for him. I wasn't the one who ran around and put Pat's name on silent auction bids, or goaded him into daredevil stunts, or went out looking for girls, or drinking late into the night. I wish it were otherwise, but I just can't get that glint of mischief in my eye.

Howard, Lewis and I fly to Chicago for the wedding. We are only going for the day. It is an Irish wedding, complete with bagpipers and kilts. Pat has capitulated and one of his brothers stands up for him. There is no chair. As the bagpipers play and the guests surround them, I pray that Gary is up above somewhere sharing in his friend's happiness.

❧   ❧   ❧

Despite putting thousands of teddy bears on the chairs at the memorial service, I have not even made a dent in our teddy bear stores. We decide to have a private event for our families, specifically, those with children. Howard underwrites it, and we rent out the Chelsea Piers ice skating rink for December 2nd. The volunteers and I bring down our quilts, letters, cards, posters, books and pins. We use everything kind people have sent us to decorate the rink and the surrounding rooms. Children and adults have written us from all over the world and I want our families to know that they are not alone. The cards are touching. The sentiments are beautiful. The rooms look magical. We will allow the families to take home any decorations they would like. I especially love an enormous mural sent to us by a school in California. Each eighth grader has decorated a white heart with a picture and a message meant to convey love and hope. The hearts are glued onto red oversized poster boards, laminated and then tied together with ribbon. It covers the length of a full wall. As with all of our events, we have grief counselors available in a special room if any are wanted. But this event is different. Children are skating and eating cookies. Cantor gets known athletes to come and sign autographs for the kids, and they are being bombarded. One Euro Brokers widow has her heart set on a quilt that another family has taken. Juliet asks her if she can get her a different one, and the wife declines. But then the wife looks over and says, "Oh my G-d…Stephen Baldwin!!" Juliet asks, "Do you want to meet him?" Stephen graciously comes over, hugs her, signs autographs and takes photos with her. When she says she wishes she had her cell phone, Juliet hands hers over. The widow calls her friend and says, "Guess who I'm with?" She then puts Stephen on the phone to talk to her friend.

The Relief Fund gets food and cookies, popcorn and cotton candy machines donated for the day. And always there are the bears. Our volunteers are at a desk up front and we give each person a bear when they come in, along with a ticket for a free skate rental and a disposable camera. I have a walkie-talkie and in my red oversized ski jacket, over Gary's sweater; I am running everywhere. Howard teeters out in shoes to the middle of the ice rink. We hand him a microphone. He greets our families, thanks our guests and announces that Cantor Fitzgerald will match any donations that the Relief Fund receives through the end of the year, up to $5 million. Children are everywhere having NHL players sign whatever they can find, but mostly teddy bears. And they are laughing. Parents come up and thank me. It is the first time they have heard their children laugh or seen them smile in almost three months. We have received a donation of hundreds of teddy bears that are identical except for color. There are blue, yellow and pink ones. I decide to pile them up in the corner of a room, like a huge pile of leaves and let the kids jump in them. It's wildly successful. I walk into the room and I see three little girls, jumping into a mosh pit of teddy bears. They are laughing uproariously and the bears are flying. It is the first time I genuinely smile since September 11th.

Family members are requesting that we make donations to different organizations that are willing to memorialize their loved ones. We decide, once again, that our families are in the best position to decide how their loved ones should be remembered, and that we shouldn't choose which individual charities to support on their behalf. The remembrance of each of them is important and personal. It is a way to "pay forward" the kindness that people have shown us. Howard agrees to send each family $1,500 with a letter explaining that this is a grant to allow them to memorialize their loved one in any manner they see fit. We distribute more than $1 million for the future philanthropy of our families. Additionally, I begin helping families that want to establish their own charities, instead of donating the money to others, by getting not-for-profit status.

THE VICTIM
COMPENSATION FUND

Soon after 9/11, on September 22nd, to be exact, Congress established the 9/11 Victim Compensation Fund (VCF) as part of the Air Transportation Safety and System Stabilization Act. Basically, if all the victims' families sued the airlines, the plethora of potentially lost lawsuits might cause the airline industry to fail. As a way to save the airlines, Congress set up a fund whereby, in exchange for forgoing their legal right to sue potential defendants, the 9/11 victims' families would be compensated. The fund would have no cap. This was very important because so many of the World Trade Center victims were in the top 2 percent of wage earners in the country. The recovery for plaintiffs would be the same as if they had sued, but the process would be easier and less time consuming, and the potential defendants would be spared. For those who chose to sue the airlines, or were ineligible for the fund, recovery was capped at the insurance coverage of $1.5 billion for each incident. On November 27th, Ken Feinberg, an attorney with mediation experience, was appointed the "Special Master of the VCF." This fund was supposed to be easy on the families and fully compensate us for our economic and non-economic losses. We looked forward to trying to restore at least some financial stability to our otherwise shattered lives.

Howard started having town hall meetings to explain what the VCF is and how Cantor could be involved. Lawyers, specifically airline crash attorneys, had been soliciting our families and charging 10 percent or higher for their services. Howard warned the families that no attorney had any expertise in this, and that the families should "keep their pens in their pockets" until Cantor figured it all out. Cantor would do the leg work and keep the families informed.

On December 20th, Feinberg issued interim regulations for the VCF, stating, "It is important to ensure that people have a sense of what they might receive from the program before they decide to apply."[15] These regulations did not, however, mirror what we were led to believe was the intent of Congress. The right to sue the airlines was taken away by Congress in exchange for the recovery of "full economic loss." Feinberg took that right away from the victims. Full economic recovery would only be given to those families whose loved ones earned under $231,000. Any family whose loved one earned more than that would be required to show "extraordinary circumstances" to be compensated based on what they actually earned. In death, Feinberg demoted every high-wage earner. This ruling would deny hundreds of millions of dollars to at least one-third of our families.

Many families and family groups take exception to the interim regulations, and there are almost as many comments (2,687) as there were victims. Cantor had previously been instrumental in having charitable contributions exempt from VCF awards by showing how a corporation or charity would in fact be helping the government and not the families if their charitable contributions resulted in a decreased award.

But while other family groups fight about the reduction of an award by the amount of life insurance received, Howard understands that the exclusion is part of the statute and will not be changed without an act of Congress. Therefore, he shifts Cantor's focus and energies to the areas where Feinberg has made unilateral decisions without congressional mandate or intent.

Feinberg will be looking at three years of the victims' lost income in calculating economic damages. Cantor focuses on getting 2001 included and having the option of a two-year calculation. This change is vital for all 9/11 victims, but specifically for the younger ones who may have come to their jobs from college or from training programs.

The interim regulations only award each family $250,000 and $50,000 for each child for their non-economic loss. In wrongful death cases in court and as anticipated by Congress, non-economic loss includes pain and suffering, mental anguish, loss of enjoyment of life and consortium, and any other nonpecuniary losses of any kind. In court, these losses usually result in awards in the millions of dollars. Howard takes the position that, if families are forced to come in and recount the devastating loss that the death of their loved one has caused, then every family—no matter what the award—has lost, because the emotional toll will be incalculable. He advocates for a much higher dollar award for non-economic loss for everyone.

Cantor further argues that pre-tax income should be used in calculating earnings and that the heightened consumption rate being applied to single victims is improper. Cantor's largest and most important argument, however, addresses the disparity between what is being offered to those who earned less than $231,000 a year versus those who earned more.

The problem is that Feinberg has unilaterally instituted a "needs test," and a showing of "extraordinary proof" never contemplated by Congress. He is discounting by millions of dollars the awards that high-wage earners are entitled to as a matter of law because he has decided that these families don't "need" that much money.[16] This is a different, more onerous and subjective standard.

A woman raises her hand and says that her husband was in his 30s and, made $500,000 a year, and that she has three children. She asks why she is being treated differently than someone in the same circumstances whose husband made less money. We are at one of Howard's town hall meetings in Uniondale, Long Island, and Feinberg has come to persuade us to enter the fund. He tells her that she doesn't have to be treated differently. She can accept the formulaic amount indicated for someone that makes $231,000. If, however, she feels she wants to receive more than that, she will have to come in, schedule a hearing and explain the circumstances of her life that are extraordinary. "Wants?" What she "wants" is to know why the fact that her husband made $269,000 more isn't enough, and what extraordinary circumstances he is referring to? Isn't the murder of her husband by terrorists when they flew a plane into the World Trade Center extraordinary enough? Does the pain their incineration on national television caused need to be explained?

But Feinberg is telling us that we are going to have to parade in our children, our nightmares, our therapy bills. Wives are going to have to tell him how lonely their beds are without their husbands. Mothers will be forced to recount what it has felt like to lose a child after nurturing him for 30 years. Or that this child, the first in the family to achieve financial success after familial sacrifice to send him or her through school, has been the financial mainstay for not only his wife and children but also for his aging parents. Children will have to explain what it is like to have Daddy or Mommy not come home at night, or tuck them in. Is he really going to make people, who are enduring the unthinkable, prostrate themselves in order to receive the compensation that anyone whose loved one earned less than $231,000 is getting as a matter of right?

As I process what is happening here, I become more and more distraught. I remember what it was like to lose my father, have two younger brothers and have our income source disappear. I remember being forced to sell our house and have Gary change schools at a time when stability was what he needed most. I know what it was like to plead and fight for student loans to finish college while being told, "perhaps you should drop out until you can find the money." I remember what it was like rationing my coins to put together enough money for food. Being thrust into an untenable adult role when I should have been able to still be a child isn't something I chose. This "methodology" is not going to be good for my families, and I find myself uniquely qualified to understand what they are going through.

Feinberg makes it clear that, even with extraordinary circumstances, he does not feel that any of our loved ones' lives are worth more than $4 million, and that the average awards will hover around $2.5 million. For some, that is less than one or two years of earnings. He's not supposed to be allowed to put a cap on the amount of an award, but he has just told us there will be one.

I understand that to most, $4 million sounds like a lot of money, and people's relationship to the rich is one fraught with controversy. This is how Feinberg is going to get away with denying the families of people who were successful what is rightly theirs. Large monetary numbers won't play well on television and will not engender sympathy. I have already heard people say we are "greedy" if we think we should get more than that, or "if my husband gets hit by a car crossing the street, no one is going to give me any money." I've heard people say these women shouldn't have been shopping at Prada anyway.

The reality, however, is that people make choices. These young men and women made a choice to endure financial hardship to pursue an education. They then went through training programs, lean years, and worked extraordinarily long hours in order to rise in the ranks of their chosen professions. They became the best at what they did in a field that compensates highly. They made choices. They made sacrifices, and they were rewarded with a lifestyle many of us covet. But a bill is a bill. If you have a $20 delinquency or a $200,000 delinquency, the credit card company pursues you relentlessly and the bank puts your house into foreclosure. It doesn't matter at what economic level you live. The problems are the same. If your husband's salary or your own allowed you to shop at Prada, then it wasn't irresponsible to do so.

In a city where a small one-bedroom apartment costs more than $1 million and private school tuition can run $40,000 for each child, money doesn't go very far—$4 million for a 32-year-old, not reduced for present value, results in his family receiving $133,000 a year, instead of $500,000 or $1 million or $8 million. The families of victims who earned more than $231,000 a year will not be able to maintain the stability in their life if they have to rely on this award.

This is going to be an enormous problem. I already envision the calls from mothers who will no longer be able to see their grandchildren because their daughters-in-law are being forced to move out of state. The calls about children who will need additional therapy as they are uprooted from their routine and their friends, as all shreds of normalcy are ripped from them. If I can see this so clearly, I'm wondering why Feinberg can't. Is it really possible that he just doesn't care? Rumors— that I will never have the access to substantiate one way or another— are that he has cut a deal with the Justice Department to deliver the families at an average of $2.5 million apiece, the amount that is paid to the families of foreign diplomats killed overseas. No matter what his reasoning, the "no fault," "easy, pain-free for the families" compensation fund is anything but.

It's hard to miss David Egan, a six-foot six-inch, strapping older man with light hair and a graying beard. David's two daughters, Samantha and Lisa, were murdered on 9/11. The confluence of emotions we all share marshal themselves into David Egan's face. As Feinberg continues to defend his right to value human life, subject Cantor families to a self-created "needs test," rigorous hurdles, and deny them their congressionally mandated VCF awards in exchange for forgoing their legal rights, David Egan is silently stewing. After Feinberg finishes his presentation, David, with rage all over his face, runs toward Feinberg to confront him. How can Feinberg tell David that he is going to "decide" the value of David's daughters' lives? Feinberg sees David coming and is visibly afraid. David is a huge man, but like the friendly dragon who has fire spewing from his mouth and a heart of gold, he is all uncontrolled rage but no physical menace. Feinberg doesn't realize this and turns and hurriedly leaves the room. His "methodology" hasn't left any of us with a very good impression. After he leaves, Howard once again tells everyone to keep their pen in their pocket. If these are the rules, this isn't the time to enter the fund. I, on the other hand, wait for David, throw my arms around him and try to calm him down.

On March 13, 2002, Feinberg announces the final regulations for the Victim Compensation Fund. High-wage earners have not won the ability to be treated like everyone else and Feinberg has instituted a de facto cap. No one at Cantor is pleased with this result. Howard has been successful in getting a two-year calculation inclusive of 2001 and a pre-tax income calculation for the earnings component. These changes will result in millions of additional dollars to the 9/11 victims' families, but still nowhere near what they are entitled to.

On December 22, 2001, a man attempted to blow up American Airlines Flight 63 from Paris to Miami by placing a bomb in his shoe. Airport security in the United States changed forever as a result. When he was sentenced to life in prison on October 4, 2002 he called himself " a soldier of G-d (Allah) under the command of Osama bin Laden." The judge responded, "You are not a soldier in any army, you are a terrorist … You see that flag, Mr. Reid? That is the flag of the United States of America. That flag will be here long after you are forgotten."[17]

2002

MOVING ON

The holidays are tough. Every year, Howard, his best friend Doug Gardner and Gary threw a New Year's Eve party in New York City. Even though I never could afford to pay my share of the costs, I was always allowed to invite my friends. My brothers and I spent every New Year's Eve together. I can't bear the thought of having a party or being in New York City. Howard and his family, Jennifer Gardner and hers, and Lewis and I head to Florida. New Year's Eve is a somber occasion in a restaurant.

Even after 10 years of New Year's Eves without Gary I still cannot participate in celebratory events without an overwhelming sense of sadness and loss.

No matter how hard I try, even being away, 9/11 consumes my every waking thought. Howard and I talk about how the donations coming into the Relief Fund have slowed, and what else we can do. I express my frustration with the United Way. After raising $425 million in four months, it stopped soliciting donations on January 16th, but still received an additional $76 million. The public's belief that their generous donations would reach the 9/11 victims' families was erroneously placed. Ultimately, the 9/11 families each received a payment of $10,000 from the United Way instead of the more than $150,000 that should have been distributed. To try to justify its refusal to help, the United Way conducted an "ordinary person" poll of approximately 1,100 people with the majority agreeing with their usual distribution strategy.[18] I don't see the civilian families receiving the financial support they need.

Howard thinks we should hold a fundraiser. It's a way to get additional assistance to the families that we have not yet tapped. I agree to start working on it shortly after our return to New York.

The New Year also brings lots of changes. While September 11th is still in the news all the time, the world around us is moving on. The country starts coming out of the recession that it officially entered back in March 2001.[19] Barbara Lamb, who has been so instrumental in setting up the Relief Fund with me, needs to find a paying job. Fish & Neave also needs its space back. They move us to a smaller conference room and one office. Most of my volunteers have gone back to their lives, or moved onto paying jobs. It's hard to see so many of them go, but they remain at my disposal if I ever need them. They are so young and so bright. I have fondly watched them go out at night after a hard day's work, in search of girls or the latest hot spot. Their dreams are so big, their hearts so open, and their lives ahead of them. They are the beginnings of balm for my heart.

Thankfully, the core volunteers remain. Planning for our first fundraiser begins. At first we start thinking along traditional benefit event lines. Howard will contact a friend at the Pierre Hotel and we will have it there. We start thinking about performers, dinner and music. It doesn't take us very long for Howard to verbally mirror my own silent sentiments, "I don't want a party." None of us know exactly what this event will become, but we do know that we have to get donations of items that we can sell in a live and silent auction. We start focusing on that. I draft a donation letter and Allison, Howard, Jennifer Gardner, myself, Lewis's mother, all our volunteers and Cantor's senior staff start contacting everyone we can think of for donations. Once again, we are making lists: people to call, donations pledged and donations received. We make a dream list and start chasing down those items.

Shortly thereafter, Howard makes the decision to hold both a live and a silent auction of everything we have acquired for sale. He approaches Sotheby's about holding our auction at their location and they agree. At our first meeting it becomes clear that there will be a tremendous amount to do. A team of amazing volunteers take care of all the details and they, along with Howard and Allison, are wildly successful at getting magnificent high-end items donated—designer clothing, prestigious artwork, jewels, trips, one-of-a-kind experiences, tickets and more. With a million other things to do, because nothing has stopped when we decided to do a fundraiser, I need to focus my energies elsewhere especially since my senior staff are wholly focused on the auction.

I think by now that when my phone rings I will have some idea of what the person on the other end will say. I couldn't be more wrong.

"I need your help. They won't consider him dead. Can you get me phone records from Houston?" In the orthodox Jewish religion, for a person to be considered dead, and the family allowed to observe the attendant rituals, you need a body. Without a body, the Rabbinate needs to decree a death. Here, there is no body. The family has to prove that their child was in the building. They know that he was talking to the Houston office of Cantor. "Were the calls taped?" Yes. "Do you have floor plans of the building?" I think so. "Can you show where he was sitting?" That's going to be harder. "Do you have records proving he worked for you?" Yes. I tell the family not to worry, and I jump right on it. That means calling Heidi Olson, one of many employees who left Cantor before 9/11 and came back right after. Not for the first time, I think that the only thing predictable about my days is their unpredictability.

At the first snow, I look out at the unsullied white church courtyard that can be seen from my apartment window and know what I want to do. I bundle up in Gary's winter jacket and go outside. I carefully place my booted feet away from my entry steps and then about a foot apart from each other. I bend my knees and fall backwards. I flap my arms again and again from my head back down to my thigh in an arc. I carefully stand, jump back to where I was originally standing and survey my work. I have made a snow angel. I write "GARY" above it in the snow. I take a picture. When I get it developed, I put it in a frame and place it by my bed.

HEROES

Bill Doyle is not an obvious family leader, but that doesn't make him any less effective. Father of our victim Joey Doyle, he also worked on Wall Street in his former life. Now Bill decides to take on an enormous informational gap in the system. While we have effectively compiled contact information for our families, no one has taken on the daunting task of consolidating the email contact information for all the victims' families. Bill asks for my help in getting every Cantor family to send him their information. He will ultimately have more information than the city and his will be the list they will go to when they want to contact the families. The failure of government information collection and coordination remains a problem on numerous fronts and is one of the country's largest holes in disaster preparedness.

Bill also takes on the issue of health care. While Howard has pledged 10 years of health care for the Cantor families, other firms have not been as generous. There are hundreds if not thousands of widows and widowers without health insurance. Bill tried to get the United Way and the Red Cross to fund health care for the families. He told me that an annuity of $190 million would provide this benefit for the remainder of their lives. The United Way once again refused, despite raising more than $500 million. Bill also said that the Red Cross told him that it was not in the business of long-term relief. With Bill's persistence, however, it did agree to step into this void temporarily by having its Liberty Fund pay insurance benefits for two years. In response, I tried to get our Cantor families covered in the Red Cross program. It refused coverage to our families, claiming that because Cantor provided health insurance, it did not consider paying for our families in their calculations. If it had agreed to extend the same coverage to our families that it extended to the uninsured, Cantor's distributions to its families each quarter would have been larger, or our health care program extended by two years to

2013. As a result of Cantor's largesse, our families received less from the Red Cross than other victims' families did. Bill Doyle, knowing that the Red Cross Project Liberty health insurance project would have a finite end, continued working on a permanent health care program to cover all 9/11 victims who had insurance before 9/11. He also became the seminal source for the dissemination of information affecting all the families.

While I have been solely focused on the well-being of our families, issues springing from 9/11 and family members to address those issues have moved to the forefront both locally and nationally. Some are focused on the recovery effort. How the debris, which contains human and ashen remains, will be handled. How the attack on the World Trade Center, the Pentagon and the White House could have happened both from a political standpoint and a building structure standpoint, and of course, what should be done with the World Trade Center site now and how the victims will be memorialized. The Pentagon and Shanksville have these issues to resolve along with others. It is more than one entity can possibly resolve. I decide to stay focused on the World Trade Center.

POLITICS

Prior to 9/11, when it came to politics, I considered myself to be fairly ordinary. I read the newspapers and watched TV. I tried to acquaint myself with candidates and what they stood for before I voted. Then I pretty much let the processes of government take over unimpeded by me or my thoughts. I lived my life. I paid my taxes, abided by the law, quietly grumbled about things I didn't like and equally quietly praised things that I did. Once in a while my friends and I would engage in political discussions, but usually I lived by the tenet that religion and politics are better kept to oneself and most of the time would just listen and try to learn something. So when Mayor Giuliani, who had become a symbol for 9/11, finished out his term as mayor of New York City, and was replaced with businessman billionaire Michael Bloomberg, I really wasn't thinking this had anything more or less to do with me than any other mayoral election. With an all-consuming 9/11 life, I didn't even exercise my constitutional right to vote. It would seem to me that both Mayor Giuliani, while he held office, and Mayor Bloomberg, during his tenure, were staunch supporters of their employees. The needs of the civilians, however, despite the fact that they were members of their constituency, weren't high on their agendas.

Unlike me, Christy Ferer has a very political life. On February 11, 2002, New York City Mayor Michael Bloomberg names her "special liaison to work with the relatives of those killed September 11th."[20] Christy Ferer is not a Cantor family member. Her husband Neil Levin ran the Port Authority and had a close relationship with Governor Pataki. Newly elected Mayor Bloomberg and Christy Ferer are close friends. She has been having meetings with some of these newly emerged "family leaders." They claim to represent the bulk of the 9/11 families. Christy's assistant lost her brother at Cantor, and tells her that none of the people she is meeting with speak for the Cantor families. My name leaps to the forefront. Christy contacts me and invites me to a meeting at her Vidicom office on February 21st. She is very nice to me, but it doesn't take long for me to figure out that I am being brought in to combat the more "militant" positions being espoused by family leaders from various groups. Unexpectedly, I am being thrust into the world of 9/11 politics.

At the meeting I learn about the Lower Manhattan Development Corporation (LMDC). The LMDC was formed in November 2001, and was controlled predominantly by Governor Pataki and secondarily by Mayor Giuliani. This is the entity charged with overseeing the development of the World Trade Center site. The governor had ultimate control because as far as both the governor and then mayor were concerned, there would be a Democratic mayor (Mark Green), and this distribution of power was a political block.[21] There is a Family Advisory Council to the LMDC and all of the people attending the meeting in Christy's office are on it. I can't help but wonder why Cantor Fitzgerald hadn't been contacted to join. I get myself appointed to the council and in return I get a valuable gift, peers.

⌄   ⌄   ⌄

I am talked into doing a "Public Lives" interview with Robin Finn of the *New York Times*. Having guarded my privacy, I don't really want to, but planning for our first fundraiser is under way, and she agrees to put our donation information at the end of the article if I agree to do it. I am wearing Gary's black cable sweater when she comes to the office and we begin to talk. She asks me about my past and feeling vulnerable and exposed, I tell her about the death of my mother to cancer when I was 18 and the death of my father a year and a half later. I tell her about raising my younger brother and how we had no money. She asks about my education and I walk her through attending Jericho High School, the University of Rhode Island and then Syracuse University for my law degree and MBA, and how I graduated early from all of them out of necessity. I tell her that I worked multiple jobs in addition to pursuing my joint degree from Syracuse while Gary lived with me. When it becomes apparent that circumstances dictated my path, she asks me what I would have been if things had been different. I say, "Maybe a comedian." The irony isn't lost on either of us. I like Robin. She is the first media person that seems to "get me." I'm petrified of the outcome because of O'Reilly and Rosie, but I am as honest, open and as trusting as I can be in spite of my fear. She asks me about the Relief Fund. She sees the nonstop activity around us. This is comfortable terrain for me and I tell her about everything we are doing for our families. I tell her all about soliciting donations for upcoming fundraiser. While she is there the phone rings constantly. The amount of family members that want to talk to me has not lessened.

As I recount our activities she says to me, "Edie, you do realize that you can go home?" She means literally that I can go home and that I don't have to spend all my time at the office. I look at her blankly. This is the first moment in my entire life that it has ever dawned on me that this commitment is a choice. From the safety that comes from being behind my desk, I say, "When the phone rings and you answer it, and someone is in pain, do you get off the phone? When you hang up, and the phone rings again and you *know* that the person on the other end is in pain, do you not answer the phone?" For me, there is no choice. There never has been.

They take my picture. At about 3 am, Lewis and I go home. The next day, when I am at my usual, unshowered, curly bird-nest hair everywhere, puffy-eyed self, in my second-favorite Gary sweater, the black and white one, they call and say the photographs from the day before didn't come out, they need to come over now and shoot them again. Are they kidding? Whatever bit of vanity I have left is appalled, but I don't say no. Instead I grab the Cantor Fitzgerald baseball cap that is a staple in my office, and plunk it on my head.

She is a "hollow-eyed woman of 42 ..."[22] Robin Finn has my number, but not the Relief Fund's. The donation information for our fund isn't in the article. Neither are the activities the fund is engaged in. This is all about me. The portrait is accurate, but I have spliced myself open for no reason. The new picture captures it all. My friend Shari Clayman-Kerr posts the February 26, 2002 article on the bulletin board in her office under a sign that says, "NO WHINING" and makes anyone who comes in complaining read it. The article comes out on the anniversary of the 1993 bombing.

❧　❧　❧

On February 25, 2002, we send out 772 checks. This is Cantor Fitzgerald sending each family $6,118.93 as the first installment on its five-year commitment. In the face of the murder of two-thirds of his employees, the devastation of the World Trade Center headquarters, lack of cooperation from competitors and the one-sided negative media onslaught, Howard's ability to revive Cantor Fitzgerald, with his surviving and new employees, and begin making good on his promise is nothing short of remarkable.

Every year, Boomer Esiason (retired quarterback for the Jets and Bengals and analyst on the CBS pregame show *NFL This Morning,* as well as radio for *Monday Night Football*) holds a fundraiser to benefit Boomer's Cystic Fibrosis Foundation. Boomer's son, Gunnar, has Cystic Fibrosis and his charity focuses on medical research. Howard met Boomer years ago and they became good friends. Howard gave Boomer, along with Sarah Ferguson, the Duchess of York, office space on the same floor as me (101) in Cantor's offices for their charities. Fortunately, neither the Cystic Fibrosis Foundation nor Chances for Children staff were in the building the morning of September 11th, but Boomer's best friend Timmy O'Brien, and many other friends and supporters from Cantor were. Fundraising for any non-9/11 charity in its wake is near impossible, but Boomer's fundraiser is an annual event and he decides to hold it anyway. This year, however, will be different. We are asked to submit a picture and a bio of Gary. On March 9, 2002, Howard, Allison, Lewis, myself, Jennifer Gardner, Lisa O'Brien (Timmy's wife) and others attend the charity event. Unbeknownst to me, Boomer has put together a tribute to all his charity's supporters who passed away on

9/11. It is a film, and there is a book with all of their faces and bios at our seats. There isn't a dry eye amongst us. I go up to Allison and I congratulate her for the good job she has done capturing Gary. She looks at me, positively dumbfounded, and says, "Edie, you wrote it." With all that was going on, and my utter lack of sleep, I just didn't remember. We got two copies of Gary's photo enlarged and Howard and I hung them in our respective offices.

ANSWERS

Elise Fraser is looking for answers. While most of our families have been trying to piece together what happened that day, Elise needs answers from above. She is looking for faith. Elise, who is Jewish, even contemplates becoming Catholic because they seem to know what happens afterward. She wants to know if there is life after death. Elise is the wife of Stuart Fraser, Bernie Cantor's nephew, Cantor senior partner, and one of Howard's closest friends. Stuart survived by not being at work that day, but Elise's brother Eric Sand was not as fortunate. Like many who struggle after a death, Elise starts going to psychics. One after another. She is trying to find out what Eric's purpose was in life and why he had to die. She goes to one psychic and is taking notes. The psychic says something about a waffle. Elise thinks that this has gone far enough, but writes it all down anyway. Several days later she is talking to Eric's wife, and she is telling her all the things that the psychic said. She tells her about the waffle. Eric's wife stops her. "Waffle? Really? Because they just opened a new playground in the mall, and I took Aaron to it. It's all made up of breakfast foods. Aaron was jumping on a waffle."

Lisa O'Brien, Elise Fraser and I are having this conversation. Lisa tells us that for weeks after September 11th, her son insisted that "Daddy" (Timmy O'Brien) was in the room with him when she came in to tuck him in at night. Her son couldn't understand why Lisa couldn't see him. Elise then tells us that she went to see a psychic in Florida. The reader tells her that she is going to see Bozo the clown and that will be her brother. Elise is thinking, "Yeah, right." She is in the mall and walks into Spencer's (a kids' novelties shop) and in the back is a huge Pez dispenser of Bozo. Elise starts loudly saying "Bozo, Bozo," to those she is with. She then says "Hi, Eric?" They, along with many other family members have asked me if I have gone or am going to a psychic, after recounting their experiences to me I smile and reply that it would never work. There would be so many souls trying to get at me to give messages to their loved ones that it wouldn't be fair to make them trample over each other. Besides, there isn't a single name that a psychic could mention that wouldn't be the name of someone that I know.

Elise and Lisa are just examples of many stories I heard from family members through the years. So many of us had paranormal experiences even if we might have previously been skeptics. One of our widows wrote a book about the phenomenon. We all still want to feel connected to the person we loved. I view anything that makes me feel Gary's presence as a positive. Repeatedly I have said that however our families choose to deal with 9/11 is okay. Some people derive comfort from psychics. Some do not. It's an individual choice. Once at a party many years ago that Gary and I attended, a psychic was present and doing readings for the guests. After Gary's reading, he came up to me and said, "Edie, I have some terrible news." "What is it Gary?" "Our mother needs an operation!" As he waited for the words to set in, a smile was forcing its way onto his lips. Our mother had been dead for more than 20 years.

⌄   ⌄   ⌄

I am invited, along with other family leaders, to attend a meeting at Gracie Mansion, the mayor's official residence, in order to discuss the Tribute in Lights. Before September 11th, I never imagined that I would see the inside of Gracie Mansion, a stately residence I have passed a thousand times while walking along the East River. This is my first introduction to the mayor, who smiles, shakes my hand, and asks me how my brother Howard is. We are all sitting around an enormous conference table. Mayor Bloomberg wants to see the Tribute in Lights, two blue lights shining from the WTC up into the skies representing the absence of the two buildings, as the temporary memorial for the six-month anniversary. Most family members are not opposed to the idea. I have a few concerns and I voice them. I am worried that the presence of the lights this early will force people to confront 9/11 at times when they are not prepared to do so, like when they are driving in their car across a bridge. For those people who don't want to see the lights, they will not be able to avoid them if they live in certain areas. And, last, as one family member said to me, "What happens when the lights are shut off? Will it feel like a new loss?" March 11, 2001, the six-month anniversary, is less than two weeks away and the mayor obviously wants this, so I don't pursue it beyond making my concerns known. Christy Ferer selects a 12-year-old who lost her Port Authority police officer father to flick the switch to illuminate the lights.

REMAINS

By late September or early October 2001 the next of kin of each family had been issued a *P* number by the medical examiner. The need for a number to identify each victim arose when the medical examiner's office realized that there were multiple victims with the same name. When a family came in to give DNA evidence, for example, and said it was for Michael Francis Lynch, without a picture of the victim, which of the four victims with that name did the toothbrush or hairbrush belong to? Next of kin were invited to come to the medical examiner's office and get a victim's photo ID, which had a *P* number on it. That number and ID, which had no expiration, became our entry and invitation into all things 9/11, such as the six-month anniversary ceremony.

Some families like the lights. Some do not, but no one can ignore them. For me and most of my families, March 11th is an artificial milestone. I know personally, as a survivor, I'm not yet ready to see two lights highlighting where my life used to be. Someday, maybe.

The overwhelming thing I feel the morning of March11th is an inability to be comfortable in my skin. I don't know what to do with myself. I don't know where I should be. I look out the window and I see a gathering of construction workers two blocks farther north on First Avenue, hard hats in hand, standing under an enormous American flag. They blow what sounds like an air raid horn at 8:46 am, the time that the first plane hit the North Tower. They stand there silently and somberly, remembering. I know this is where I want to go. I pull on a pair of jeans, Gary's black sweater, my Cantor Fitzgerald baseball cap, a pair of sneakers and race out the door. I leave my building and, head held high, join the gathered. It is almost with an air of defiance that I stand among them. I am not of them, in theory I don't belong, as it is a gathering of construction workers, but it feels right. They are honoring our shared loss. As they sound the next horn, I raise my eyes to the sky and tears march their way through every hard-earned wrinkle on my face. I hear my name. "Edie?" Can't be. But then I hear it again. "Edie?" I turn around and there is a woman, with eyes as puffy and a countenance as unhappy as mine. "It's me. Sherry Partridge." "Sherry?" The question isn't so much about who she is, as much as a "What are you doing here?"

I used to volunteer delivering food to the homebound elderly in my previous life. For everyone, life is now squarely divided into before and after September 11th. Sherry was the volunteer coordinator before she moved on to work at Cabrini Medical Center. We liked each other almost immediately, and became more than just acquaintances. As life marched forward, we lost touch. Now she stands with me, and we both unabashedly let the tears fall, as we maintain the next set of moments of silence. When those surrounding us go back to work, Sherry comes with me back to the outdoor playground in my building, the same space where Gary's death was affirmed by the collapsing of the buildings.

Sherry is a fiancé. She isn't one of Cantor's, but she lost her fiancé in the towers at another company. She tells me how she loved him, how he loved her and how they were getting married. 9/11 took his future, but it took hers also. My heart breaks for her. We sit in the backyard talking. She says to me, "Can you feel them?" A strong gust of wind, like the one that blew Gary's picture down the street, envelopes us. "Every time I feel the wind I know it is him surrounding me."

˅ ˅ ˅

Christy Ferer says that "after March 11th it feels like some weight has been lifted off my head. Sure you all must feel the same."[23] My emotional connection to my brother is so strong that six months without him is just an indication of how much more time stretches out in front of me. I contact Allison and ask her to include Sherry, even though she is affiliated with a different company's loss, in her fiancé support group. Milestone or not, work continues as usual.

I start to attend the LMDC Family Advisory Council (FAC) meetings. The FAC, along with eight other advisory councils, began in

January, so I am coming to the process a little late. 9/11 family groups have solidified by now and many have picked their issues. Several have become well-known voices in the press on 9/11 issues, and figures often seen in the company of the governor, mayor (past and current), senators and congressmen. Seven groups, realizing that their voices are not being heard, have banded together into the Coalition of 9/11 Families. The vocal advocates for this group are Anthony Gardner, whose brother Harvey was killed at General Telecom, and Patricia Reilly, whose sister Lorraine Lee died at Aon Corp. They are formidable and very smart. The other players who make an immediate impression for differing reasons are Monica Iken, a leggy blonde with obscenely long fingernails who started September's Mission; Mary Fetchet, whose coiffed hair, conservative dress and political demeanor make her seem like she is vying for a congressional seat, and Beverly Eckert, a laid-back blonde, who are the founders of Voices of September 11th; Lee Ielpi, a soft-spoken and always diplomatic, highly decorated retired firefighter who lost his firefighter son Jonathan, and Marian Fontana, a firefighter widow, represent the 9/11 Widows' and Victims' Families Association. Cantor family member Bill Doyle, who I first met at the Feinberg town hall meeting in Uniondale, is there representing Give Your Voice and the Coalition of 9/11 Families. There are probably 20 people in all at the meetings. I come into the process optimistically. Because we represent a quarter of the victims, I am sure our voices will be heard. The process itself and the dynamic within quickly disabuse me of that notion.

While I am once again brought in to combat the voices of the other family leaders, the positions they are taking do not strike me as unreasonable. Almost all of the family leaders are in agreement that the 16-acre WTC site is sacred ground and that nothing that goes on the site should be inconsistent with that. The Coalition of 9/11 Families wants the "bathtub," which is the land representing the Twin Towers' footprints, the plaza in front of it and what was the Marriott, preserved down to bedrock. Monica Iken wants the full 16 acres dedicated to a memorial. Beverly Eckert wants to ensure that there is no vehicular traffic across the site. Sally Regenhard, whose young probationary firefighter son was killed, probably has the most overtly forceful personality of the group. She has formed the Skyscraper Safety Campaign. She focuses on the safety of anything being built going forward. She claims the exemption of the Port Authority from New York City building and fire codes contributed to the collapse of the buildings. While I can understand that there would be cost considerations to doing away with Port Authority building exemptions, and that 16 acres of prime real estate dedicated solely to a memorial is probably unlikely, preserving the land where 2,479 people were murdered and treating it as sacred ground, down to bedrock, which is where the majority of the human remains were found and are the historic ruins of the building, not allowing cars to drive across what is in essence a massive cemetery, and ensuring that no matter what goes on top it is constructed safely, doesn't strike me as patently unreasonable. I know that some of the deliveries haven't been refined, but I'm having a hard time figuring out what I'm supposed to oppose.

The first LMDC Family Advisory Council meeting that I have a clear recollection of attending involves a discussion about running the PATH train (the train from New Jersey to Lower Manhattan) and subway lines 1 and 9 through the site. Lee Ielpi, a retired firefighter and someone who has been "working the pit" looking for remains, is agreeing to allow them to build train tracks over the exact location of where his son Jonathan's body was found. Lee is taking a stand against his personal interest to show the LMDC that the families are not unreasonable, as they have been quick to label us, but rather willing to compromise in order to move the process forward. We quickly learn, however, that the decision to proceed with this plan has already been made. Like with the tribute in lights, we are being consulted after the fact.

The problem is philosophical. The governor, mayor and LMDC (who are appointed by the governor and mayor) don't believe that the families have a place in the redevelopment of the World Trade Center site. The name of the agency is a telltale sign. It is the Lower Manhattan *Development* Corporation, and that is exactly what the WTC site is perceived as. It is a development project. New York City has received $21 billion in federal aid and $2.783 billion became the LMDC's budget to address 16 prime real estate acres in Lower Manhattan.[24] There should have been plenty of money to build a 9/11 memorial and museum, but the LMDC cast its net much wider, spending hundreds of millions of dollars on parks and waterways.[25] To some, it is not a sacred site and a memorial is not their focus. One of Mayor Bloomberg's agendas is to connect the street grid through the site. This forces the family leaders into a never-contemplated situation. We must pay attention and be involved in every decision that is made on the site, because with each decision, the area within the 16 acres that should be sacred ground is eroded.

Shiya Ribowsky comes to see me. I am the gateway to the information that the Cantor families possess and he needs. Shiya works for the medical examiner and they need tissue samples from all of the next of kin of the 9/11 victims. He explains the swabbing process. This entails taking a sterile Q-tip and rubbing it on the inside of your cheek, returning it to a test tube, which is then sealed and identified as yours. Either the family members need to come in and get "swabbed," or we have to send kits to the individual homes and explain carefully (done wrong and it is useless) how to complete the process and send back the samples. Shiya knows that Howard and I are never going to be able to come in, so he has come to meet me, explain what he needs and to swab me. I will help him get all of my families, even those in other countries, swabbed. Shiya is a handsome man, a little younger than I, with brown hair and kind eyes. He is a cantor at a temple in Gramercy Park when he isn't working at the medical examiner's office. He speaks in a scientific language that I do not want to understand. I know that without this tragedy, our paths would never cross, but we become friends. He is compassionate in a wholly different way than I am. He is not a hugger per se, but he is trying to make death palatable. His matter-of-fact style when talking about things that belong in a Stephen King novel, make everything so surreal that somehow I can absorb it. Shiya explains to me that to match one sibling to another sibling given the circumstances is very difficult.

The chances of Howard and I getting identifiable remains of Gary back are very, very slim. With our DNA, matched against a partial profile, it is just as likely that Gary's DNA will match Shiya's or anyone else's as mine. Parents are the best DNA for a match. Siblings, without parents' DNA to also test, not so good. I get swabbed anyway. So does Howard. We have nothing to lose.

I get a call from Cantor's attorneys that the U.S. Attorney's Office wants to meet with our families. They are preparing for the trial of Zacarias Moussaoui, the so-called 20th hijacker. He was the man arrested after taking flight lessons prior to 9/11. On March 27th they want to interview individual families to obtain victim impact evidence that could be used in the event the government seeks the death penalty. Each family would meet for 30 minutes privately with a prosecutor and an FBI agent and tell the story of their loved one. Currently the interviews are scheduled to take place in a hotel in Manhattan. We ask them to consider satellite locations in New Jersey and Long Island as well. Some of them agree to meet with the prosecutors and tell their stories of loss. As a result, some of our families testified at his sentencing trial four years later.

SACRED GROUND

The Family Room is a small space reserved for victims' families that can be decorated by us and is dedicated to memory and remembrance. It is being opened on the 20th floor of One Liberty Plaza on Broadway, down the hall from the LMDC's offices. Howard urges me to go. It's difficult as I have not yet been back downtown. It will overlook the WTC site. John Whitehead, the chairman of the LMDC board, Governor Pataki and Mayor Bloomberg are attending, as well as the family leaders and selected families. Mayor Bloomberg is now appointing eight people to the LMDC board and will be an equal partner with Governor Pataki. The room is both lovely and gut-wrenching at the same time. It houses so many missing flyers, memorabilia and mini-altars that visiting families have left. I look out the window and I'm a bit numb. It's just a massive ditch, the rudimentary beginnings of a construction site.

The Family Advisory Council has an hour-long meeting with the mayor. Christy has set the agenda from suggested items culled from the families. The mayor will only discuss what is on the agenda, and we don't get anywhere. He talks at us instead of to us. His lack of compassion is becoming a real obstacle for us.[26] Christy starts to lay the groundwork for the mayor that a 16-acre memorial is off the table.[27] The family leaders begin to realize that Christy is not the family liaison *to* the mayor, but rather the family liaison *for* the mayor *to* the families.

I didn't form a clear idea of what I wanted to see at the site, nor did I ever believe that was my role. I spent 10 years keeping my personal opinions out of discussions and representing only the wishes of the majority of our families. I did share our families' position that the memorial should have driven the development project. It wasn't that I ever thought the full 16 acres had to be a memorial. Rather, it was that the things that were important to the vast majority of families should have been respected, and at least a reasonable attempt made to accommodate their considered requests. Specifically, I wanted to protect their view that where the vast majority of remains were found should remain sacred ground, that no vehicular traffic should run through the site, that the full 16 acres should be recognizable as such through the use of architectural elements, that a bus depot shouldn't be built in the tower footprints, that whatever was constructed be done so safely with a better eye toward security, that significant artifacts such as the tridents and Koenig's Sphere (which used to stand in the mall area between the two towers) be returned to the site, and that all the victims should be treated equally in death with the names of the murdered victims listed the way that the families wanted.

While being touted as "open and transparent," the LMDC was making important decisions behind closed doors and talking to the families at the Family Advisory Council meetings about things like the gauge of the steel that should be used in the fencing.

I look across the table and catch the eyes of Darlene Dwyer. Darlene is not a family member, but she runs Windows of Hope. This is the charity that takes care of the restaurant workers, most of whom were Hispanic and indigent. The prestigious WTC restaurant, Windows on the World, was on the 107th floor of the North Tower. Similar to Cantor, no one who was on the floor when the plane hit survived. Darlene rolls her eyes in disbelief at the steel gauge conversation and I smile. We connect at the meeting's end and realize that we have overlapping victims in the 21 Forte Foods employees. Forte Foods was the food service provider at Cantor Fitzgerald. We had a cafeteria on the 101st floor manned by Forte Foods employees, as well as some that worked on the 105th floor. Darlene and I decide to work together to address the needs of these families, many of whom are being forced to pay fees or percentages of their checks at check cashing facilities to access the funds we are sending them.

While the LMDC is keeping us engaged (pun intended), they are creating blueprints that run vehicular traffic through the site. This is something I have spoken with my families about and know they strenuously object to. The objection is grounded in the fact that the

World Trade Center site should be respected as a sacred site as a whole and not carved up by anything other than pedestrian roads. The scale of the tragedy will be lost to the public. Most important, human remains have been found where they are proposing the roads be built. Most families, across all groups find the thought of cars running over their loved ones' burial ground tough to stomach.

We had previously met with Governor Pataki, who assured us that there would not be vehicular traffic, so the fact that the roads have resurfaced on the blueprints is unexpected. We fight the battle. We win the battle. The win is ignored. Beverly Eckert demanded that LMDC Board Chairman John Whitehead reassure us that these vehicular traffic streets would immediately be taken off the blueprints for the site.

The blueprints were altered, but it didn't change the outcome. The reconnection of the street grid became a requirement for the site plan competition, and ultimately all of our reality. I think most families still would have preferred that the traffic across the site be pedestrian. When the memorial opens in less than a month, idling buses on the newly created streets are of major concern to residents.

FAMILIES IN THE WAY

It seems to me that the LMDC and the mayor have come up with several strategies to use against the 9/11 families when they don't agree with us, and we fall prey to them repeatedly. When we are asked to decide on fence gauge while they divide the site for nonmemorial purposes behind closed doors, that's obfuscation. The second is to announce a contentious topic or decision at a Family Advisory Council meeting. When the family leaders, who all have strong personalities, voice their initial reactions, which almost always differ from each other, the press is waiting outside to capture the divergent opinions. Then they take the position that since the families cannot agree amongst themselves, the mayor, the governor or the LMDC must take control of the situation and make the decision. If even one family member can be found to disagree, this strategy is used. The democratic concept of majority rules, does not apply to the family interaction with the government bodies overseeing the WTC development. As the mayor has a small handful of family members in his corner—Christy Ferer and Paula Grant Berry chief amongst them—this is very effective.

Next, the families fight an issue and they either win or the issue is ignored. The issue then disappears from discussion. At some point down the line, the previously won issue resurfaces on a document, under its original or different name, as if the "win" never occurred or objections had never been raised. The battle has to be fought all over again. Then there is the "not my job" or the "you are in the wrong forum" defense. This involves having the families chase after different agencies. The LMDC will say the issue isn't their province, rather it falls to the Port Authority. The Port Authority will point to the city, the city says the governor, and he turns it back to the LMDC. This is an effective way to stall long enough to get what they want implemented while the families chase their tails. A slight variation to this is not to pass the problem to another agency, but rather to state that the comments are in the wrong forum and therefore dismiss them as if they have no merit. Then there is patience. If they wait long enough, the families, but, more important, the press and the public, will get tired of the battling, and of the families demanding to be heard, and lose interest. This will impede the family leaders' ability to get press for positions, no matter how meritorious. The last, and most difficult to accept, is the concerted effort to paint the families as overemotional people who cannot effectively handle grief. Statements are made to the effect that we want our loved ones back, which the mayor cannot do, and therefore we can never be satisfied.

The work of Mothers Against Drunk Driving (MADD) has resulted in major changes to the law. Megan's Law is the result of a family demanding a law be changed after the death of a child. The list of victims' families that have brought positive changes to our lives is endless. The 9/11 families are not, however, seen as such a vehicle to change. We are seen as people who cannot control our emotions and therefore cannot be entrusted with important decisions. The process is like seeing a train coming right at you, and just not being smart enough to figure out how to get out of the way. The family leaders are trying their best to make a positive contribution, to have something productive come from the loss, and yet are consistently being victimized. Sometimes the genuineness, openness and naiveté of the families is our biggest undoing.

In theory, having one person, or a small committee tasked with speaking for and unifying the voices of the families makes sense. However, when the Coalition of 9/11 Families tried to do just that, their seven individual group voices were only considered one vote. When I brought all of the family groups together and we spoke with one voice, we were still dismissed. Only when an issue could be framed in a national or political way that caught the attention of the wider media circuit were we able to gain any traction.

On May 13th, I am one of several family leaders meeting with Governor Pataki at his office on Third Avenue. Anthoula Katismatides, a Cantor sibling whose brother John died on 9/11, works for Governor

Pataki. While her job and loyalty to the governor come first, we are kept in the loop. The family leaders don't believe it is right that the LMDC board of directors does not have a single family member on it. Anthoula and I discuss this at the meeting. She tells me that the problem is that the family leaders are too volatile. She uses Monica Iken's threat to chain herself to a bulldozer if we don't receive the full 16 acres for a memorial as evidence. I listen and, objectively, I guess I can understand the governor's position. But I tell Anthoula, "Listen, tell the governor that he can find a family member that is not as outspoken and radical as these family members. Howard is a family member. I'm certain the governor can find a family member among the tens of thousands that exist, that has the education, experience and temperament that he wants to sit on the board." I can see the light bulb going off in her head.

Subsequently, the governor appoints Tom Johnson, the outgoing CEO of Greenpoint Bank and father of Scott, killed at Keefe, Bruyette & Woods. His wife Ann already sits on the Family Advisory Council. His daughter worked for Bloomberg. As a bank president, Tom is mild-mannered but firm, and has dealt with politics, bureaucracy and disgruntled employees. He's a perfect choice for the governor and the mayor, because Tom Johnson states that "he would not be able to solely represent the narrow interests of the family survivors—important as they are." His allegiance, he said, would have to be to the "whole of the institution and all of its constituencies."[28] And while he is not the choice the leaders would have preferred, and he isn't going to be a voice or advocate solely for the families, no one can really complain, as they have technically now gotten what they asked for.

SUPPORT

I get requests from money managers all the time asking to be put in touch with our families. If they are being solicited by attorneys, families are being courted even more frequently by money managers. I start receiving calls and emails about a financial advisory plan for families through the 9/11 United Services Group. The top charities have joined forces under this name to share information ensuring that distributions aren't being made to victims' families by multiple charities for the same things. While I understand the philosophy behind it, I don't like that it is allowing charities like the United Way to say that they no longer need to distribute money to this pool of victims because "needs" have been met by other charities.

The reality was that the financial needs of our families were not being met in their entirety. I fully supported the concept that families should be given money and decide for themselves how it should be spent. Federal monies allocated to create grief camps, for example, when several effective camps already existed was, in my estimation, a misallocation of funds. As monies were allocated for that purpose, they couldn't be used for anything else.

Goldman Sachs COO Steven Wisch calls me about the Cantor families entering the United Services financial program. I bring the matter to Howard's attention. He tells me that he has been thinking about this. He will bundle the Cantor families together and negotiate an institutional instead of individual rate. The cost to any family that wants it will be much lower.

Three of our widows, Mindy Kleinberg, Laurie Van Auken and Patty Casazza, join with a fourth from another company to seek information from the government of the United States of America. They are leading a charge of 9/11 families calling for an investigation into the events of September 11th. Mindy contacts Howard, and he passes off to me Mindy's request that we post a flyer on our website and send out an email to our families informing them of a rally in support of Senators Lieberman and McCain's bill S1867 calling for a 9/11 commission. The Jersey Girls, as they become known, are ultimately successful in having a 9/11 commission appointed.

˅　˅　˅

There are 103 pregnant women whose husbands have been killed in the World Trade Center, and we have 43 of them. The Infant Care Project has received a lot of positive press for its program to assist these women and their new babies. The White House has seen the positive press and President Bush wants to send a letter to each of the new mothers. They assure Judy Hill, who runs the project, that they will destroy the list, but file copies of all presidential letters are kept. I would love our new mothers to get letters, but I need assurances that they will not be contacted about testifying in terrorist trials or anything else along those lines. I don't want these new mothers upset any further in any way. I contact Allison for birthdates since she has started the new mothers' support group, as well as contacting Cantor's insurance company. I compile a new list. This one, at least, has life associated with it.

I get a call from Judith Glaser. She was a producer on a documentary I was interviewed for, and she sits on the board of a new charity started by Nile Rodgers and Nancy Hunt, "We Are Family Foundation." Judith is a leadership consultant to CEOs and their teams. She has been discussing with some of her influential female clients how they can positively contribute to 9/11. Judith's story is different from anyone else's I have heard so far. On September 11th she left her doctor's office with a breast cancer diagnosis in hand. She hit the street more deserving of sympathy then she had ever been in her life, and the world had fallen apart around her. Comparatively, she felt that her diagnosis was "nothing," because as my father always said, "Where there is life, there is hope." When Judith comes to me with an idea they have been bantering around, she is fighting for her life. If she hadn't told me, I'd never have known.

While undergoing chemotherapy, Judith starts an organization called Women in Transition Helping and Healing (WITHH). They will offer training, support and internships to our widows who now find themselves needing to enter or reenter the workforce. They will have coaches, stress counselors and confidence-building facilitators work with them. When the women are ready, they will be placed in paid internships. I love the concept and give them ideas on how to better tailor the program to the needs of our families. They start small, with openings for 10 women. I send the information out in a letter, post it on our website and have Howard talk about it on one of his family conference calls, which he holds every few weeks. The women who participate are so excited. This is the opportunity for a new beginning for them. Initially it is open only to widows. WITHH then expands to fiancés and mothers.

I receive word from a family member that she is trying to establish a sibling support group in New York City. I have had several siblings come see me on a regular basis, and I think this group can have some teeth. My volunteers secure us space in the basement of St. Vincent's Parish. It's very important to me that two of our female siblings, both of whom were extremely close to their murdered brothers and are having a very difficult time (one who quotes a statement that the sibling relationship is the longest and most important relationship in your life) attend.[29] They will only go if I do. So, I agree. On March 19, 2002, I find myself dragging a reluctant, tall, blonde "drink of water" to her seat. The group begins. Sibs are sharing their experiences with other support groups that span different types of victims and don't really focus on their issues. They have what I have come to call the hierarchy of grief problem. The widow or widower with children tops the pyramid, followed by the children, then wives without children, then parents of unmarried victims, fiancés, parents of married victims, siblings, friends, colleagues. The doling out of sympathy by friends and society is proportionate to where someone falls on the pyramid, as is financial assistance. In actuality there shouldn't be a hierarchy of grief. Your pain is your pain. The closeness of your relationship and the depth of your loss and how you deal with emotion aren't necessarily dictated by the category you fall within. The siblings, who often times are called upon to shoulder the feeling of loss of their aging parents, are feeling forgotten, their loss unacknowledged.

This group provides a respite for siblings only. In these sessions they do not have to fight their way up the pecking order. First they eulogize, then they talk about their individual feelings. Then they get to me. They don't really want to know about my personal feelings. They want to know about my feelings in relation to Howard. "How is Howard dealing with 9/11?" "Gary's loss?" "Do you see things the same way?" "Does he get angry?" "I'm not seeing eye to eye with my brother, do you and Howard?" "Do you and Howard fight?" Of course we fight. We're siblings. Is there any relationship among strong-willed people where they don't argue sometimes? There is no rift between me and my brother and this is not the time, the place, nor the people with whom to air our spats. I say very little. As I steer everything back to them, I realize with a start, that we are like celebrities. Our every move and thought is of interest. I can't be myself here. This is not a safe haven for me. I find myself marshaling my words very carefully. The group, however, is important and will continue to meet every Tuesday.

The next day, I hear from my oldest friend, Cynthia Aranow. Her mother and my mother were best friends, so I have known Cynthie (she's now called Cindy, but childhood habits are hard to break) since I was four. Cynthie calls to tell me she thinks it's great that I went to a support group for siblings. WHAT?? How does she know? I haven't told anybody. It was only yesterday! Apparently, one of the siblings who attended the group works at the same location with my doctor friend. When the 9/11/Lutnick/ME connection comes up at the water cooler he tells her about my participation and my utterances. "Wow, what a small world." The impulse to protect my privacy kicks in.

This sibling support group will go on for years, and will sprout an arm on Long Island started by a sister of a sibling in the Manhattan group. I will be thanked for saving a sibling's life for making her attend this support group. Unfortunately, I am not about to participate and must deal with the loss of Gary on my own.

v   v   v

Mother's Day used to be difficult because my mother died so young. Now it isn't an easy day for me for a different reason. Gary used to take me out every Mother's Day even though, by this point in his life, I really wasn't his mother anymore. Gary understood that our mother/ son relationship was still important to me, so he always invited me out. This Mother's Day I am downtown at the Tribeca Film Festival giving away *Star Wars* preview tickets to our families. It's not laughing with my brother at brunch or being taken to some extravagance or other, but at least I'm making 9/11 *Star Wars* devotees happy as they shake the hands of actors and actresses dressed in character.

A DREAM

After nine long grueling months, the rescue and recovery effort at the World Trade Center site is coming to a close. The brave men and women who have searched for our loved ones' remains at what is now called The Pile are ending their efforts. The families want there to be a closing ceremony so that they can offer their thanks. Several family leaders meet with members of the Office of Emergency Management (OEM) to discuss the closing ceremony. The family leaders request that the ceremony be held on a weekend so that the largest number of family members can attend. The gentleman from OEM agrees, stating that it will actually be easier, because traffic will be lighter on a weekend. The family leaders think the closing ceremony will be held June 2nd. Mayor Bloomberg, without consulting with the families, holds a press conference and announces that the closing ceremonies at Ground Zero will be held during the week on May 30th. When the family leaders object, the mayor states, "You can't please everyone,"[30] and tells the families if they can't make it, they should watch it on TV. Christy cautions the families to "pick their battles."[31] Over strong objections, the closing ceremony is held May 30th, with Mayor Bloomberg telling the press that the date was a "compromise."[32] Many family members who wanted to attend are forced to miss it, myself included.

The mayor's lack of compassion doesn't surprise us. At an earlier meeting at City Hall, where the recovery and identification of remains were being discussed and family objections raised, the mayor said, "So, they experienced a loss. Why can't they just get over it?!" A firefighter father quietly got up and exited the room. When someone politely let the mayor know that there were family members present, he just shrugged.

On May 28th I attend a public hearing before the LMDC. Ever since I joined the LMDC Family Advisory Council, the families have vociferously voiced their objections to the concept of vehicular traffic

running through the site. There wasn't vehicular traffic before the terrorist attacks. Why should the development opportunity be more important
than the rights of the families of the dead? I voice the families' objection to Greenwich and/or Fulton Street being reconnected as anything
other than pedestrian, because it would be too intrusive in a place where
people would be going for contemplation. Unfortunately, this is closely
followed up by a statement to the press by John Whitehead, the chairman of the LMDC board, saying, "It's almost certain that Greenwich
and Fulton will cut through Ground Zero and carry vehicular traffic." [33]
It's that win a battle, make believe the battle was never fought, revive the
original position, lose the battle thing again. I find myself wondering
how many more times this is going to happen.

The June 3rd auction at Sotheby's is tastefully done, well attended and
hugely successful. It is Wall Street supporting Wall Street. The only
"star" is Larry King, and Judith Glaser has brought him and his wife. I
still haven't forgiven him for the show about Gary.

The live auction begins. Trips on yachts, castles, an enormous
canary diamond are all auctioned off. It's fun to watch and it all goes.
I pick out a sculpture entitled *Tikkun*, which from the Hebrew words
Tikkun Olam means "repair the world." It is a glass sculpture made by
Howard's artist friend Henry Richardson.[34] It is a large globe made of
layered pieces of glass. It's fractured, but still together. It speaks to me
and I love it.

The day after the auction brings a new set of endless tasks to ensure
that everyone who made a purchase pays, receives their item and is
satisfied. Our volunteers are understandably exhausted and after nine
months, even the core volunteers need to move on. The ones who can
agree to stick it out with me until the auction tasks are complete. During
the auction, Mary Jo got really sick with pains in her stomach and,
unbeknownst to me, went to the hospital.

The week before, in our shared office, we were talking about dreams.
A woman had come up to me at one of the early town hall meetings, and
told me that she wasn't going to tell me this, and she hopes I don't think

any less of her, but after meeting me she knows I will understand. She said she had a dream. She is on the Long Island Rail Road. Sitting across from her is a very good-looking young man. They start talking and he introduces himself as Gary Lutnick. He asks her to do him a favor and tell his sister and brother that he is okay. Then she woke up. She has never met Gary, Howard or me before. Shortly after 9/11, a cousin (who isn't really a cousin but we call a cousin) told me that on September 11th she awoke out of her sleep and saw Gary sitting on the edge of her bed. She said, "Gary, what are you doing here?" She said that he looked really disoriented. Her sister had the same experience. Mary Jo asked me if I'd seen Gary in a dream yet. Even though Gary is in my every thought, he doesn't make it into my dreams. I said no and that it bothered me, because I wanted to see him so badly. She then told me that the night before she dreamed that she saw her husband Bob. He had aged and told her that he had been waiting for her. He looked great. She found the dream comforting. Bob had passed away when they had only been married six months. It's the main reason Mary Jo came to work for us. She understood what the young 9/11 widows were going through and wanted to help. She hadn't seen Bob in a dream before. Eight months after the Sotheby's auction, Mary Jo died of pancreatic cancer.

Romina is willing to help with closing up the auction but the sabbatical she took from work is almost up, and she needs to return to her life and her paying job. I, alongside the volunteers, put together what we have earned. With the Cantor match we raise just shy of $4 million.

FRESH KILLS

A lot had happened before I became involved. The city needed a place to bring the debris and the human body parts that they were removing from the World Trade Center site. Mayor Giuliani authorized the WTC land to be brought temporarily to Fresh Kills. It is on Staten Island and, at 2,200 acres, is the largest landfill in the country.[35] No change to the name of the dump was made, which was unfathomable to the families on top of the reality that this was, in fact, a garbage dump.

Adding insult to injury, both Mayors Giuliani and Bloomberg decided to sell the World Trade Center steel before it was examined for human remains. They sold more than 185,000 tons of WTC steel to salvage yards in New Jersey over the objections of 9/11 families. The salvage yards cut up the steel into 3x5 girders, loaded then onto ships and sold the steel to manufacturers overseas in China and India. The steel was then recycled into things like toasters, alarm clocks and cans.[36] New York City sold the steel for $120 per ton. 9/11 families aren't going to get back human remains of their loved ones to bury because the City of New York got $120 per ton? Were we so numb from the carnage that confronted us that no one was willing to address the moral implications of these actions?[37] Mayor Bloomberg's only response regarding the destruction of evidence was that if you wanted to take a look at construction and design, that's what computers were for.[38]

Diane Horning's 26-year-old son Matthew worked and died as an information technology "cog" (Matthew's word) at Marsh & McLennan on the 95th floor of One World Trade Center—the North Tower. Her mission is to get the human and ashen remains of the 9/11 victims out of a garbage dump. Diane has had to fight repeatedly for access to Fresh Kills. Her walks through the dump have turned up evidence of overlooked human remains and artifacts countless times. She has found wallets with pictures inside and shoes. The medical examiner signs an affidavit that remains still exist at Fresh Kills. The public claims that there is nothing left to be identified prove false, but go unheeded. She cannot understand how, as a society, we can possibly allow this to happen. She can (and does) fight for what is still in the garbage dump, but the human remains that were attached to those beams are now tin cans with "made in China" stamps on them, and are lost forever to the people who loved them. Each one of the families would gladly have donated $120 to the city instead.

One day, I hear Diane Horning give a speech. She begins by showing a beautifully gift-wrapped package, one we would all wish we were receiving. As she talks, she carefully undoes the tape, preserving the paper and bow. We wait with anticipation as she opens the lid to see what gems of delight are hidden within. Diane turns the box over and spills out a box full of garbage. Her point? No matter what you call it, or how you dress it up, garbage is still garbage. The body parts and cremated remains of human beings should not be allowed to stay in a garbage dump. Calling it a landfill doesn't make it any less inappropriate.

Once again, I'm having a hard time understanding why the mayor does not take action to support this understandable position. I also can't understand why every member of the clergy from every religion isn't actively protesting against this. When Diane Horning confronts the mayor, he comments that he doesn't go visit his father in the cemetery and can't understand why we can't just "move on." This isn't the first time he's made the comment or the only person he's made it to. We are all being subjected to Michael Bloomberg's view of death. He doesn't visit his family, so why do any of us need a burial place for ours?

I get a call that someone has seen a portion of a letter found at the WTC site on Cantor Fitzgerald stationary on sale on eBay. We contact the police. They then open a case and win the bid. We get the letter back. The police contact us again because someone has found Cantor Fitzgerald business cards from the site and is selling them online, claiming that the money is being donated to our Relief Fund. The claim is completely untrue. We would never allow deceased employees' items to be sold. This isn't the norm for this type of personal property.

The police have found ID cards for many of our employees. We work hand in hand with them to get these cards returned to the families. I get one back for Gary. It's amazing that they survive the heat, but the people they identify don't. Personal property and photographs are another story altogether. These are being catalogued by the police and, without proof, are almost impossible to get returned. The gold chain or ring is often melted beyond recognition, or looks exactly like the one that someone else wore. Howard and I could get the serial number of Gary's watch and chase it down, but we choose not to. Being told about his contaminated and destroyed car that sat in the WTC parking garage, which I know also has the umbrella that he made a special trip back to the U.S. Open to retrieve for me, is enough.

One family member tells me that they got an invoice for all of the contents of their son's wallet down to the dollars and cents. They were given his credit cards back, but not the wallet or the money. Dennis McKeon, another family leader who has started a group called Where to Turn and has created a database similar to Bill Doyle's, has taken the return of personal property on as his personal challenge. Despite his constant vigilance, he doesn't get very far. Another database is subsequently created with all the found pictures. There was a photo developing store in the mall below the towers. The hardest to view are the men and women photographed in front of the huge Peace on Earth that adorned the entrance to the mall area between the two towers every winter. I scroll through hundreds of pictures looking for Gary. It is an impossible and emotionally torturous task. I ultimately give up.

A NEW BEGINNING

At Gary's eulogy, I said that my heart was divided into three sections. The first section belongs to me to give as I see fit, and I have chosen to give it to Lewis. The second section belongs to Howard, and the third section—which is broken but never severed—belongs to Gary. Lewis has made me a large rose gold heart with the third section broken but still connected. From the moment he gives it to me, I never take it off. It allows me to take off Gary's sweaters but still feel like I have him near me. When Gary's very close friends Peter and Michelle invite us to their wedding, I can wear a gown. They ask me to read a poem. I know that I am the Gary stand-in. The good times without him are as difficult as the bad ones. The first time Lewis and I go down to the beach, I feel betrayed. The sun is shining, the waves are crashing, the beach is pristine. How can there be all of this beauty and all of this sameness, but no Gary? I hold onto my broken heart necklace and look out over the water and try to believe that Gary is here also.

Peter comes up to me and says that he knows that this is going to sound strange, but he has seen Gary's face in the sky, and that it was almost as if Gary had stayed until Patrick and Peter were both well settled. Gary was smiling and then faded away. Peter says he feels like Gary is now gone. I think he may be right, because as I am standing in the hotel's entryway getting ready to leave the festivities and return to my life, I also see Gary's smiling face in the sky. I can't really explain it. His face isn't in the clouds per se. It's just there. And then he gradually disappears.

It is my birthday—June 25, 2002—and the Cantor Fitzgerald Relief Fund is about to get a new home. Cantor Fitzgerald has leased temporary office space on the corner of 57th and Lexington. They are consolidating the employees who have been spread out all over Manhattan and New Jersey back under one roof. Much to my satisfaction, they have leased the lower floors. In the eyes of Cantor, prime rental space is no longer On Top of the World. Before 9/11, the senior executives were on the uppermost floors. Now, they are on the lowest floors. Howard is on the 3rd floor. Someone tells me that this is the building that gets blown up in the *Spiderman* movie. That bit of information doesn't really thrill me. We are moving to the 6th floor. Everyone is on a floor reachable by firefighter ladders.

Our move from Fish & Neave into our new space isn't without its problems. Debbie Click has designed our computer system in Access, which of course means nothing to me. Our system is incompatible with Cantor's firewalls. The system is password protected and Debbie its keeper. Every time I need something done or changed, she has to do it. No one from Cantor can. She isn't across the hall anymore, and no longer on loan to me. Fish & Neave wants her back doing the work she is being paid to do.

My first day at Cantor Fitzgerald, the phone lines don't transfer and my computer crashes. Everything I have saved personally on my computer is now gone. Just as the task of opening a bank account was an urgent first step 10 months ago, now it is having someone from Cantor figure out our computer system. I plead with Debbie Click and she begins coming to my office after work and between her long commute to Pennsylvania, to show Cantor's IT department what she has done, and how they can do it instead. It starts sounding more and more as if Cantor is going to have to rewrite our entire program. In the meantime, I am worrying about what our families are going to do when they can't reach me. It's not an easy first day.

I am contacted by the Mercy Band Company. This company made POW style bracelets with the names of victims on them. They sold them online and I believe they donated the proceeds to charity. They call me and say that they aren't going to sell them anymore, and that they have extras that they would like to give to my families. I agree to distribute them. When they arrive, there are so many of them. There are differing amounts for different victim's names. I guess it depended upon how many were sold. I receive five with Gary's name on it. Some families get 12. Some get none. We send them to each family. The bracelet gives me comfort. "Gary Lutnick, WTC" on my wrist, like my broken heart necklace, becomes part of my uniform.

THE CHILDREN

Children are having problems, no matter what their age. Some Cantor children are in college, or will be entering college in September. They are away from their families, and they are struggling. The evidence is seen when they return home for breaks and in their grades. We start contacting the colleges and universities where I know we have attendees, not only about financial aid, but to see whether there is some way they can quietly "put together" 9/11 kids if they have more than one attending the university. I know where a lot of my kids are going, but I don't have that information about children outside of Cantor Fitzgerald. Some children see themselves as 9/11 victims and don't mind being identified as such. Others are overwhelmed by the event, and just want to be "normal." Some are still numb. None of their friends' fathers die over and over again in the newspapers. One mother comes to me about her teenage child, telling me that "he put his fist through the wall." She tells me that he is being "killed with kindness." These young men and women are being thrust into adult or parental roles while they are grieving and wholly unprepared, just as I was when I was their age. And they aren't talking. The teenagers are carrying their anger and rage inside and letting it build until it bursts forth in wholly unanticipated ways. These children hear: "You are now the man of the family. Stay strong for your mother." "Take care of your sister." "If you need anything, call us. Your mommy might not be able to."

I make a note to see what programs I can get put together for teenagers that will allow them to vent their physical aggression. I find a swimming program started by a sibling. I talk to him. I try to find a karate class. I contact other family groups to see whether there are support groups or children in need in outlying regions we can pull together to make a group.

Then there are the younger children. One day a mother tells me that a firefighter came into her child's classroom, and the class was told that he was a hero because of his actions on 9/11. Her elementary school-aged child came home and said to his mother, "Mommy, how come my daddy wasn't a hero?" She had to explain to him that there are different kinds of heroes. "Since Daddy was only with all of his friends, they were heroes to each other." Another mother went to her child's school and alerted them to the fact that they had a 9/11 child in the class, and that the teacher was not to give a September 11th assignment. She was horrified when she learned the teacher did it anyway. Her son wrote, "My daddy died on 9/11" and could write no more. He handed his paper to the teacher and started to walk out of the room. The teacher frantically pulled the papers back from all the other students and changed the lesson.

I receive a call that says, "Do you know where I can get scholarship money for my daughter?" I know the answer to this one off the top of my head. Families of Freedom has been raising money from the general public to pay the educational needs of the 9/11 families. They have raised well over $100 million. I send her there. A few weeks later I get a call back from the same mother. "Families of Freedom tells me that I am not qualified to receive funding from them." "Huh?" "They say my husband made too much money. Because of the money I am receiving from you and will receive from the Victim Compensation Fund, I am ineligible to get funding for my daughter." "Then where is the money going if you are ineligible?" "I don't know." "Okay, thanks for letting me know. I'll get back to you."

Here we go again. I take the elevator down three floors. I march into Howard's office, pat his face (an occurrence that warrants his explaining to anyone he may be meeting with that this is his sister and that she needs to do this—errant employees do not just walk in and touch his face), and rant to him that we have another United Way on our hands. Howard tells me to set up a meeting for him and me with Families of Freedom. When we meet with them, Howard tells them that if they are going to exclude all of our families on the basis of income then they have misled the public who gave donations expecting it to go to these families. They need to remove this requirement. They tell us they will get back to us. They don't.

The inability to get educational funds from Families of Freedom transcended the Cantor families. It became a problem across the board. Bill Doyle put together a conference call of frustrated representatives from most groups helping the 9/11 families. Ana Coronel from Senator Clinton's office and Laura Graham from Bill Clinton's staff were on the calls. Both President Clinton and Senator Bob Dole engaged in fundraising for Families of Freedom. The concerted attempt to get them to give the donated money to the 9/11 families continues almost 10 years later. Because of the artificial "needs" test they incorporated, they were able to use the VCF awards to exclude the vast majority of 9/11 children. The latest excuse given to Bill Doyle is that they have an actuarial table of the educational needs of all the 9/11 victims and won't be able to help those in the future if they dispense all the funds today. It's a sophisticated way of saying that the newly named Scholarship America is still not disbursing the money. While they claim that the money will assist more than 4,500 9/11 victims' children, this organization, which has raised more than $116 million from a generous public, has become a source of frustration to the constituency it pledged to help. Two years later it had only distributed 1 percent of the monies raised.[39]

The scope of issues that Bill Doyle is involved in is astounding. He has taken his compilation of 9/11 family resources and become a one-man information clearinghouse. He castigates me for not keeping up. I don't know how I possibly can. The issues run from notifying us about goods and services, like camps and scholarship monies; media opportunities, national and local issues like lawsuits he's helped begin against the Saudis and Iraqis, an extension of time to file against the Port Authority; visits and meetings with John McCain and President Bush; the city's and other memorial services, rallies and vigils; calls to action for federal bills that need family assistance to be passed; and information updates from the LMDC and the city. He tells us of meetings he has had with the property clerk of the NYPD and sends us information on what the process is regarding the return of our loved ones' personal effects. Sometimes he gives his opinion or solicits opinions from others; sometimes he just passes along information. He asks me to do things, like get him the demographics of the Cantor families to assist in the health care plan he is close to getting implemented. Looking back at what Bill has accomplished, I imagine the contribution his son Joey would have made if he hadn't been taken from us all.

*1. Jane Lutnick, November 1978 **2.** Solomon Lutnick, circa 1960*
***3.** Gary, Howard, and Edie, circa 1971 **4.** Howard, Edie, and Gary at Edie's graduation*
*from college, 1980 **5.** Edie and Gary at Lincoln Center, Mother's Day 1992*

6. *Howard's birthday celebration, Gary, Howard, and Edie, July 2001*
7. *Allison, Edie, Gary, and Howard Lutnick, July 2001*
8. *Gary and his cat Bocchi at Edie's summer rental, September 8, 2001*

6

7

8

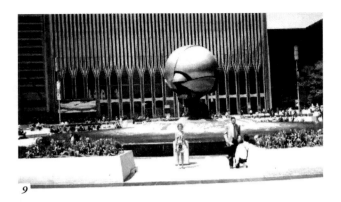

9 *Koenig's Sphere in front of the WTC, 1998* **10.** *Gary at Cantor Fitzgerald with John Delaney, who left the firm before 9/11* **11.** *Howard's office on the 105ᵗʰ floor of WTC. Sculptures are Rodin's, December 18, 1998* **12.** *In front of the WTC every winter, December 18, 1998*

13. *Setting up for Cantor Fitzgerald's memorial service in Central Park, October 1, 2001*
14. *Gene Arbeeny, Edie, and Anthony Larocco, whom Edie has said she will always hug when she sees them* **15.** *Howard speaking at the first Cantor Fitzgerald memorial service, October 1, 2001*

16. *Gary's birthday celebration—he would have been 37—on marathon Sunday, November 4, 2001.*
A. *Lewis Ameri* **B.** *Howard Lutnick* **C.** *Patrick Troy* **D.** *Peter Farmer*
Front, Edie holding Gary's picture

17. *Relief Fund volunteers after our children's event on December 2, 2001.*
A. *Lewis Ameri* **B.** *Romina Levy* **C.** *MaryJo Olson* **D.** *Juliet McIntyre* **E.** *Arlene Rich*
F. *Sharon Lefkowitz* **G.** *Edie* **H.** *Juan Godoy* **I** *Donna Dudek* **J.** *Barbara Lamb*

18

20

19

21

22

18. Edie and Howard, New Year's Eve 2002 19. Assistant Marianna Taaffe in Edie's office. Donated handmade flag quilt became the centerpiece of every office Edie had. 20. Relief Fund, White Party Clambake in Memory of Gary Lutnick, Amagansett, New York, August 9, 2003 21. David Egan with Edie at White Party Clambake August 9, 2003 22. Lewis Ameri, and Edie in front of the Tikkun sculpture at Cantor's fundraiser, June 6, 2002 23. Lauren and Greg Manning at a benefit, November 25, 2005

23

24. *Family leaders and now Edie's friends, Debra Burlingame and Lee Ielpi, 2005*
25. *Steel from Hangar 17 at JFK Airport twisted like a pretzel, October 20, 2005*

26. *Family leaders at the National Press Club in Washington, DC, battling the proposed International Freedom Center, June 29, 2005.* **A.** *Edie.* **B.** *Jack Lynch.* **C.** *Bill Doyle.* **D.** *Diane Horning.* **E.** *Mary Fetchet.* **F.** *Anthony Gardner.*

27. Trailer at Fresh Kills landfill. The engine and landing gear from one of the planes is mixed with Cantor's destroyed Rodins, May 20, 2002. Photo courtesy of Joan Inciardi 28. Cantor family members at a WTC site rally to remove remains from Fresh Kills, September 9, 2006 29. Rally to bring in JPAC after human remains are found in a manhole on the WTC site, November 2, 2006

30

United Airlines FLIGHT 175

31

32

30. Mock-up of names with ages and ranks, in alphabetical order with affiliations shown to media during Save the 9/11Memorial press conference, January 29, 2007 **31.** Edie's interim layout for the Cantor names after Howard Lutnick proposed a change **32.** Jake Loveless with the 715 Cantor names layout in the executive boardroom March 16, 2010 **33.** Names of people split across seams at the National September 11th memorial built to scale mock-up at the Brooklyn Navy Yard **34.** Gary's name being stenciled into bronze at the fabrication plant in New Jersey, January 31, 2011

33

34

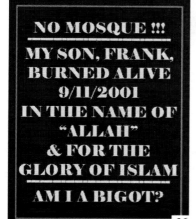

NO MOSQUE !!!
MY SON, FRANK,
BURNED ALIVE
9/11/2001
IN THE NAME OF
"ALLAH"
& FOR THE
GLORY OF ISLAM
AM I A BIGOT?

35. Edie at the permanent memorial standing in front of Gary's panel, June 8, 2011

36. Sign carried at rally against the proposed mosque 600 feet from the WTC site, September 11, 2010. Photograph courtesy of George Reisman.

37. Eli Manning and Lady Gaga at Cantor Fitzgerald/ BGC Partner's Charity Day, which to date has raised over $65 million. Photograph courtesy of Amy Fletcher

38. President Obama signing a book he tells Edie to sell to raise money at a meeting with families after Osama bin Laden's death, May 5, 2011 **39.** Cantor survivors visit the memorial before it opens and stand at the "Survivor Tree." Second from the right is Ari Schonbrun, August 19, 2011. Photograph courtesy of Amanda Zapp

PART II

Edie, after speaking about forgetfulness at a rally to keep the
Memorial Quadrant about 9/11, bombarded by the media, June 25, 2005
Photograph courtesy of Lower Manhattan Development Corporation.

NO ESCAPE

When he walked into my office to introduce himself, I recognized the shattered quality in his eyes. I didn't know who he was, but he was clearly one of us. He was in good physical shape, in a conservative Brooks Brothers–looking suit with a full head of brown hair and Gucci loafers. He told me his name was Ron Bowman. It was his company that most of our construction contractors worked for. These were his friends and his colleagues. He attended our first memorial service in October 2001.

Ron was down at the site and saw the carnage. Like Howard, his life was in danger although he never processed or talked about that. He has the survivor's hell, which is different from what most of my families face but no less devastating. He told me that he had stood on the street while he was on the phone with one of his guys. I asked him where his guy had been. He responded, "on the roof." "But I thought the roof was locked? They couldn't get on the roof." "No, Edie. My guys were on the roof. I was talking to them while they were on the roof."

His employees were on Cantor's floors and some of them got onto the roof. This was something I hadn't known before that moment. Looking at the situation now, I'm not sure that was a blessing. To this day, it still upsets me that an alternative escape plan wasn't in place for the upper floors. It seemed to me that the possibility of extreme heat from a fire or heavy winds were conditions that should have been anticipated long before 9/11.

I wanted to help both this man, who felt the weight of this responsibility, and his families. We were already assisting them financially and giving them access to all the goods and services posted on our website. I decided to make sure that every contractor was included in our memorial service and that their families were invited to attend. As with Euro Brokers before them, the contractors are now squarely in my fold.

When Anthony Gardner considered the bombing of the Federal Building in Oklahoma City, the similarities between the losses the families had suffered was obvious. He started the Oklahoma Exchange program so that 9/11 victims' families, rescue workers and survivors from both tragedies could interact. On his first trip, Anthony heard the story of a grandmother who fought and won the right for her deceased daughter's unborn child to be recognized at the Oklahoma City Memorial. Anthony never forgot. He subsequently lobbied the LMDC to include "and her unborn child" in any names arrangement at the 9/11 permanent memorial. He was ultimately successful. Cantor's two pregnant victims have "and her unborn child" after their names.

∨ ∨ ∨

When the *New York Times* started running a series called "Portraits of Grief," they captured both the public's and the families' attention. The articles are powerful, brief glimpses into the lives of the 9/11 victims as provided by their families. Howard and I were so focused on rendering care that sometimes the things being done to memorialize loved ones fell through the cracks when it came to Gary. I still wasn't ready to share Gary with the world, or paraphrase his character succinctly, so Howard gave the interview. He described Gary as a confirmed toy lover, and a people magnet. "From kindergarten on, he had best friends who stuck to him like Velcro." He went on to tell them about how Gary loved Howard's children, played with them every Saturday and how his boys nicknamed him, "Uncle Gary with the TV games" because they often played video games together from his extensive collection. Howard said that if Gary had been a stock, "He'd be the one you'd always want to keep around, always want to bet on. He went in one direction: up." He described the close relationship between the three of us by saying, "We fit like a puzzle." The portrait of Gary, aptly named "One-Third of a Trio," came out on Howard's birthday, July 14, 2002.[40]

BLOOMBERG

Despite our attempts, we continued to have a very difficult time finding common ground with Mayor Bloomberg. His comments both to the press and to us out of their presence didn't do anything to make us feel that we had an ally in city hall. When he said the "size of the memorial … should not overshadow the needs of downtown residents and businesses," and went on to say that it shouldn't feel like a cemetery because that would hurt the real estate market,[41] it only confirmed our belief that a considered memorial wasn't driving this development project. In a meeting in April 2003, when families tried to enlist his help in getting our issues considered, he responded that he didn't lose anybody so didn't have an emotional attachment to the site. He told us that if it were up to him, he would build schools and housing instead of a memorial … but that, thankfully for us, it wasn't up to him.[42]

Ironically, when he had the power to build schools and low-income housing in Lower Manhattan, he didn't do it. When Congress approved $8 billion in interest and tax free bonds, referred to as Liberty Bonds, to revitalize Lower Manhattan, the city gave most of the money to developers of prime real estate in midtown Manhattan and Brooklyn—including $650 million to erect a tower for Bank of America near Times Square and $113 million for a Bank of New York tower in Brooklyn. One of the few projects downtown went to Robert De Niro to build a high-end boutique hotel in Tribeca. Even John Whitehead criticized those awards, saying that Congress did not intend the Liberty Bonds for the more prosperous precincts of midtown. He said that the bonds would be "needed for the World Trade Center site itself and the surrounding area."[43]

Previously, the LMDC had held public forums to discuss the urban planning competition for the WTC site. This public announcement let us know that the site was being divided up for multiple uses, and that a preserved 16 acres was no longer an option. On behalf of the Cantor Relief Fund Families, I said the following at a public hearing on May 23, 2002:

> *We polled our families to see what it was that they wanted, and what they said was they wanted the memorial to be where the people that we loved and lost lived. They would like the memorial to be the footprints of the two buildings and the mall area in front of it.*[44]

I went on to declare that there should be no vehicular traffic through the site. Last, I said that however and whatever they decided to build, they should make the site architecturally compatible, so that even though they were going to make the World Trade Center site appear smaller by breaking it up into various uses, a visitor should be able to tell by the architectural elements (i.e., streetlamps, signage) where the original 16 acres were. When the competition designs were whittled down to six, they were deemed uninspired and were universally panned by both the media and the public, which claimed they all looked the same, and they all looked like Albany.

Despite the critiques, the LMDC chose a winner, and then yielded to public pressure, and scrapped the winning design. As with most 9/11 issues, the battle to get the winning design thrown out was long and arduous and took up way too much newsprint. So, when the second competition commenced without all the fanfare of the first, almost no one from the general public was paying much attention. The LMDC narrowed the design choices down to two, "Think" and Daniel Libeskind's. Both plans connected the street grid as Bloomberg had "required" and both ignored the family leaders' adamant pleas not to run vehicular traffic across the site. When the LMDC picked "Think", and limited public response concurred, Governor Pataki and Mayor Bloomberg overrode them and announced that Daniel Libeskind's design had won the competition.[45]

The public, families and Libeskind himself believed that he was designing everything but the memorial, which in a separate competition would have to fit into his urban design. This was not in fact the case. The LMDC president at the time, Kevin Rampe, told us to disregard Libeskind's building designs because they were "merely placeholders." This was very confusing to us because we thought that was why he had won the competition. Weren't the designs of the buildings the element that drew people to his design? Much to his and everyone else's confusion, the only thing Libeskind appeared to have won was the ability to set the "quadrants," meaning what would go where.

Even after a Memorial Quadrant was defined, the mayor's office eroded that quadrant even further by trying to discredit the Coalition of 9/11 Families position that the land underneath the WTC towers was significant. I, along with all the other family leaders, got an email from Michael Cartier of the organization Give Your Voice. Michael lost his brother in the South Tower. He said this:

> *A representative from the mayor's office has stated that they are in contact with the majority of family members and that "majority" agrees that the grounds below the footprints of the North and South Tower are not in fact sacred. We are interested in exactly how the mayor's office has contacted you and come to such a determination.*[46]

This was news to me. I wasn't contacted, nor was I aware of any family who didn't view the WTC site in its entirety as sacred ground regardless of what was ultimately built on it. Thanks in large part to strenuous and constant vigilance on the part of Anthony Gardner and the coalition, much of the tower footprints below ground have been preserved, especially when you take into account the amount of tower footprint on which the PATH train station was built. But the preservation position was bastardized into a justification for putting both the memorial and the museum below ground, with nothing visible above. This had never been the aim of the vast majority of families or the coalition, and was contrary to the wishes of most. Besides, Governor Pataki, in his campaign for reelection for a third term as New York State governor, promised that there would be no commercial development on the tower footprints.[47]

On July 2nd, the LMDC appointed Anita Contini as vice president and director of the memorial, cultural and civic programs. Specifically, her job was to oversee the process for creating a memorial. The LMDC described her as "an advocate for art in the public realm."[48] One of the initial things she did was take the members of various advisory committees on a tour of local public monuments. After seeing many memorials, including the Maine Monument in Columbus Circle, which has no historic markers, discernible connection to the deceased it honors and hence no emotional power, Ms. Contini said, "Maybe they shouldn't have long-term relevance. Not everything should be remembered forever." She asked, "Do we want to celebrate the culture of death, instead of the culture of the living?"[49] This disconcerted all of us who wanted a memorial with a connection to the lives lost.

During this time, there was a juxtaposition between what was happening in response to personal travails, local politics, and what was happening on the national front. Every once in a while, I would have to step outside my role as family advocate to make a decision for my own family. The court decision which allowed families of 9/11 victims to watch the trial of the 20th hijacker, Zacarias Moussaoui, on closed circuit television at various locations was one of those times. The trial began in August 2002 and continued for four years. Many of our families were interested in watching the trial and we made all the information known to them. I chose not to watch it. It was too painful for me and I had too much to do. Families reported back that the hijackers practiced slitting the throats of the pilots by slitting the throats of sheep. The pain and rage this must have brought to those families incenses me still.

A NEW PHASE

With the passage of time, and the incredibly frenetic pace of the previous months, it wasn't surprising that most of our volunteers moved on. Three were given full-time jobs at Cantor and it was a joy for me to still be able to see their faces. Others went back to their old paying jobs. The only person left was me. I became a one-person relief fund, and often felt overwhelmed. I told Howard that I needed help and could no longer accomplish anything with a volunteer staff that, along with contributions, had dwindled to almost nothing. Cantor's CFO was there while I was complaining. He said he had an employee he was going to have to lay off. She had lost her sister-in-law at Cantor. He asked me to meet her. If I agreed, his department would continue to pay her salary for her accounts receivable job but she would work for me. To me, family is family and she was one of mine. I would have taken her if she had two heads. She didn't. Marianna Scibetta was sweet, young and pretty. We immediately became a Relief Fund of two. The first time she asked me if I wanted her to get me something to eat, I looked at her blankly and started to fall in love.

There was comfort in the world I came to know. If Marianna is little, Phyllis Frank isn't much taller. She has shoulder-length, curly black hair and can fit under my arm. She has an open and kind face. To meet her is to immediately be drawn to her. She was walking by our offices on 57th Street and, on a whim, decided to come see me. As she sat in my office, our conversation flowed easily. She told me about her son Morty and how he loved his job as an equities trader. She asked me about Phil Marber, the boss of equities. Then she asked me if I knew John Law. John and Morty were desk partners for nine years. They lived in the same building on Prince Street. Both Phil Marber and John Law are alive and still work for Cantor.

"Come on. I'll take you to see them." I brought Phyllis upstairs. She was amazed to see all of those young people up there working. I brought her over to John's desk. It was a warm and touching moment for them. John introduced Phyllis around and it was a turning point for both. The Frank family has a benefit golf outing every year in Morty's memory. They give scholarships to children so that they can attend college. Because of their meeting, John Law attends the benefit every year. Because of the Frank's charity, Phyllis gave me a place to send some of the mothers denied help by Families of Freedom. Cantor families helping other Cantor families—it remains a common theme.

When Lewis insisted that we go to the Hamptons for the weekend, I agreed. He was trying, without much success, to restore some degree of balance back into my life. Now married, Peter and Michelle invited us to the bay-front house they were renting in South Hampton. As we sat on their rock beach enjoying a balmy summer evening, a lone swan swam by. It was beautiful. We stopped our conversation to watch it. The swan stopped swimming in front of me, changed course and started swimming straight toward us. Then it walked out of the water and up the beach toward me. We looked at each other. I said, "Hi, Gary?" The swan stood at full height and flapped its wings. It then turned around, moved gracefully back into the water and swam away, leaving four flabbergasted humans in its wake.

❧ ❧ ❧

Shortly before the first anniversary, Mayor Bloomberg said that he tried to call the families of the approximately 400 uniformed workers who died on September 11th. He recounted that most had moved on with their lives. Then he said, "There were 15-odd families where the spouse, I think it was probably all women, they just kept crying and crying…. It's not my business to say that to a woman, 'suck it up and get going,' but that is the way I feel."[50]

At the Relief Fund, with our second Cantor memorial fast approaching, we started working on hotel rooms. Family members began calling us requesting to come in from out of town for what would now become our annual memorial service. I called my friend Shari Clayman-Kerr, who works for Le Parker Meridien, and got rooms donated. I called another friend, and asked her to use her Four Seasons connections to try to get us donated rooms. We started cold-calling all the hotels in the city. Many of them were already booked up. We spoke to the Red Cross. They started securing hotel rooms and offered assistance with travel costs. We blocked rooms with them for families coming from England, France, Australia and Japan, as well as from out of state. In my August 16th letter to the families, along with their quarterly Relief Fund distribution of 25 percent of Cantor's profits, which this quarter was $6,703.41, and their health care costs, I told them about the hotel rooms and the details for our memorial service in Central Park.

Every year Cantor held a picnic for the families of its employees. Howard decided to continue the tradition in spite of 9/11. We invited all of the Cantor Fitzgerald Relief Fund families to the picnic. After all, their loved ones were gone, but to us they are still very much a part of this company. We continued to give away everything that was sent to us from the general public: pins, CDs, books, letters, hearts, memory boxes, bears, quilts. Like the Chelsea Piers event, it was another place where children, in spite of their loss, could safely be children.

After all the ups and downs that surrounded manually trying to create an electronic check, my hands finally got a reprieve. ADP would now do our quarterly check run processing electronically. Juliet, who went to work for payroll, became involved with this process on the Cantor side. After handwriting 8,883 checks, a significant portion would now be written by a computer and reviewed by us. I joked to Marianna that if I ever had to sign my name that many times again, it better be on traveler's checks!

CHARITY DAY ⬩

Howard made the decision to turn September 11th into something positive and created Charity Day. All employees who wanted to could come to work on September 11th and donate their day's pay. Those who didn't want to work, didn't have to. One hundred percent of the revenue the firm earned that day would go to the Relief Fund. We scheduled our memorial service for the late afternoon so that any family member or survivor who wanted to attend the city's service at the World Trade Center site would not have a conflict, and any survivor who wanted to work until the market closed could do so.

We are more prepared for this first anniversary memorial service, but it doesn't make it any easier. Kent has co-opted my friend Donna Dudek and made her his second-in-command in charge of production. I make my way to SummerStage in Central Park early. Setting up with my friends and volunteers is good for me. I need to keep busy. It's that "nowhere in the world feels right without Gary" feeling that I am trying to stave off, or at least make manageable. My friends and volunteers come and help Lewis and me. We place whatever left over teddy bears and quilts we have on the chairs, along with grey or white t-shirts bearing the phrase "United We Stand." Fish & Neave's receptionist has made pins out of red, white and blue ribbon in the shape of the breast cancer ribbon for each of us. When the enormous tent has the sense of warmth I want it to have, and it starts getting late, I go home to change.

Lewis and I, once again dressed in black, make our way to Central Park. I look at the registration desk, on which I have supplied each volunteer with a list of all of our 768 victims, who include the 658 from Cantor, the 61 from Euro Brokers and all 49 of our contractors. The core volunteers have all returned. Friends I haven't seen in years are there manning registration. True to their word, the Fish & Neave core are sitting expectantly behind a desk, awaiting the faces of the families whose loved ones' names they have come to know so well.

For me, it is overwhelming to realize how many people I now know, and how many more recognize me. Here are the numerous family members I have spoken with, physically touched, assisted with a problem, advocated for or sent a check to. They are grateful. I wrap my arms around every person, be they family member or survivor.

When Greg and Lauren Manning walk through the front of the tent to take their seats, my heart goes wild. This is the same Lauren Howard visited in the burn unit, the same Lauren who was in an induced coma, the same Greg who had to act for Lauren. I am so happy to see her. Lauren is burned over 82 percent of her body, but her face was spared because she covered it with her hands. She looks amazing—slightly worse for wear, but still Lauren. I gently encase her in my arms. She tells me I am her inspiration. I look at her and say, "That is ridiculous. You are mine." To me, Lauren Manning is the embodiment of strength.

The colors are posted and then retired by the U.S. Marine Corps, the Boys Choir of Harlem sings "God Bless America" and "The Star-Spangled Banner." Jennifer Gardner tells us about her husband Doug. Frank Aquilino tells us about his son. When Carole King, who at the request of Congresswoman Carolyn Maloney first sang at the crisis center, again sings "You've Got a Friend," I dig my nails into Pat Troy's palm as we, along with everyone else, helplessly cry. Lauren Manning sits up on the stage next to Hillary Clinton. Their mutual admiration is palpable. Whether or not you agree with her politics or policies, Hillary Clinton has been a friend to the 9/11 families and she is here to speak. This is not about politics. It is about support. Family members speak as do members from three clergies. Judy Collins sings. Senator Schumer speaks. Calvin Gooding's widow LaChanze sings "I Will Remember You" and we unabashedly sob. Last, Howard comes forward to speak. Thousands of people, in the throes of their grief, applaud.

Marianna's first task as my new assistant was to help me collect a picture of the person who was loved and is now gone from every family. Cantor's IT department put them into a PowerPoint presentation, and

Kent erected huge screens for the memorial recitation of the names. As hard as it is to listen to the names, seeing their vibrant smiling faces, some in head shots, some with their families, one catching a monster fish, all of them engaging, punches you in the stomach. For me, the names on my master list with multicolor highlighter lines through them marking the checks that have been sent for different purposes—holiday distribution, child care runs, charity set up, parental assistance, quarterly distributions—now have very real faces attached to them. As Cantor's surviving employees begin reading the names, and these young, handsome and beautiful faces (the average age is 36) fill the screen, a huge, and I mean seriously enormous, gust of wind comes up out of nowhere. We wonder whether it will blow the tent down. Other family members, who have not had the conversation I had with Sherry Partridge on the six-month anniversary, are inexorably drawn to the same conclusion. It must be their souls. They are here with us now.

Kent has gotten doves. In truth, they are white homing pigeons, but, to our untrained eye, they pass as doves. They are released into the sky as the names are being read and fly away. As we come to the end of the last names that begin with L and Gary's name starts to be read, a lone homing pigeon flies back to the stage, sits on the speaker and refuses to be shooed away. I stare at the bird. The bird stares at me. I say, "Hi, Gary." The bird looks at me, almost in acknowledgment, and, as the next name starts to be read, flies away. Okay. I guess if Sherry can have the wind, I can have a lone bird.

After significant prodding, I was scheduled to take my first vacation, which a friend and I purchased at the Cantor Sotheby's auction, to Bali. Two weeks before we were supposed to leave, 200 people from 21 countries were murdered during a terrorist attack in Bali.[51] We were shocked and appalled as we watched the horror unfold. It is the devastation in Bali that finally causes the terror of 9/11 to start penetrating my numbness.

As I look back on that first year, from a vantage point of 10 years later, it's hard for me to imagine how much we accomplished. I really just wanted to crawl up in a ball and not move. Having a purpose larger than myself—caring for our families—was the only thing that kept me going. I never actively thought about what I was doing or how it would turn out. I just reacted, over and over again. It was never about strength. It was always about survival. Not just mine and Howard's, but all of ours.

FLASHBACKS

When the thick black smoke started racing toward us as we sat in our Lexington Avenue offices, we ran. People were screaming and racing toward the elevators. No one had the courage to voice it, but we all had the same thought, "Oh my G-d, this is happening again." "Howard! HOWARD! Where is my brother?" I was numb with fear. I ran down from the sixth to the third floor looking for him, all the while thinking, "Please G-d let him have gotten out." Juliet's boss in payroll started screaming for everyone to get out of the building. When I saw Juliet outside, she told me she saw Howard and another employee carrying wheelchair-bound Tommy Tedford down the stairs. When Howard finally emerged from the building, my heart returned from my throat to its rightful place in my chest. I threw my arms around him, kissed him and ran my hands over his face. We subsequently learned that there had been a crane accident at the Bloomberg building, which was being built across Lexington Avenue. Juliet's co-worker, a 9/11 survivor, couldn't handle it and took a medical leave of absence. No one at Cantor was physically hurt, but this was just a little bit too familiar. As is expected with victims of post-traumatic stress, our memories were revived.

❧ ❧ ❧

While many families anxiously awaited any word that their loved one had been identified, many others came to dread the knock at the door or the phone call. When an identification was made, a police officer was dispatched to inform the family or a staff member from the Office of the Chief Medical Examiner placed a call. Most of our families already had a memorial or funeral service for their loved one. Friends and family already made the shocked and numb foray to the cemetery, watched the coffin being lowered into the ground. Now what were our families supposed to do? Should they have another service? Quietly bury the remains in a different box in the same plot? Should they pull up the empty, memorabilia-filled, or single-bone coffin and add the newly discovered "piece?" And how were they supposed to deal with the emotional ripping open of the cautiously closing seams of their lives that this new discovery brought?

Not knowing what would be on the other side of the door, or what would confront them when they said hello on the phone carried its own brand of anxiety.

Would this be the day or night you learned that another fragment of your child or spouse would be returned to you? And would you be a bad person if, after the fifth or sixth time this happened, the seventh time your remaining family saw you turn around with no color in your face, the eighth time you went with the funeral director to the cemetery plot, that you wished they wouldn't knock anymore? When an official identification is made the first time, by law the family must be notified. They should be, because a Freedom of Information Act request requires the Office of the Chief Medical Examiner to publish the name of every victim found. So, if the police or medical examiner didn't inform the family first, they or someone they know would likely find out the news in the press. But when one of our families was notified over 100 times, enough was enough. The families had to be given a choice as to whether they wanted to continue receiving notification of identifications. I asked Shiya to prepare a form, which we sent out to every family, allowing them to articulate in what manner they wanted to be notified, and whether they wanted to cease receiving identifications.

Years later, Shiya told me that some families didn't want to be notified, even from the beginning. When the last reported identification was made before the ME's office ceased testing, the brother-in-law commented that the family now knew that their loved one was not out there somewhere suffering from amnesia. Remains removed hope, and for some that was an unacceptable way to live out the remainder of their lives.

Howard began his fourth round of town hall meetings. This time the meetings were to update the families on the VCF. He explained that Cantor had negotiated with top law firms to provide each family with legal services either pro bono or at 1 percent, rather than at the 10 percent airline crash attorneys were charging. He also told our families that he had hired Chicago Partners to prepare an economic analysis for every Cantor victim. They would analyze the mathematical model Feinberg was using and do an analysis of each Cantor victim's earnings to present each of the 658 cases in its most positive economic light. At least now the families would be able to go to their hearing prepared, and argue with Feinberg using his math instead of just emotion. Cantor Fitzgerald would also fill out the required affidavits. In short, he told our families that Cantor would fully prepare them to present their strongest possible case. He reminded them that anyone whose loved one earned more than $231,000 would be treated less favorably and therefore the next of kin had to participate in a hearing. In fact, he advised every family to request a hearing, regardless of income. Howard assured them that Cantor was still fighting the methodology and that at this point no one should enter the fund. Paul Pion, an auditor who came from Deloitte and Touche and now works for Howard, started putting families together with attorneys.

New Yorker magazine published an article on Kenneth Feinberg on November 25, 2002. Feinberg reiterated what he had already told us, that "except in extremely rare cases," he would not give out awards of more than $6 million. (Howard's changes to the calculations forced the increase from $4 million to $6 million.) The law was clear, the families give up their rights to sue the airlines, and in return the government steps in and makes the victims' families whole. Full economic loss for a lifetime of earnings is what a victim who proved liability would get in a court. With the VCF, the government stepped in and capped the airlines' liability at their insurance, saving them from bankruptcy. But Feinberg was completely manipulating the law. When the author asked him to respond to comments that "Feinberg is supposed to determine economic loss, not to make value judgments about different groups of income earners," Feinberg responded. "[The law] gives me discretion to do whatever I want. So I will." When she raised the point that there are clients that deserve $16 million and $17 million, he responded, "You've lost your fucking mind! This guy should file suit…. And do me a favor—hold a press conference. Say I wouldn't give sixteen million dollars—tax free! Who's going to fight? No one's going to fight."[52] These people were *supposed* to be made economically whole, live in their same houses, send their children to the same schools, stay financially the same. Feinberg, worrying how he would look, changed it all. After Feinberg called Staten Island a third world country, the congressman from Staten Island, Vito Fossela, approached the Justice Department about having Feinberg removed.[53] He was unsuccessful.

Sometimes, emails, letters or phone calls brought good news in the midst of all the controversy. On October 24th, Anthony Gardner of the Coalition of 9/11 Families sent an email suggesting that the damaged but not destroyed Koenig's Sphere, which used to be the centerpiece of the mall between the two WTC towers, and is now a temporary memorial in Battery Park City, be restored to the WTC site as part of a permanent memorial. I used to sit with so many others in front of that sphere and listen to music at lunchtime or just enjoy the sunshine. In the winter, I loved the enormous Peace on Earth sign you always saw in front of it at the mall's entrance. On behalf of the Cantor survivors, I joined him in his quest to have the sphere returned. In the email he told us that he and his wife Lorraine were expecting a daughter they would name Lia Hope Gardner after his brother Harvey.

The battle to return Koenig's Sphere to the WTC memorial site, and specifically the Memorial Quadrant, still rages 10 years later. Mike Burke, who lost his firefighter brother, took the lead on this battle. He consistently advocated that the story of 9/11 should not be buried. On behalf of a wide cross-section of families, he has fought for the return of the sphere and taken the position that artifacts should be displayed above ground on the WTC site. To date, Koenig's Sphere still remains in Battery Park City, because the land is now controlled by the City of New York and not the Port Authority, and the mayor will not allow its return.

Nor has Community Board 1 budged on its position that no emotional reminders of 9/11 should be on the site.

ᵛ   ᵛ   ᵛ

As hard as it was to contemplate, we had to address Gary's belongings. Howard made arrangements with his storage facility. They spread out all of Gary's belongings, the remnants of a life in one large room. We invited all of Gary's close friends to attend. Howard and I came to the storage facility early, putting the things we wanted to one side. I took Gary's socks. He had work socks (men's dress socks are nothing like women's) in conservative colors, but with personality affirming designs. Each pair is different. I knew that when I wanted to feel him near me but couldn't get away with wearing his sweater, I could sneak on a pair of socks. I kept his iron bed, and the bedspread in that masculine green/brown that will never be quite right in my house. I didn't have a place for them, but I wanted them anyway. I kept the barometer filled with water and blue glass balls that tells you the temperature, and the chess set he and Lewis used to play on, as he furrowed his brow in concentration. I took a few jackets (which I discovered had sunglasses stuffed in the pockets), button-down shirts (sometimes I still sleep in the one I have from my father—it's very sexy now that most of the buttons have fallen off), and the pictures. I filled a suitcase with the pictures. I took the African art wooden gazelle that had been in my father's house, then in Gary's. I looked at furniture that had made the rounds to all three of our houses and apartments in no particular order, as it shuffled between us as if we were one.

Howard became an auctioneer. "Okay, we have a tuxedo, a barbeque, golf clubs, jet skis, a cashmere coat, a jean shirt." He physically sized up Gary's friends and announced that Mark Gallagher, who was once mentored by Gary and is now a success in his own right, and can always be counted on to send you the card that says just the right words, should try on this jacket. John Stefanelli, Gary's "wild child" friend, took his bachelor-affirming black leather couch. Since Peter had the boat, we decided he had to take the jet skis also. I'm not sure Peter actually wanted eight-year-old jet skis, but he went with it. It was cold. Gary's friends were taking off their coats in this cement clad room, to try on Gary's clothing—as if fit had anything to do with it. I forced clothing on Lewis that he would never wear. Lewis's arms are longer, his shoulders bigger. I just wanted to see it hanging in the closet. Sometimes I was laughing. Sometimes I was crying. But, it was like one of those cartoons in fast motion when pieces of a room quickly disappear. Howard made arrangements to have all of Gary's belongings delivered to the eight or 10 close friends who were in the room. Whatever wasn't chosen, we donated to charity. It's hard to accept that you can't hold onto everything. But if you give yourself enough time to get it right, the things that you do hold onto end up being enough. Howard and I walked out of the storage facility, our arms around each other.

❤   ❤   ❤

When Howard decided to rent out the Big Apple Circus in New York City for our families and for Cantor's clients, we got the word out to our families that they could have as many tickets as they wanted. When they walked in the door, they received tickets for free refreshments as well. We took all the donated toys we received and separated them by age and sex. We gave each child a gift. The children laughed when they saw the clowns. Howard and Allison brought their children. When Howard went into the center ring to greet the families, he was as popular with the parents as the circus performers were with the children. Cantor Fitzgerald now has two annual events where parents can bring their children and safely know that they can just be kids.

Meanwhile, the LMDC divided the Family Advisory Council into two committees charged with drafting a memorial mission statement and a memorial program, the purpose of which was to set the parameters for a competition to choose a memorial designer. This wasn't an easy task, because opinions differed on how to express what we wanted. It took up a lot of my time. Perhaps the easiest way to describe how difficult and time consuming this was would be to talk about the discussion that surrounded the word *murder*. Almost all family leaders believe that our loved ones were murdered on September 11th. Tom Roger, whose daughter Jean was a flight attendant, does not. He along with Nikki Stern, who lost her husband, were doing the drafting. Tom sent us an email:

"Murdered" vs "Perished or died"—our anger demands that we call this a mass "murder" but in fact all of these people were not "murdered"; the pilots and a passenger on my daughter's plane were murdered by the hijackers but my daughter and many others died as a consequence of the suicide hijacking and airplane crash; and many died because they were trapped in a burning building that collapsed; and some died because they jumped out of a building..." [54]

Stephen Push from the group Families of September 11th (a group Tom Roger was a member of) wrote back:

All 3,000+ people who died as a result of the terrorist acts committed that day were murdered. It doesn't matter whether the weapon was a box cutter, a plane, or a collapsing building. All of the killings were deliberate, were not in self-defense and lacked any other extenuating circumstance recognized by law. In fact, our loved ones' deaths were murders under Islamic law, as well as western law. [55]

Carol Ashley, of another 9/11 family, then wrote,

In the mission statement, rather than "murdered," I would prefer to use the word "killed." It is less angry than "murdered" and more powerful than "perished." Although I totally agree that the terrorists planned to murder as many people as possible, and I feel the same anger as others, in keeping with our goal of reverence and peace at the Memorial, "killed" is less strident.[56]

A similar conversation ensued about the words *patriotism* and *heroes*. After numerous months, countless emails and drafts, the Family Advisory Council came up with a memorial mission statement and programmatic statement, which were submitted to the LMDC. They included the word *murdered*, which I felt appropriate because it reflected the position shared by most.

Our work and careful conversations, however, proved moot. A week later the LMDC announced that they were appointing two committees encompassing members of all the advisory groups and others to do exactly what we had just spent months doing. The families that could always be counted on to parrot Mayor Bloomberg's positions— Paula Grant Berry, Nikki Stern, Tom Roger and Christy Ferer—were all appointed to the committees. When Monica Iken, along with other family leaders, started publicly complaining that no family member who had expressed divergent opinions had been appointed to a committee and that the influence of the families was waning, the governor had the LMDC appoint Monica to the Memorial Program Drafting Committee.[57]

CHANGE

Lewis is a beautiful person, inside and out. He has large features that somehow work on his face. His long, brown curls flecked with copper make women want to come at him with scissors and take his hair home for themselves. But more than any of that, he has a wide open warm smile, and hazel brown eyes that make you know that he is a safe place to fall. His friends all call him Sweetness, and you don't have to spend more than five seconds with him to know why. Any tranquility in my life I owe to Lewis, but I was systematically removing all peace from his. His unstated job, which he still does instead of being an artist, and took on without request or objection, was to watch me and anticipate my needs. There were days when it was a struggle to get out of bed. I was gaunt, and while normal activities were creeping back into our lives, no one would have described me as a happy person. I robbed him of every holiday that used to give us joy. We spend every Thanksgiving at his parents' house and they would always go around the table. His parents, his sister Jill and nieces Vicky and Erika, all of whom were a bulwark of strength for me, stated the things that they were thankful for. Even in the midst of all the pain, I never forgot that I still had so much to be grateful for.

September 11th tested the foundations of many relationships. It either made them stronger or ripped them asunder. Friends of mine told me that it made them realize they didn't want to stay with their spouses any longer. Others, believing time was precious, sped up their marriage plans or starting trying to have a baby. Still others decided that this wasn't a world to bring a baby into and scrapped their plans. Parents who lost their children found themselves among the statistics as their marriages dissolved along with their family lives. I was one of the lucky. My relationship, seven years long before 9/11, had only grown stronger.

I let Lewis into my heart in a way I didn't before. Howard and Lewis are alive and healthy. I have a roof over my head, food on my table and clothing on my back. When construction finally finished, I moved into Gary's apartment.

Our families were slowly coming out of the numbness that their brains kindly allowed them. More and more of them were starting to "accept" and individually trying to put a semblance of a life back together. Their well-being is my life. That Thanksgiving, just over a year after 9/11, I looked at the faces of Lewis's family around the table. I tried to get words out expressing my gratitude but I just couldn't. They stuck in my throat. Gary's absence was still too profound. "Please just skip me." I left the table in tears.

ᵛ   ᵛ   ᵛ

On December 5, 2002, a week after her appointment to the Program Committee, Monica Iken sent us the following email:

> *All members of the programming committee have been asked to keep what is discussed in the meetings confidential so that when the draft program is ready, it can be released to the public without prior bias and at that point, public meetings will be scheduled to allow all interested parties to voice their opinions. That means that unfortunately I will not be able to discuss my work or the committee's work in preparing this document with the families.*[58]

When the LMDC committees released their finished product, the word *murdered* was nowhere to be found.[59] Neither were most of the things the families fought so hard to safeguard.

The new memorial mission statement went before the LMDC board for ratification, and a battle we never saw coming ensued. Madelyn Wils, the forceful chair of Community Board 1, up to this point had been fighting the return of any artifact to the neighborhood, including the battered but recovered Koenig's Sphere. Now she objected to the use of the word *sacred* in the phrase, "Respect this place made sacred through tragic loss." Wils wanted the "record to reflect a specific, limited definition of the word sacred, one that would not make the site as a place apart." In short, she didn't want any space designated specifically for a memorial. She wanted to make sure that the phrase allowed "secular uses on the memorial site."

The LMDC held off on a competition for a memorial until all of the space for other uses had been planned out. Rather than having the memorial drive the process, it was given the space that was left. Now that we had already lost the sacred nature of the entire 16 acres, and were fighting for the space that the towers once occupied, Ms. Wils advocated for allowing secular uses on that site as well. Thankfully, another board member, prepared for her objection, faced it down by saying that sacred comes from the word *sacrifice*, which "means really to make sacred by the loss of their lives, how they perished. So sacred is consecrated, it's holy. It's hallowed."[60] The board resolution went forward without a limitation on a jury's interpretation, but her objection and position had been heard by many.

LOVE

The winter holidays brought an abundance of Christmas cards. If a family decided to send out a card, I think I got one. Just as the pictures at the memorial made the victims real, so did the cards with the faces of the 805 Cantor children they left behind. Families sent letters of thanks and some even sent gifts. I was humbled by the thoughtfulness and generosity. I put the letters and cards up all over my office. On days that were oftentimes frustrating and thankless, this was my reminder for why I persevere.

Cantor Fitzgerald was now operating at a consistent, albeit smaller, profit. Institutional Equities—where Cantor helped money managers like Fidelity, pension funds like California Teachers, and hedge funds across America buy and sell stocks in bulk sizes—had been rebuilt with the hiring of about 150 people. eSpeed, Cantor's electronic U.S. government bond exchange, continued to operate very well, but now had tougher competition from ICAP/Brokertec, which still sought to profit from the events of 9/11.

Our first widow remarried on December 28, 2002. She was the second wife of one of our victims and he had children from both marriages. The two from his current marriage were 13 months and six years old on September 11th. Four months later, our first widower got married. He has three children, who on 9/11 were 16, 10 and five. Some people (including his 16-year-old son) viewed it as too soon, others saw it as his right to find a new happiness. Everyone deals with loss differently. There are no right or wrong answers. These are young men and women with children and it wasn't surprising that they found love again. I have heard from many of the wives that they don't want to parent alone. But not everyone was or is in the same place. Some wives and fiancés started dating. Some started thinking about it. Some are offended by the suggestion, and others will never contemplate the idea no matter how long they live.

As with everything else surrounding death, remarriage comes with its issues. What is the role (if any) of the dead spouse or fiancé's family in the newly formed familial unit? If there are children, will they be adopted? Will names be changed? Will the ex-daughter-in-law move to another state? Will the victim's parents still have the right to see their grandchildren? Will the lost parent be forgotten? How will the children deal with a new presence in their lives? Will an old fiancé still be embraced in her deceased lover's family now that she is remarrying, and will she want to be? Can the parents deal with a daughter-in-law that has moved on with her life without them? How will the new spouse deal with their partner who, in the recesses of the heart, will always have loved another? How will parents of married victims face the fact that the money left in a will or awarded to their ex-daughter-in-law will now be spent on another man? As these newly married begin their lives afresh, I wish them well. The road won't be without its bumps.

2003

GIULIANI

On January 15th, I went to the LMDC Joint Advisory Committee Meeting at the Merrill Lynch Building in the World Financial Center. The meeting was open to the press. To me, something about this building was eerily reminiscent of the World Trade Center. I'm not sure whether it was the marble or the escalator up, or what exactly, but it threw me back a bit. When I read the new mission statement and programmatic statement I became very concerned. This was the structure on which the jury rules would rely. Nikki Stern, who drafted the original mission statement, told me that what she wrote didn't survive in any form. I had multiple points I wanted to make, but when I took the microphone and raised the first one, it dominated the conversation for the remainder of the meeting. The newly drafted mission statement no longer stated that the 9/11 memorial should memorialize the dead. Instead, it included the acts of heroism and kindness of the living. I forcefully asserted that the stories of the living belonged in a museum and not on the memorial. Someone else cautioned that by continually co-opting space for nonmemorial purposes, the LMDC was effectively limiting an artist's vision for a memorial. Nikki and I just looked at each other and shook our heads. I'd been saying this consistently and repeatedly for over a year now as they continued to build and co-opt space.

I went with other family leaders to meet with Rudy Giuliani at his new offices in Times Square to try to enlist his support regarding the World Trade Center development downtown. Although as the ex-mayor he didn't have any official power, as "America's mayor" because of his role on 9/11 and its immediate aftermath, our hope was that his support in the media might be persuasive. He had been vocal in his position that the entire 16 acres be preserved as a park. When I entered the building I went to the security desk. They asked me for my identification, and I smiled while a camera at the security officer's desk took my picture. "Where does my picture go?" "Excuse me?" the guard said. "Well, when you take my picture, do you have a record of it somewhere?" He pointed to what looked like a computer tower off to his side. "It's backed up here." I took my newly printed ID card, good for one day, walked toward the elevator and thought, "That's pretty dumb. What if the building gets blown up?" This is how I think now.

When they were doing long-term construction in the road in front of my apartment (Gary's), which is over an MTA substation, I wondered whether we were going to be like that gymnasium in Chechnya, and explosives would methodically be planted as the site was open and unguarded at night. I see post office bags left unattended in buildings as the postman makes his rounds, and think how easily these could be bombs left in every apartment building. It didn't stop me from going to my meeting with Rudy Giuliani, or entering my apartment building, or even sleeping at night. These are just thoughts that go through my head now, as easily as thinking, "I think I'll get a cup of tea." When people ask me, "Aren't you afraid to fly?" I respond, "No. I should be afraid to go to work." The innocence with which I look at the city was taken from me.

We have sent $1,500 checks to the victims' next of kin, as well as $500 to parents of married victims twice, in order to allow them to set up charities or make donations in their loved ones' names. As a result, we received numerous requests for Howard's and/or my participation in their charity events or fundraisers as attendees or speakers. While these were much more positive events and oftentimes enjoyable, like the memorial services before them, it was not humanly possible to attend them all. We started canvassing employees who lived in the areas where the events were held to see if they could attend. Here is one I forwarded to Kent.

Dear Mr. Lutnick

I am writing to you because my brother, Andrew Alameno, was killed in the World Trade Center on September 11. He worked for Cantor on the 104th Floor. We are holding our 2nd Annual Polar Plunge on March 9 in Wildwood Crest, NJ. All the proceeds go to a scholarship set up in Andrew's name.

My family is so very overwhelmed at your companies [sic] kindness and generosity that you've shown to all the families. You also had to deal with the loss of your brother. For that we are very sorry.

We would love it if you or someone from your company could come down on March 9. It would mean so much to our community. You could bring copies of your book, sweatshirts, or whatever to sell that day. We also would love to support your fundraising...

We tried our best to honor as many requests as we could.

THE FAMILIES VS.
KEN FEINBERG AND THE VCF

On January 27, 2003, the Cantor families filed a class action lawsuit against Ken Feinberg and the Victim Compensation Fund, challenging his implementation of a cap as well as the other issues raised in the 80-page document Cantor Fitzgerald submitted in response to the proposed rulings.[61] Feinberg's staff had shared with Howard in writing, what the award amounts would be for those who earned more than $231,000 if the methodology being applied to everyone else were also applied to them. Feinberg's proposed awards were significantly less than that—by millions and millions of dollars. In some cases his proposed awards don't even amount to one year of salary to the family of the deceased, who would have had another 25 years to work before retirement.

On April 14th, I went to Judge Alvin K. Hellerstein's courtroom at 500 Pearl Street in Lower Manhattan to hear oral argument on the case. I went with Stephen Merkel, Cantor's general counsel, Paul Pion, who matched families with attorneys, along with other Cantor families and legal staff employees. As the arguments proceeded and I carefully listened to both sides, I heard Judge Hellerstein say the following:

> *I have known Mr. Feinberg for a long time, and I share the view that Mr. Moller expresses. There are few people in the United States that I would want in that job other than Mr. Feinberg...*[62]

I turned to Stephen Merkel and said, "Why didn't he recuse himself? We've lost."

Judge Hellerstein subsequently issued a ruling that basically said, because Feinberg hadn't yet made an award to these plaintiffs, one couldn't say he had instituted a cap. We lost. The catch-22, however, was that once Feinberg did issue an award, by law, that award was not appealable, so prior to its issuance was the only time the "methodology" could be challenged. Despite actually saying that he would not give high-wage earners full economic recovery, Feinberg got the green light to deny hundreds of millions of dollars to the families of top wage earners, money that had been promised to them by Congress. I was thoroughly disheartened.

Unfortunately, as it turned out, Feinberg was correct when he said, "Who is going to fight this? No one is going to fight this." We had no recourse but to enter the Victim Compensation Fund. Cantor Fitzgerald is still awaiting recompense in its litigation for the terrorist attack of 1993. The insurance recovery amount on each WTC tower has been capped at $1.5 billion for a total of $3 billion. If the families chose not to enter the fund, they would have had to stand in line for this recovery alongside every company that was damaged, had their business interrupted or destroyed during the attacks. We would likely recover only pennies on the dollar years later, because the $1.5 billion would not be enough to fully compensate all who experienced losses.[63] This same scenario wasn't true for the families of those who died on the planes. Those who sued the airlines from the planes recovered significantly more than those who entered the fund. It isn't what the results should have been, but Feinberg made up unfair rules and, despite Cantor's valiant attempts, we weren't able to stop him.

So, we did the next best thing. Cantor Fitzgerald prepared each family to fight on an individual basis to ensure the highest possible award within the given limitations. Cantor senior executives appeared and testified, over and over again. Howard testified at countless victim's compensation hearings. Before having our families enter the fund, Cantor Fitzgerald's legal team chose test cases, to see what the range of awards would be, how these hearings would go, and what information our families needed. Irene Boehm's husband, an equities trader, was at 49 older than the norm. She and her attorney, along with Cantor General Counsel Stephen Merkel and Howard, presented her husband's case at a hearing that all parties agreed would not be binding. The test hearings helped Cantor prepare its families and their attorneys.

As the deadline of December 22, 2003 approached, very few Cantor families had entered the fund. When Howard had exhausted all avenues, legal as well as personal persuasion, to move the methodology upward, when all of the paperwork was completed, and we knew what to expect, Howard gave the command—100 percent of the Cantor families entered the fund. This entailed Paul Pion's flying down to a remote area of Florida to get the last family entered—they don't even own a telephone—but we got it done.

MEMORIAL

While I was concentrating on the Victim Compensation Fund and how to appropriately memorialize the dead at the World Trade Center site, huge antiwar demonstrations were erupting all over the country. On February 15th, protestors outside the United Nations in New York City spanned more than 20 blocks. My life was very insular and singularly focused, so while I recognized that these events were happening on a national level, I stayed committed to the issues where I hoped I could effect change. My sympathies ran to the mothers and wives whose loved ones were overseas protecting our liberties rather than to judgments about whether we belonged there. Family members had strong political leanings on both sides, so I always remained cautious to stay neutral or avoid voicing my opinion. I never forgot that many of them enlisted because of what happened to my brother and his colleagues.

I had been speaking with Susan Herman, the director of the National Center for Victims of Crime, on and off over the past year. She invited me to participate in a roundtable they were hosting in Washington. Once again, this was a room full of the experienced and powerful. I still didn't feel like I was one of them. Josh Gotbaum was there representing the United Services Group, a group put together by three major charities (United Way, Red Cross and Salvation Army) and funded predominantly by the United Way. Present were representatives from charities from all over the world. A woman from a charity in Australia told us how they gave one victim a cruise and another a computer. A powerful leader grumbled that we would "never do that in the United States." I couldn't help myself. I raised my hand and said,

What if I told you that there was a mother who, because of the death of her child, didn't leave her house? And the best way that

she can stay connected to the goods and services that are available to her is via computer. But she doesn't have one and she'll never go out to get one. Would you say it was inappropriate for her to be given a computer? Now how about a woman whose husband was murdered in the towers, and her apartment is across from the WTC site, and she has seen the unthinkable. In fact, she's having a hard time figuring out how to live, let alone get up in the morning. Her therapist believes that she needs to get out of here, go to an environment that she has never been in before, where no memories can intrude, where only new ones can be made. Would you deny her a cruise?

I reiterated that we believe our families are in the best position to determine what they need. We, as the charity, should facilitate the attaining of those needs, not dictate what they are. It was here that I learned that there were federal monies specifically allocated for grief camps that cannot be spent on more pressing unmet needs.

The governor, mayor and LMDC announced that there would be an international competition to choose the World Trade Center Memorial. On a jury of 13, there would be only one family member. That family member was, once again, Paula Grant Berry. May 29th was the deadline to register for the competition. June 30th was the deadline to submit a design. Howard and I contemplated having someone submit a design but then decided against it, letting those with experience in memorial design submit.

A group of firefighters and firefighter families led by John Finucane started an organization called Advocates for a 9/11 Fallen Heroes Memorial. They wanted a separate memorial built at the World Trade Center specifically for the uniformed service workers—firefighters, police officers, EMS, court officers—with all the information that would go on a plaque at the location of any fire that claims their lives. The idea of two distinct memorials ran afoul of everything the families had been discussing for over a year. Michael Cartier of Give Your Voice summed it up when he said that the memorial must "honor the loss of life equally and the contributions of all without establishing any hierarchies." The equal remembrance of all victims was an LMDC board resolution as well as part of the memorial mission statement. This battle played out in the press.[64]

This issue came on the heels of the battles the families had with the LMDC, the mayor and the residents regarding a bus depot. On their blueprints, the LMDC placed a bus depot underground in the footprints, on the location where a significant portion of the remains had been found. They claimed that because buses can't be left idling on the streets, this was the only place, given all the infrastructure they wanted to build, that the bus depot could be located. This was another argument the families thought they had already won, when, after a meeting with the governor, he claimed that there would not be a bus depot in the "bathtub" area (the tower footprints and the Marriott hotel). But the issue resurfaced, and we fought it again. Win a battle. Issue resurfaces as if it were never won. Fight the battle again.

The LMDC hosted public meetings so that the memorial jury could hear input from all constituents. On behalf of the Cantor Fitzgerald Relief Fund families I said this:

> *Hi! My name is Edie Lutnick. I'm the executive director of the Cantor Fitzgerald Relief Fund. As all of you know, we lost six hundred and fifty-eight families [sic], including my brother Gary. My office was on 101 of Tower 1.*
>
> *The Cantor Families and the Relief Fund families, which make up approximately 900 families, have been incredibly consistent in what they have said that they wanted from a memorial. They have said it at the beginning and I will reiterate it now, although it runs afoul of some of the things I've already heard this evening.*
>
> *The Cantor families would like one memorial that is dignified and respectful.*
>
> *I think the one thing that you have to remember is that you are not dignifying and respecting the lives that we have lost if*

you run roughshod over the people that they loved the most in the world, which means that I would charge you to listen to the families and listen to them very, very carefully.

Their needs are tantamount here. And I'm sorry if other people don't agree with that. But in point of fact this is the final resting place for these families and that cannot be ignored. That's number one. We want a dignified and respectful memorial that honors the lives of those that we have lost.

Number two, the families have asked that the remains—and that includes the land from Fresh Kills—somehow be returned to this site and be interred there so that the remains of our loved ones are, in fact, on the memorial grounds where they lost their lives.

And we understand that this isn't going to be a cemetery and the families aren't asking for that. But they are asking that the remains of their loved ones be returned where they were lost. That's number two.

Number three, the families have asked consistently and repeatedly and have not wavered from the fact that they do not want any vehicular traffic running across the site. This is where they lost their lives. This is where the remains were found.

None of you have vehicular traffic across your loved ones' gravesites.

Make it something else, call it something else, but respect the fact that to these family members this is, in fact, sacred ground no matter what you put there. So don't make it a place that these families do not want to come to.

We are going to be here. Our children are going to be here. Our children's children are going to be here. And they are going to visit repeatedly.

And that includes a bus depot below one of the towers.

And these are things that were discussed and agreed upon and everybody thought we were in the same place.

All right. So these are the major points.

Now, I don't want to say that this is everything that the Cantor families want because it isn't. And now that we know that we have a forum where potentially our voices will actually be heard, I will tell you that the Cantor families are meeting on this. I have already told this to Tara. And we will have a complete and comprehensive thing that the united Cantor Fitzgerald Relief Fund, 900 families, agree on when I come forward and I talk to you the next time.

But these are fundamental propositions that everyone has heard from us time and time and time again. And I think that it's uniform across all of the families.

And I hope that you'll listen to it very, very carefully.

Thank you very much.[65]

THE HAMPTONS

Lewis and I decided to rent the house in Quogue that we rented before 9/11. We hoped that my coming to the Hamptons on the weekends would give me some balance. We hung a hammock out by the serenely landscaped pool. I used to lie in it and enjoy my favorite pastime, reading. It was a fabulous way to escape into another world. But September 11th was an historic event, shared not just by our families but also by the world. It has been captured not only on television and in the newspapers, but also in books. I thought that by picking up a book and reading a jacket that had nothing to do with September 11th (best friends trying to seduce each other's husbands, or something equally mindless), that there would be no reminders of my life. I was wrong. The first time the planes went into the towers, a character confronted her loss, or missing flyers were everywhere, I knew that reading novels was a problem. Even a book about Victorian times had magnificent weather on a Tuesday morning before a tragedy befell all assembled. I confined myself to books that were published before September 11th.

Around this time, I also started watching television again. Not any programs you would imagine. I became part of the dumbing down of America I heard so much about. I could only watch TV shows that I knew would have no relation to my life. Reality dating shows were the best. They helped me sleep. The more ludicrous, the better. There was absolutely no chance of any life overlap. I watched Flavor Flav and Miss New York try to find love. I counted the words they said that weren't words. My favorite was when she said she was in her "blist." Mindless was all I could handle.

One weekend after a long week of work, I took the last bus out of the city to the Hamptons. I didn't know that it was the last bus. When I walked into the house and tried to turn on a light, I discovered we had no power. When Lewis got through to LIPA they told him the outage was from Canada all the way down South. The extent of the outage created the immediate feeling that this was terrorism. Howard was in the city, and I couldn't get through. I called Allison and she said she had spoken to him and that he was okay. It made me breathe a little easier, but I still needed to hear his voice. I received other calls from people who walked up the Manhattan streets in an eerie silence that mirrored that of 9/11. When I finally got to speak with Howard and knew that he was okay, I could take in the stillness of the surroundings. As long as Howard and Lewis remained safe, everything else was manageable.

Michelle and Peter Farmer wanted to hold a fundraiser for the 932 children of the Cantor Fitzgerald Relief Fund in Gary's memory. I thought it was a great idea. We decided to host a white party clam-bake on the beach. We were criticized by the local paper for copying P. Diddy's famed White Party, but his party had nothing to do with our decision. Michelle knew that white was easier to decorate with inexpensively. Michelle got permits for Indian Wells Beach in Amagansett. I got the required insurance through Cantor. Michelle tapped the drumming master class that plays on Sagg Main beach in Sagaponack every Monday night to open the event. We rented tables and chairs, and found a caterer who agreed to provide the food at a reduced rate. We used items we had in inventory and donated items for a silent auction and a raffle. We scheduled our event for August 9th and we sold tickets for $150 apiece. I asked my core volunteers to help and they readily agreed. Michelle got a band. We got alcohol donated. Howard underwrote the whole thing.

When it threatened rain and we had no rain date, we didn't know what to do. After going back and forth whether to try to change locations and move it indoors, at the caterer's 4 pm deadline, Peter made the decision. "That's it. We're having it on the beach." I said, "Okay." I looked up at the sky and said, "Gary won't let it rain."

The volunteers, Lewis and I caravanned to the beach and set up the First Annual White Party Clambake in memory of Gary Lutnick. Michelle made centerpieces out of what she found on the beach and filled lunch bags with sand and votives. Lewis's mother got lanterns donated from Super Deals in Cedarhurst and beverages from a local beverage barn. She also got the ingredients for s'mores donated for a bonfire. Lewis took the Flag of Honor flags and made wooden flag posts for them. We outlined our beach site with them. Flags with our loved ones' names in the stripes flapped in the wind. Because the weather was iffy, we knew most everyone who came. Friends, then Cantor employees, and family after family start walking up the lit path—I was overwhelmed. This was supposed to be *for* the Cantor families, but they came out in force.

When Howard and Allison arrived, Howard was hugged, kissed and thanked over and over again. He threw his arms around me and whispered in my ear, "This is the best event ever. I didn't have to do anything, and I get all the credit." But Gary and Doug and all of our 658 got the credit, because the sky cleared and we were treated to one of the most beautiful sunsets any of us had ever seen. The event was warm and inviting in a way that most benefits are not. Lewis took out his guitar and people sang around the campfire. People started calling it a "heart" event. Whatever it was, it was very special and we knew it. We raised $13,000, matched by Cantor to $26,000, and I sent out a "child care" run with the money. Child care check runs were an additional amount of money sent to a parent with children specifically designated for the care of each child. These distributions were above and beyond the 25 percent sent to every Cantor family.

We held our White Party clambakes for seven years, and there were many memorable moments within them. At the fourth annual clambake, Greg Manning who plays in a Rolling Stones cover band called the "Rolling Bones," asked if his band could play. I readily agreed. Howard, Lauren Manning and I were talking when the band started playing, "(I Can't Get No) Satisfaction." Lauren said, "Excuse me" and ran through the sand toward the stage to hear her husband play. As Howard and I watched her run, we turned to each other and smiled. Lauren doesn't have it easy, and surgeries are a regular part of her life, but she has come a long way from that burn unit bed. It was arguably one of the best moments in my life.

As we were setting up for another clambake a few years later, one of our volunteers heard people yelling for help. Two swimmers out at Indian Wells beach had gotten caught in a riptide and were drowning. All dressed in white, Lewis and his sister Jill Gordon, both strong swimmers, jumped in to save them. As they carried them back to shore, Greg Manning and Glenn Zagoren waded in to take them from an exhausted Lewis and Jill. By the time the paramedics arrived the rescue was already complete. The clambake started later that year, and Lewis, Jill, Glenn and Greg were very wet all night, but two people slept safely in their beds.

The events where Gary should have been at the center don't abate. When Pat and Sheila Troy have a baby girl and ask me to be her godmother, I am honored, but know that once again, I am standing in for Gary. When they had their second child years later, Howard became their son's godfather. Gary loved children. He always said that every family needed at least three children, because if my parents had fewer than that, he never would have been born. Even in our happiness, his absence is palpable.

RULES

I was approached by a New York City school teacher who taught in the summer school program. She came to me when she was asked to sign a document at the end of the summer attesting to the fact that she had been a grief counselor to her students. Her school is in Brooklyn. Her children were not 9/11 children and her summer program had not been modified in any way that summer, versus any other summer. She refused to sign. Her principal told her that New York City was using the 9/11 FEMA funds to pay summer school teachers. If she refused to sign, she wouldn't be paid for working for the summer. She was outraged. So was I.

If there were ever a "whoooosh" day that sucked you right back to September 11th, the release of the 911 call transcripts and radio tapes made by the Port Authority police was it. On August 28, 2003, in response to a lawsuit filed by the *New York Times*, 2,000 pages of dispatcher recordings were released. The new emotional devastation to families was incalculable. Sally Regenhard, founder of the Skyscraper Safety Campaign, and I found ourselves squarely on opposite sides of this argument. Sally believed that all tapes, no matter their content, should be released in order to show blame. She wanted to "show that operators are untrained to tell people how to save their lives."[66] Up to this point, she had tried to show the failing of the radios and the communication systems that were in place. She believes that firefighters, like her probationary firefighter son, needlessly died as a result. She thought the release of this information would further her cause. While not disputing her premise regarding the communications systems, I could only see what this did to the families who turned on the news almost two years later and were confronted, without warning, with the terror their loved ones had faced.

Communication with the public was a huge problem. In the days following September 11th, public officials such as Mayor Giuliani and EPA administrator Christine Todd Whitman, in their quest to stabilize Lower Manhattan, were quick to assure the public that the air quality was safe. Mayor Giuliani refused assistance from several federal agencies and assigned oversight of the cleanup to the largely then unknown Department of Design and Construction (DDC), which never required the recovery workers to wear respirators. In 2003, the investigator general of the EPA issued a report stating that the EPA did not have enough information to give the public the assurances made by Ms. Whitman.[67] Later in the year, she resigned from the EPA. She was ultimately sued for her statements, but was shielded because she acted within her official capacity.[68] Mayor Giuliani, making his bid for the presidency in 2008, in large part on his reputation for his management of 9/11's aftermath, also found that his assurances of safe air and the failure to mandate federal safety standards such as respirators had become a blemish rather than a star on his record.[69]

UNITED

On Veterans Day, Louise LoPresti, a VP at JP Morgan with disaster and facilitator experience, put together a panel discussion of group leaders and survivors to improve communication and to share what we learned to date. I invited the Cantor survivors to attend, but most were still not talking. They dealt with 9/11 the same way Howard and I did. They worked. Ari Schonbrun, who survived by helping Virginia DiChiara to safety, agreed to sit on the panel with me.

We were asked what our biggest challenge since 9/11 had been, what helped us get through it and what insight we had going forward. A Lower Manhattan resident said seeing the ferries bring the families and the recovery workers, and the courage of people impacted so much worse than her, made her think, "If they can do this, so can I." I responded that the biggest hurdle initially was the lack of information, and dealing with the overwhelming emotional toll. Two years later, however, I said that it was getting the needs of the families met and their voices heard. Ari responded that the biggest change for him was in his priorities. "Work will be there tomorrow. My kid's play is only once." Monica Iken said that, after being in denial for two weeks, she thought, "OMG, they are going to build over dead people. I have to stop them. I'm going on a mission." So she started September's Mission. Her biggest challenge was proving to herself and others that she could do it.

Then Louise asked, what gave us hope for the future, or would be our best advice for others. The resident responded—seeing the worst and doing the best; finding commonality and taking the media into our own hands. A family member said she hoped more people would listen, learn and respond, and that people would try to see the goodness in other people. I said that nothing about September 11th was okay except how you choose to handle it. Ari agreed with me. Monica said she hoped to see a beautiful memorial someday, and that her advice would be to live your life. Don't live it according to a terrorist. Someone else said he derived hope from his child. Another family leader said that when George Bush gave his annual award to Ted Kennedy, he knew anything was possible. Many people said no one should be afraid to ask for help.

When Saddam Hussein was captured on December 13, 2003, we were proud of our military and thought that perhaps this would lead to an end of our involvement in a controversial war. It would be another three years before an interim Iraqi government would convict him of killing 182 Iraqi Shi'ites and sentence him to death,[70] and still our involvement in Iraq did not end.

2004

PLANS FOR REVIVAL

Monica Iken pointed to a model Kevin Rampe, the president of the LMDC, was showing the Family Advisory Council and said, "Kevin, what's that?" She pointed to a box that was sitting on the Memorial Quadrant. "Oh, don't worry about it, Monica. It's just a placeholder." "What is it holding a place for?" "Nothing. It's not important." "Then why is it there?" That "nothing" turned out to be an acre-by-acre cultural center that would overshadow and take space away from a 9/11 memorial.

It was located in the bathtub area (the area from the slurry wall to the PATH train that encompasses the footprints of both towers and the former location of the Marriott Hotel) that the families were fighting so hard to preserve. Did he hope it would just slip by our notice? It was just a box on a large model that changed every time we were shown it. It could have very easily gone unnoticed. In fact, up to this point, the LMDC had led us to believe that the cultural center building *was* the 9/11 Memorial Museum. This was the first time we had an inkling that this was an entirely different entity, serving a completely different purpose. The LMDC decided on the size and placement of a non-9/11 cultural center on the WTC site in the bathtub area, behind closed doors and without any input from the families. They engaged in obfuscation when they told us it was the Memorial Museum, and told others it was a cultural complex. We were once again frustrated and infuriated, and we had a big problem with it. The families wanted and were led to believe that the Memorial Quadrant would be dedicated to a 9/11 memorial and museum. At no time, before Monica saw this new "building," had a non-9/11 cultural center ever been discussed with the family leaders.

By far the strongest lobby group regarding what should be built at the World Trade Center site was the residents, headed by Community Board 1 leader Madelyn Wils.[71] On more than one occasion, she made inappropriate comments to and about the families that raised their ire. So no one was really very surprised when the winning memorial design selected by the jury, "Reflecting Absence," two large waterfalls, one within the footprint of each tower, was entirely underground.[72] The residents' lobby was steadfast that they did not want anything sad, nothing like a cemetery; in sum they wanted no reminders of 9/11 above ground. They wanted vehicular traffic through the site, and they didn't want a memorial to impede their commute in any way. The sentiment echoed in many different ways by the mayor was that a memorial should not impede a visitor's desire to spend money in Lower Manhattan. Countless meetings had been spent discussing the proposed 600,000 square feet of retail space and where it would go. The desire of the Coalition of 9/11 Families to "preserve bedrock, the tower footprints, and the box beam column remnants," which was what was left of the 16 acres after it had been whittled away for other purposes, had been twisted to the unwanted extreme that the families had consented, which they clearly had not, to everything being placed below ground. On the contrary, the coalition consistently advocated that there be preservation and access to the box beam columns, and that it might potentially make an excellent lower floor in a museum. The families did not want an underground memorial or an underground museum.

The selection of "Reflecting Absence" also wasn't surprising because it had the unwavering support of Maya Lin. In 2002, long before the memorial competition, Maya Lin, the Vietnam Memorial architect and memorial jury member, sketched out her vision for a memorial for Herbert Muschamp of the *New York Times* ("Masters' Plan"). One of her designs "showed a park with two reflecting pools in the footprints." On the final day of deliberations, the jurors were leaning toward the selection of one of the other finalist's designs, all of which had "done much more to render the human victims as unique." But Maya Lin made an 11th hour impassioned plea for "Reflecting Absence" and persuaded the jury.[73] Based on our experience with the process, the family leaders knew what it meant and looked at each other with knowing glances when an unknown architect was selected. Unknowns were far more easily manipulated and, as this was a reputation-building project, would be easier to control.

Debate on what the memorial design "should be" raged. People were very vocal with their opinions. Greg Manning, Lauren's husband and a talented author, wrote an op-ed advocating for the rebuilding of the towers. Ultimately, an entire movement formed behind Donald Trump's plan to scrap the design and build an aboveground memorial that would do more to memorialize and recognize the losses from multiple countries. When families asked me—and they did, repeatedly—what I thought of the memorial design, I told them that it wasn't my place to decide and therefore my opinion should have as much or as little weight as anyone else's. I did everything I could to impart on the jury what was important to our families. Unlike in Oklahoma City, where two-thirds of the jury were family members, here the composition of the jury did not allow for our true representation. But this was the design that the jury chose. This was the design we were bound to move forward with.

The design had its flaws. "Reflecting Absence" provided no context. As one family member said to me, "If a visitor from another planet arrived at the memorial he or she would have no clue as to who all these people are, and why their names are underground around these massive squares." Nowhere did the design allow for any explanation, words of solace, or create any understanding of what happened that day. The voids were 30 percent smaller than the actual footprints, so they wouldn't represent the size of the buildings. And if the intent was to represent the buildings lost, nothing would tell you that seven buildings were destroyed that day. The planned design called for no American flag, nor did it allow for the placement anywhere of the dates September 11, 2001 or February 26, 1993.

It is precisely because of the absence of context in the design that the listing of the names became so important. With the museum underground, unfinished and unconnected to the memorial, it was even more essential there be a logic to their placement, and that they convey the story.

What I found most disturbing and unacceptable about the names arrangement of the 9/11 victims was that they were listed randomly throughout the footprints of the towers. Michael Arad, the architect of "Reflecting Absence," stated that this was a "random" act of "haphazard brutality."[74] But it wasn't random or haphazard. This was a carefully orchestrated attack on the center of capitalism (the WTC), the center of government (the White House) and the center of the military (the Pentagon). Listing the names arbitrarily would dehumanize the people who died, and deny the visiting public an emotional connection to them. Making believe that this was a random act belies history. The 658 people at Cantor Fitzgerald had a connection to each other and their names should not be scattered as if they didn't. Surviving employees should not be made to go to a representation of an outline of a building they didn't work in to find their deceased colleagues' names. Worse still would be to make these families, who are still looking for the remains of their loved ones, search for the names of their dead at their final resting place.

The jury, before the announcement of a winner, met with the eight finalists and the LMDC made changes to each memorial design. I could not understand how Paula Grant Berry, knowing how strongly opposed the families were to a random listing of names, could have ever let this stand. When I had the opportunity to ask Paula about it, she replied, "It was never my job to represent the families. It was my job to make the best memorial I could for everyone." I can count the number of times in this process I had been angrier on my fingers. So we had no advocacy on any committee that Paula ever sat on, and at the behest of Mayor Bloomberg she was the chosen voice for all of us. Why, if her job wasn't to specifically represent the families, didn't they just put someone with more memorial and urban design experience in her place? This was more public pretense of family and victim representation without any actual voice. How the names of the dead are listed at the place of their murder in a memorial that was supposed to honor them should fall to the families of those who died. I needed to fix this. For two and a half years I had followed the rules, allowed the process to proceed and been a voice of reason from the shadows. The issue that I was being compelled to spearhead found me—appropriately remembering those who died.

On January 14, 2004, Governor Pataki and Mayor Bloomberg made an announcement that shocked us. The names of the 9/11 dead would still be listed randomly, but insignias (shield designations) would distinguish the uniformed service workers. This was obviously being done to placate Advocates for a 9/11 Fallen Heroes Memorial, who didn't get their separate memorial. They weren't any happier with this compromise than we were. The Memorial Program stated that the victims would all be treated equally; this guiding principle of the memorial competition and the LMDC board resolution were being tossed aside. The requirement for equality was a principle shared across all family groups. If you had enough power, there were no hard and fast rules here. Unfortunately, the civilians didn't have any. The names situation just went from bad to worse. I asked to Coalition of 9/11 Families Leader Anthony Gardner, "Why not have a little Rodin Thinker insignia next to all of the Cantor names?" That was the symbol of Cantor Fitzgerald. We weren't asking for that. It was just to make a point.

When I sent the quarterly check distribution of $6,233.50 to each of our families on January 22nd for a total of $4,400,850, I alerted them to the current names/insignia proposal. I asked them to communicate their objections if they had any to the mayor, governor and LMDC. They did. En masse. The Cantor families were firmly united in opposition to the way the names of their loved ones would be listed at the memorial. Despite making the announcement, when families called Mayor Bloomberg's office, they were told that the mayor, "has nothing to do with it." The governor's office and LMDC kept transferring them to different numbers.

On February 6, 2004, Governor Pataki and Mayor Bloomberg announced that they had appointed a nine-person search committee to select a new chairman of the World Trade Center Memorial Foundation. That person would replace John Whitehead, who had also been the chairman of both the LMDC and the World Trade Center Memorial Foundation. The World Trade Center Memorial Foundation is the not-for-profit that was set up to fundraise for the memorial and museum. Michael Bloomberg previously appointed Paula Grant Berry to the World Trade Center Memorial Foundation Board, and he now appointed her to serve on the search committee, along with Monica Iken.[75] John Whitehead had timed the announcement of his retirement in a way to ensure that the Republican governor and mayor would select his replacement. Governor Pataki was likely to be replaced by a Democrat and this way the Republicans could solidify control of the site and keep the Democrats from changing it. He would not actually retire for another two years.

When Kevin Rampe told me the reason the firefighters couldn't have their ranks next to their names on the memorial was that the civilians would insist on their titles, I'd had enough. When I told him that the current arrangement was not something a quarter of the victims' families could live with, he told me to have my families keep fighting. I called a meeting of all of the family group leaders to be held in Cantor's offices on February 17th. The gathered were almost all the leaders who to that point held any sway with the families. We had never all met together before. I told them that I was tired of hearing that I was opposed to people I had never had a conversation with. I watched the LMDC manufacture a rift between the families of the uniformed service workers and the civilians that I did not believe existed, for their own gain. I proposed that we have meetings, with a press gag order, to see whether we had grounds on which to agree, and what, if any, our differences actually were. My goal was to mediate, and come up with a proposal that all of the family leaders supported. We would then present it to the families and see whether it was something they wanted. Once we were all on the same page we could speak with one voice and nullify the divide and conquer strategy that had been working so well for the governmental bodies. No one in attendance wanted the names listed randomly.[76] No one wanted the insignias.[77] Everyone wanted the victims all treated equally. It was a place to start.

The meeting was contentious. The firefighter families were furious that the insignias didn't convey battalion, ladder or engine company and rank. Everyone had a different idea how this should work. I started writing down emerging themes. The leaders wanted the dead remembered as individuals, not just as a stream of names, and absolutely no one wanted our families to have to search through a random sea of names to find their loved ones. Ages seemed to be important and so did pictures. As they say, though, the devil is in the details.

It was a long slow process, requiring a lot of meetings and effort, but I saw the commonality between the uniformed service workers and the civilians. We never wanted to deny them their ranks, or being identified with their brethren. We never asked for or wanted titles next to the civilian names. We did, however, want to be listed all together in the appropriate tower and identified by our affiliation and floor. The next day, I was called when Tom Roger, one of the Bloomberg lockstep families, ignored our imposed gag order and gave a quote about our meeting to the press. On February 19th, an article about the memorial names ran in the *New York Times* Metro section.

When 190 people are killed and 2,000 injured in yet another horrific terrorist attack, this time in Madrid, we were stunned into silence. We could not stop the tears from flowing or our own pain from returning.

After yet another long and arduous process, the Victim Compensation Fund awards started coming down, and families were having a very hard time with them. The numbers weren't what we had wanted, but we were resigned to build the best futures we could with what we received. The families fell into three categories. The first group took the money and structured it for the future of their families and themselves. The second group spent all or part of the money as if it burned their hands. The third group considered it blood money, or the award insultingly low, and couldn't touch it.

ECHOES

Howard held another round of town hall meetings to help our families become more financially self-sufficient. He presented his layman's guide to investing. He said that if we followed these fundamental tenets, as investors, we would be in the top half of 1 percent of all investors. He held up and spread his fingers and told us we should be diversified across five things: stocks, bonds, real estate, alternative investments and cash. He continued by saying that quality of life purchases were not only allowed, but encouraged, and that if we felt like we had to watch a stock rise and fall then we had too much money in it. He told the families that Cantor had negotiated a fee deal with a money management firm to accept our families' investments at the much lower institutional rate, for any family that wanted the option.

I don't know when I first met the Horwitz family, probably at our first memorial service, but it's as if I have always known them. Their young son Aaron was being mentored by Gary. Mr. Horwitz (he would chastise me for not calling him Allan, but in my brain he is always Mr. Horwitz) has a shaved head and large eyes and glasses. He talks a lot and very very quickly. If I can point to one family member to articulate the depth and breadth of familial loss, it would be Allan Horwitz. He wanted answers I couldn't give. He started every conversation with me by going through a recitation of my lifetime of losses in order to convince me that I would be able to understand whatever he was about to tell me. His need for solace was endless. He thought by making me a surrogate child in his family that it would help him heal. He asked the one thing of me that I couldn't give.

Aaron's family opened their hearts to me. They offered me all that they are. When Allan's father died, he asked me to come to the funeral, and I did. They taught me about Aaron and about their living children, and invited me to the milestones in their lives. They were the first family I called when we had tickets to events. When they began traveling, they brought me souvenirs from any place they went. Their apartment is across the street from Gary's, where I now live. Allan used to call me when he hadn't seen lights go on and off in my apartment for a while. He invited me to meals. He crushed me with kindness. Liz, Allan's wife, speaks slowly and is patient. She understands her husband, how big-hearted he is, but how sometimes he emotionally taxed me despite my strong feelings for him. He didn't understand why they were going to run vehicular traffic through the site when they said they weren't. The same for the bus depot they proposed be built on the South Tower footprint, or why the memorial had to be underground. He didn't understand why he would have to search for his son's name at the memorial. He can't comprehend why it can't say Cantor Fitzgerald under Aaron's name, or what would be wrong with the world knowing that their son was only 24. He can't fathom a mayor who won't take the remains of human beings—some who are called heroes—out of a garbage dump. He wasn't alone, and I had no answers except to listen, or join in the rant.

Really though, what hurt him the most was the monetary award with which Feinberg valued his son's life. It took the Horwitz's an inordinately long time to complete the VCF paperwork. I worried that they wouldn't do it at all and I had to prod them each step of the way. When the award came down they felt only anger. They wanted to appeal, but beyond a review by Feinberg of his own decision, none legally existed. Allan Horwitz took the Victim Compensation Fund check and put the "insultingly low" award in a drawer. He refused to cash it. Just like Patrick with the empty chair, I had to convince the Horwitz's to deposit the check. I hate the words move on and move forward at least as much as they do, but they needed to let this money work for them. He ultimately put the check in the bank.

I want to tell you that his behavior was absurd, but in truth I was only one step farther up the ladder than he was. To me, this was blood money. I couldn't touch it. I didn't want to think about it. I couldn't write checks or spend it. Compared with what Gary's award would have been had we received full economic recovery, it also was insulting low. It wasn't the number, however. Whatever the amount, I had a hard time having anything to do with it. Howard had given me his half of Gary's award. He took nothing from the fund. It was because of Gary and Howard that I could remain the full-time unpaid head of the Relief Fund.

Howard and I had long talks about what he considered to be my ridiculous position regarding Gary's money. "It isn't Gary's money, Edie. It's your money." It just didn't feel that way. This should have been Gary's life. Not mine. Howard said, "Look, you aren't a jewelry, car, clothes kind of person. But if you could have anything in the whole world, what would it be?" That's easy. My dream had always been the same. "A beach house. Someplace with space for a barbeque and a hammock." Howard called his broker. "My sister is buying a beach house. Call her and find out exactly what she wants. Just make sure you find her one that's not too far from my house."

On April 29, 2004, I attended a "9/11 in Transition" seminar. The purpose of the meeting was to tell us that all of the major charitable initiatives would be closing by December 4th. This included the Red Cross, the United Way and the United Service Group. Most everyone would be out of the 9/11 charity business but the Relief Fund. When I learned that the United Way was closing its doors, I didn't really care. They were supposed to be the organization that helped my families the most and they did almost nothing. The United Way didn't distribute the half a billion dollars they raised for the 9/11 families to those families. I can't find a single Cantor family that received more than $28,000 from the United Way, and most received $10,000. Their own report said they distributed an average of $20,000.[78] If they had distributed the money to the 9/11 families when we had asked, the generosity of the donating public could have made a profound difference to families who had just lost their financial support. Each family would have received approximately $170,000 (big numbers become small very quickly with such a large number of victims), and this emergency relief would have been extremely helpful in tiding over the families while they made adjustments for their losses. But the United Way later announced that they divided their fund into two, calling one the September 11ᵗʰ "telethon" fund and one the September 11ᵗʰ Fund. At $20,000 per family, the United Way didn't even distribute the contents of the telethon fund to the families and came nowhere near distributing the total amount of funds they had collected. Instead, the United Way held onto the money and then changed the definition of *victim* from the 2,979 victims' families in order to continue making the usual United Way distributions. Donations made by a public intending to help the 9/11 families ended up being scattered far and wide.

Shiya called. He wanted to see me and Howard. This could only mean one thing. We met in Howard's office. They had found 10 of Gary's bone shards. I was confused. I thought we weren't going to be able to get remains. Shiya explained that the best evidence came from the victim himself. The hairbrush and tooth brush, and secondarily our swabbings, were enough. Shiya tells us the story of his best friend. His office was the center of the bull's eye for the first plane that hit the North Tower on the 96ᵗʰ floor. His back was to the window. He never saw it coming. "They found two small bones on the roof of Building 5. The top part of the leg bone was charred, the rest pristine—so we could tell." The plane immediately turned his body into hundreds if not thousands of little pieces. Howard and I quietly listened to his recitation. None of us cried. Howard told me later that the most amazing thing about that meeting was that I didn't go out the window.

The thing was that by this point I was numb. I had so many conversations with so many family members that in any other context would be completely bizarre, but for us were totally normal. We had an ongoing relationship with a medical examiner for goodness sakes! We talked about these things all the time. "Did they find any of Gary?" is a usual question. That you won't get a full body was a foregone conclusion. It's only when we forgot and didn't check ourselves in conversations with non-9/11 families that we realized that we walk apart, and that what we were saying shouldn't be discussed over lunch, if at all.

Family members compared findings, matter of factly. "I got a leg bone. You got an arm. Why do you think that is?" "First I got his wrist, then his torso. Why should that be?" "X got a whole body. I got an ID card. They worked next to each other. What do you think that means?" "The bottom half of his body was in great shape, but when we got the top half it was a mess." The first time you watch the planes fly into the building, it stops your heart in your chest and you sob uncontrollably. Second time, maybe the same response. Third, a little less, fourth, a little less still. By the 50th or 100th time, it doesn't make you cry anymore. That's what happened to the families. It was just another fact with which we live.

▾   ▾   ▾

On June 10, 2004, the LMDC announced that after a review of 113 potential institutions, they selected the Joyce Theatre, the Signature Theatre, the Drawing Center and the International Freedom Center to occupy the cultural center on the World Trade Center site, which is actually within the Memorial Quadrant. The placeholder on the model would now have non-9/11 occupants. The family leaders continued to fight any non-9/11 entity on the Memorial Quadrant. Everything associated with 9/11 was being placed underground and out of sight, and here was a 300,000 square foot, aboveground building that would clearly attract attention for institutions that had nothing to do with 9/11.

One day when Marianna and I were in the office on 57th and Lexington, the fire alarms went off and we were evacuated. As everyone was leaving, I went to the third floor and told my brother that we were being evacuated and would he please leave the building. He said, "In a minute." He was working. I went downstairs and outside. The building was quickly being surrounded with fire trucks. I was patiently waiting and Howard wasn't coming out. I knew he would stay inside until the last employee was out, and the systems secured for the tens of billions of dollars of business Cantor was doing. When it had been long enough, I called him on my cell phone and said, "Howard, I am pulling the sister trump card. Please come out of the building, now." With a laugh in his voice, he said, "Okay, Edie-Pie, I'll be right down." A few minutes later he came strolling out.

❤ ❤ ❤

When New York City made a bid for the 2012 Olympics, Fresh Kills centered prominently in their plans. Mayor Bloomberg wanted to turn it into an equestrian park. His daughter rides horses. The families were outraged at the further indignity. He was proposing that people ride horses where the remains of the dead are located. They also added a bike and BMX course. Obviously, nowhere in the presentations did it mention the 9/11 dead are still in Fresh Kills mingled with garbage. The plans didn't allocate funds to remove them or to honorably bury them. WTC Families for a Proper Burial had suggested a burial ground be created on Governor's Island as an alternative. The mayor refused. It would not surprise me if Mayor Bloomberg wanted Governor's Island for his private foundation once he leaves office. No alternative was acceptable to the mayor other than to leave them exactly where they are and ignore their existence. He stated that Fresh Kills is the place "where New Yorkers dumped the things that they didn't want … and now it's a place for us to build the things that we do want to fulfill our ambitious dreams."[79]

NAMES

After meeting repeatedly over a span of eight months, the participating family leaders from both the civilian and uniformed services organizations reached agreement. Accepting that there is never 100 percent consensus on anything, we have managed to come up with a plan that the vast majority of family leaders and families agreed to. Our proposal was straightforward. Everyone would be grouped and identified by their affiliation. Civilians would be listed in alphabetical order within their affiliation. Uniformed services workers would be listed and identified by rank. Each person who died would have their age and their floor following their name. The uniformed service workers requested an alternate third space in the memorial where their names could be listed in between the towers. This was because they didn't know where their loved ones died and, like all of us, didn't want to be listed in the wrong tower. There would be no insignias. On October 8, 2004, we sent out our proposal, signed by 32 meeting participants representing 11 major 9/11 organizations and supported by over 1700 families to Governor Pataki, Mayor Bloomberg and LMDC and WTC Memorial Foundation Chairman John Whitehead.[80] Other than a short response from the LMDC that they had received our proposal "among others,"[81] we get no response. I then sent a letter to Governor Pataki, reiterating that we were requesting a meeting to discuss a names proposal that had the support of more than two-thirds of the families. No response.

❧   ❧   ❧

Cantor Fitzgerald by the end of 2004 had rebuilt its infrastructure. It once again had proper human resources, accounting, finance and operations departments. Howard announced that Cantor was ready to grow again and to rebuild.

2005

RANDOM MEANING

WTC Families for a Proper Burial and the Coalition of 9/11 Families began the New Year 2005 with a candlelight vigil. On January 9th they held the "Justice and Honor for the September 11th Heroes Vigil" at the World Trade Center site. They started 2005 by begging. They pleaded for the preservation of the maximum area of the footprints below where the towers stood and to provide access. They beseeched that historic preservation be put before infrastructure placement. They unreservedly begged for the ashen and human remains to be removed from Fresh Kills, and they humbly plead to have meetings to discuss alternatives to a random listing of names. The New Year brought continued intransigence.

Through an intermediary, Howard and I had a private meeting with Michael Arad. Michael was trying to justify the random listing of names. After he listened to him, Howard said, "Look, you don't want random listing. What you are talking about isn't even random listing, it's aesthetically variable. If you want this to be random, you will have to put all the names in a hat, and pick them. There will be clumping of names because some letters are more common than others. So, you aren't even going to do random. You are going to move them around so that there aren't too many *Ls* together." Howard was right. What Michael was demanding was the appearance of randomness. Howard said, "Look, if all of Cantor is listed together in the North Tower and identified as Cantor Fitzgerald, I can make it look random to the world, and make it meaningful to our families. But our families need to be listed all together."

When the meeting was over, I asked my brother how our families were going to find their loved ones' names if they appeared random to the world. He told me that we would figure out a way to make sure they knew. He didn't believe that Michael Arad was going to move off this purported random position. I told Howard that I was going to continue to fight for alphabetical order within Cantor Fitzgerald. He agreed that I should, but internal meaningful relationships would be our fallback position.

⌄ ⌄ ⌄

Lewis and I had dinner with Howard and Allison for Lewis's birthday. Allison announced that she was pregnant. It made me happy. Lewis and I discussed children a long time ago. We never actually made a decision. We decided that we loved each other and that we could be happy either way. Having a baby just never happened for us. In truth, because of the early death of my parents, I felt like I had raised my children and didn't really need to do it again. The joke in my family had always been that Howard would have four, Gary would have four, and "eight is enough" so I didn't need to have any. September 11th changed my thinking on that. In 2005, Howard and Allison had three, and now Gary had none. As a result, I started going to doctors to see what, if anything, I could do to have a baby. The prognosis wasn't good. I was already older, and though I could subject myself to a barrage of painful tests, the results would probably not be any different. I had all but given up hope. The thought that there wouldn't be a baby named after Gary tormented me.

HANGAR

The first time I met Susan Esposito was at a meeting at the Marriott Hotel on Long Island after one of Howard's town hall meetings about three years ago. She has a bright smile and is a bundle of energy. She just exudes maternal caregiver from every pore. She approached me in the hallway and told me that she wanted to start a charity in her father's name. I explained to her that we had been talking about this and that I would shortly be sending Stevie (her mother) a check for $1,500 to help get the charity on its way. We had decided to assist our families in memorializing their loved ones in any manner they saw fit. Susan started A Caring Hand, The Billy Esposito Foundation, and they held their first fundraiser at the Supper Club in the theatre district of Manhattan on March 26, 2003.

When Susan started seriously examining what she wanted her charity to accomplish, she and Stevie came to see me in my office. She had been toying with the idea of opening up a bereavement center for children who lost a parent. I think back on how alone and disenfranchised we were after my parents died, and I wonder if things would have been easier if the type of facility she was considering had been available to us. It's a worthwhile idea. It seemed to me the only thing Susan Esposito was missing was confidence and a push. I gave her both. She asked if I would agree to be honored at their 2005 benefit. I was truly touched and choked up. I respond, "Don't you want to honor Howard? He's a better fundraising choice." She said no, that it was me they wanted. She reciprocated the confidence and the push. She also asked me if I would become an honorary board member. This is one of our families. I agreed to it all and was their honoree at the Copa Cabana in April. Susan then committed to being one of our family speakers at our memorial service in September.

The Cantor families are split almost in half between victims who were married and those who were single. The year before, Stella Lombardi, the mother of our victim Robert Tipaldi, invited Howard and me to a luncheon she hosted for mothers of married victims in Brooklyn. While attending, I heard once again how left out of the grief process the parents and siblings of married victims felt. I started thinking bigger. There were many, many families that needed an event like Stella's.

We decided to host a luncheon for all the parents and siblings of married victims. I wanted to address their feelings of disenfranchisement and show them that there was an entire group that felt the way they did. When Marianna sent out the letter and asked for RSVPs, the response was beyond our expectations. We ended up taking over all three banquet rooms on the third floor of Le Parker Meridien. We assigned tables based on the department their loved one worked in, so that parents of colleagues would meet.

First was a reception outside the rooms. Then we sat down to lunch. When Howard arrived, we put a microphone on him and he went to talk to the families in every room. Greg and Stephen Hoffman were twins. When Howard saw Greg, he told him how like Stephen he looked, that it made him (Howard) catch his breath. Howard then started regaling everyone with stories about their loved ones. The Kirwins came. They were involved in a lot of the advocacy that affects the families and I saw them fairly regularly. We exchanged large hugs. Families that felt they had no place to go were very much at home. A mother came in from Australia. Some have driven from upstate New York and from the tristate area. One family has so many siblings that with their parents they took up almost an entire table of ten by themselves. Daniel Trant's family came from Chicago. Kathy Trant made their life very difficult when she appeared on Oprah showing how she spent all of her VCF money. One of the siblings asked if she could come out and volunteer for a clambake over the summer. I said, "Of course." She volunteered for the clambake and stayed at my house.

The first time I met Debra Burlingame was at a meeting with John Cahill. He was Governor Pataki's chief of staff, charged with oversight of all of the agencies involved in the redevelopment of Ground Zero to try to get the process moving forward. The uniformed service workers' respective unions joined our fight and demanded a meeting with Mr. Cahill regarding how the names would be listed at the memorial. This was an enormous step forward for us because, although the families had been marginalized as a small voting block (I have heard "dead people don't vote"), the firefighter and police unions were an entirely different story. They wielded current day clout. Debra was introduced to us as a newly appointed World Trade Center Memorial Foundation Board member. Her brother "Chic" Burlingame was the pilot of the hijacked plane flown into the Pentagon. In a sea of emotionally charged issues and recitations, I succinctly spelled out the unresolved issues still confronting the families. Debra and I talked briefly at the meeting's end and she said that we should speak further. Debra is a little older than I am, with blond hair and an engaging manner. There is something about her that invites confidences. She listens and she knows the right questions to ask. She didn't say much at that meeting but in our brief conversation, I got the sense that she was very smart. Debra entered this situation very much like I had, three years ago when I joined the Family Advisory Council. She has been brought onto the World Trade Center Memorial Foundation Board to support the government-appointed family members on the board and combat the positions taken by the family leaders.

I knew about Hangar 17 at JFK International Airport. It was where the Port Authority housed all of the World Trade Center steel that wasn't sold back in 2001. Shiya Ribowsky of the medical examiner's office was called there to examine the steel as well as the composite. The composite is nine floors that were crushed together to form something that looks like a meteor. There was a lot of controversy surrounding the composite. Diane Horning, on behalf of WTC Families for a Proper Burial, maintains that it is inappropriate for a museum exhibit because it contains human remains. Shiya was asked to make that determination. He told them that he could not and they would have to bring in cadaver dogs.

The WTC Memorial Foundation decided that the composite did not contain remains and they proceeded with their plans to include it as an exhibit in the Memorial Museum.

Debra Burlingame and I were invited to take a tour of the hangar with the curator. As we both had missed the date when the larger group of family leaders went, we decided to go together. Nothing prepared me for what I was about to see. I have been to Hiroshima, and I have been to the Holocaust museums, but nothing I have ever seen was as powerful to me as this was. The airport hangar was enormous, about the size of an airline terminal. This hangar was filled with steel. Crushed, bent, twisted steel. Not little pieces. Rust-colored girders, longer and taller than most houses. Steel that was once tall and straight and proud, now twisted into silly band shapes. What chance did a human being have against this kind of force? Debra and I were in tears. I turned to her and said, "Why isn't this the museum? Why isn't this steel going onto the site above ground?" The cement hangar was cold. We would have been chilled even if it weren't. The curator was kind. He had seen the kind of pain this room evoked countless times before. The first room had nothing but twisted girders. Some of them had clearly been torn out of cement. It had the tridents, which used to adorn the outside of the World Trade Center and are prominently featured in photographs of the buildings remains. It had steel in the shape of half-eaten pretzels. We walked through in silence, lost in our thoughts. We entered another room. This one had crushed vehicles. Fire trucks, police cars, ambulances, a PATH train. The radio antenna from the top of the building that made it the tallest building in the world. Then in another room, racks of clothing covered in thick white grey ash, toys, mangled signs. Last, we entered the climate-controlled tent that housed the composites—floors so thoroughly melded together with identifiable scraps of paper crushed within that they look like something from outer space. We gasped. We cried. We hugged each other. We took photographs that could never capture the enormity of what we just witnessed. We lost ourselves in our memories. I thought to myself, "every human being needs to see this." It tells you the story in a way no manufactured exhibit can. But it doesn't give you hope. It shows you raw, unadorned destruction. I left completely drained. I was grateful I wasn't driving.

ZERO GROUND

On June 8, 2005, Debra Burlingame shattered any hopes the memorial board that appointed her had that she would become a lockstep family member. She published an op-ed in the *Wall Street Journal* called "The Great Ground Zero Heist"[82] that sent everyone scurrying. No one saw it coming. Debra had provided the answer to our problem. She had seen the political agenda in the International Freedom Center (IFC)—one of the chosen occupants of the imposing 300,000 square foot cultural complex slated to sit above ground on a memorial site where the 9/11 memorial and museum would be underground—and exposed it. The issue of "what appropriately should go where" at the WTC site, for which the family leaders had received no support, had just gotten a boost of national attention. Debra characterized the IFC as a George Soros-funded, left-wing political operation and their narrative of "mankind's quest for freedom" as a ruse to hide their real agenda, which was to trash America at the place "where heroes died."

Her view was that "the public will have come to see 9/11 but will be given a high-tech, multimedia tutorial about man's inhumanity to man, from Native American genocide to the lynchings and cross-burnings of the Jim Crow South, from the Third Reich's Final Solution to the Soviet gulags and beyond." She questioned what these important historical moments had to do with 9/11. "This is a history all should know and learn," she wrote, "but dispensing it over the ashes of Ground Zero is like creating a Museum of Tolerance over the sunken graves of the USS *Arizona*." The public reaction was instantaneous: outrage.

The incestuous nature of the selection of the IFC was alarming in and of itself. Roland Betts, who sat on the board of the LMDC, was the long-time business partner of Tom Bernstein, the IFC founder and chairman who also sat on the WTC Memorial Foundation. Bernstein was also a human rights activist whose organization, Human Rights First, had filed a lawsuit three months earlier against the U.S. government on behalf of detainees in Iraq and Afghanistan. Paula Grant Berry was the vice chairman of the IFC and also sits on the WTC Memorial Foundation board. She said that "if the memorial to the victims was the heart of the site, then the IFC was the brain." Tom Roger, the memorial board member who had undermined the families' consensus on memorial mission statement, was an IFC "family advisor."

Debra called me and asked for the support of the Cantor Fitzgerald families on this issue. I told her that she had it. Debra's position was political. Mine was psychological. We were against the location of this cultural center in space that we believe should be reserved for a memorial, before we knew what was going to be in it. Now that we knew, my families continued to want the WTC site to be about 9/11.

We had already begun fighting the IFC's non-9/11 programming when the proponents of the IFC proposed that a podium be placed on the Memorial Quadrant to be used as a speaker's corner. This way, they said, anyone with a position could be heard and their statements debated. Many Family Advisory Council members forcefully stated that a public forum for advocacy on the Memorial Quadrant was inappropriate and that this podium must be located elsewhere.

I quickly became Debra's number two in command, alongside Anthony Gardner. Next to Howard, Debra is one of the smartest people I know. The phrase "Take Back the Memorial" was coined and a website with that name became the media headquarters for our fight. An online petition resulted in thousands of 9/11 family members adding their names and their support. I spent a lot of time strategizing with Debra. On June 20th, Take Back the Memorial, supported by a coalition of 15 9/11 family member groups, staged a protest at the World Trade Center site. Our position was getting a lot of attention, and a lot of supportive press. I spoke at the rally, which was well-attended. I didn't have written notes. I addressed the desire of the IFC to discuss other events in history instead of focusing on 9/11. The transcript of what I said was placed on the Take Back the Memorial website. As part of my speech, I said the following:

But now 9/11 faces a different tragedy. Forgetfulness. The 9/11 Memorial will be buried underground. Its stories, artifacts and place in history hidden underground. The fear, loss, hope and heroism of 9/11 replaced in prominence by stories from a different time, about a different day. While the memories of 9/11 are hidden underground, while 9/11 tries to squeeze between the infrastructure underground, a shiny new building is going to be constructed for the International Freedom Center. The message will not be the hope and renewal of 9/11, but a debate on world politics. The space will not be a sacred remembrance but rather a speaker's corner. When you come to the WTC site you will not be immersed in 9/11. You will be met with world politics. No one who has come to the WTC site in the last almost four years has asked about world politics. Why? Because it isn't the appropriate place. Everyone knows that. The International Freedom Center must be removed. If the museum building stays, it must be filled with 9/11 from top to bottom, There is no reason why cost or space should ever be an issue in teaching 9/11 to our children while money and space exist to debate world politics. Make no mistake, we think Martin Luther King deserves to be honored, that there is a place for Ukrainian victors to be studied, but not on the site where 20,000 body parts of 2,749 innocents were recovered.[83]

Someone sent me a political cartoon that used my statement "But now 9/11 faces a different tragedy—forgetfulness." I hung it in my office.

Many of the family leaders who had united around the names issue went to Washington to support the Take Back the Memorial campaign. On June 30th, we held a united press conference at the National Press Club. We demanded that the sanctity of the WTC site be preserved. Debra and I met with Congressmen Sweeney, Fossella and King. The three congressmen subsequently sent a letter stating that Congress would intervene and demand an accounting of federal funds applied to the IFC if officials in charge of redeveloping Ground Zero didn't "limit the memorial there to the events of September 11th." We were gaining support, and the controversy brought fundraising to a standstill once Debra's self-made PR machine started letting donors know that by donating to the Memorial Foundation they were not building a memorial but giving money to a cultural center.

When we discovered that one of the "important" financial sponsors of the IFC was the United Way's September 11th Fund, we were appalled.[84] We didn't believe that the generous public who donated to assist 9/11 victim's families knew that their donations went to a non-9/11 cultural center.

The International Freedom Center tried to make its position clear. They showed us a large poster of an Iraqi voter. When they saw our reaction, the poster disappeared from any future presentation. But their "March of Freedom" featured exhibits that had nothing to do with 9/11. I found myself wondering if Gettysburg would give up part of their battlefield to discuss 9/11, or if they would be satisfied with a complete recitation of the battle below ground while there was an aboveground museum to 9/11 or the Holocaust on the battlefield. To characterize 9/11 as just one element in the story, at the location where the event occurred, didn't make sense to me. The story of 9/11 is big enough. The only museum on this site should be a September 11th museum.

Then the *New York Daily News* ran their own exposé on the Drawing Center, another of the tenants in the cultural complex at Ground Zero. In 2002, the art gallery located in Tribeca had featured an exhibition mocking the Bush administration's policies in the War on Terror. When the center's director refused to confirm that political art would not be shown on the Memorial Quadrant, more outrage ensued.[85]

Governor Pataki supported our position when he demanded "an absolute guarantee that as they proceed it will be with total respect for the sanctity of the site." We had seen Governor Pataki backpedal from his support before so I didn't put much stock in it. But this seemed to be different.

On July 12th, the LMDC started investigating alternative locations for the IFC and the Drawing Center, both of which refused to comply with Governor Pataki's mandate. Despite having this directive, John Whitehead still insisted, "It's doubtful they will be moved."[86] I started doing research on available real estate and gave Debra several alternative locations in Lower Manhattan that could effectively house these institutions off the WTC site. On August 11th, WTC Memorial Foundation Chairman John Whitehead told the International Freedom Center that it had until September 23rd to submit more specific plans for review. Mayor Bloomberg backed the Freedom Center and bashed the LMDC for caving to Governor Pataki's wishes. His criticisms were too late. It was like watching a steamroller gain speed. On August 16th, Steve Cassidy, president of the Uniformed Firefighters Association, withdrew his group's support from the IFC. When the International Freedom Center submitted its plans in accordance with John Whitehead's directive, it did nothing to disabuse Debra of the notion that this was an "America-bashing museum," or me of the notion that this would not keep the WTC site about 9/11 and February 26, 1993.

After their presentation, Hillary Clinton, Senator Schumer and the Police Benevolent Association also jumped ship. Governor Pataki unilaterally ousted the IFC on September 28th. Mayor Bloomberg expressed his disappointment.[87] Although given the opportunity and offered funding to find an alternative site (as the Drawing Center did rather than comply with Governor Pataki's directive), the International Freedom Center chose instead to cease to exist. It wasn't about bringing the world a tolerance museum at all. It was about co-opting the World Trade Center site.

In actuality, the mounting cost overruns at the World Trade Center site were so extreme, the inclusion of the massive cultural center was probably one of the most fiscally irresponsible moves the LMDC and World Trade Center Foundation Board could make. In hindsight, they should probably thank Debra. I know we do.

The first Sunday in April, the families held a service at the Church of St. Francis of Assisi in Manhattan to thank the medical examiners. Charles Hirsch, Bob Shaler, Shiya Ribowsky and his assistant Katie Sullivan treated the families of victims with dignity and respect. They made a process that was heart wrenching, bearable. We owe them a huge debt of gratitude and it was our honor to thank them. I never would have thought I would have a medical examiner on speed dial, but Shiya and Katie were there for the Cantor families every time I needed them.

When Shiya decided to leave the medical examiner's office later in the year, I knew it was time to get Gary's remains turned over to us. Before Shiya left, I asked to see a copy of where and when they identified the 10 pieces of Gary. Each piece, with when and where it was found, was catalogued and a form was filled out by the police. Pieces of Gary were recovered in the days following September 11th at the World Trade Center site. Then I saw a form that made me ill. In the space filled in for location found, it said "Garbage Dump." Even when the recovery was going on, no one tried to pretend that Fresh Kills was anything other than it is. I gave the form to Diane Horning and tried to forget what I had read.

The bombings of London's Underground and buses, which killed 35 people and wounded hundreds more, let us know in no uncertain terms that the terrorism we faced wasn't going away any time soon. It didn't matter that we were Americans. We were now part of a horrifying global community of victims.

When I officially met with the memorial architect Michael Arad about our names proposal, he made believe that I was asking for a telephone directory. He did a mock-up that ignored his own brick pattern design[88] and listed victims' names, last name first. Instead of trying to accommodate a proposal that had enormous family support, he cited the few exceptions. When he said that the names couldn't be listed alphabetically because there was a married couple with different last names, he wouldn't recognize that by placing those two names together out of alphabetical order, but within their grouping you would automatically be communicating the family relationship between them. When we discussed that some victims did not work for companies, we said that they should be designated all together as "visitors." By saying that A-L on one pool and M-Z on another wouldn't look right, he ignored our need to be identified by the company our loved ones kept. He inserted his personal judgment that we were creating a hierarchy if we listed the corporate names, despite the fact that those personally affected didn't feel that way, and that it was the insignias that were creating the hierarchy. We wanted the names arrangement to tell a story to the memorial visitor. Who the victims were with and worked for when they died is an integral part of that story. We told Michael that when exceptions arose, the individual families would resolve them. He could easily have accommodated our plan but wouldn't try. I thought maybe he was holding onto control of the names because so much else in his design was being changed. But the mayor and governor already changed that as well when they added the insignias and created a hierarchy. I still cannot understand the refusal to accommodate the families. I found myself hoping this wasn't purely ego driven.

StoryCorps is a program that enables 9/11 familes to record, in a conversational question-and-answer format, an oral history about the person they lost.. The stories will be captured in the Memorial Museum and, if the families give their consent, the Library of Congress. I started setting up meetings for my families to give StoryCorps interviews about their loved ones. Some families found it cathartic. I also assisted the Living Memorial Project. This project asked families for pictures, letters, items to be scanned, or anything the families would like to leave behind as a record of their loved one. Each victim will then have a file that will be housed in a kiosk in the Memorial Museum. Families are also being asked for pictures of their loved ones for quilts and for museums. The requests for information and participation are overwhelming and confusing. I try to explain and simplify the process and ensure that our loved ones are remembered.

Every time I thought we had a handle on a process that was emotionally devastating, something else would happen. A little over four years after 9/11, on October 6th, unidentifiable remains were found at the Deutsche Bank building. This building had been contaminated and condemned as a result of the September 11th attacks. A little over three weeks later, the remains were identified as human bone fragments. The death of our loved ones returned to the front pages of the newspapers and onto our television sets. Diane Horning, Lee Ielpi and I demanded a meeting with the LMDC to set up protocols with firefighter involvement for searching the Deutsche Bank building for remains. Our confidence that the building had been adequately searched was gone.

Several family leaders from the Family Advisory Council asked for and received a meeting with Gretchen Dykstra, the president and chief executive of the World Trade Center Memorial Foundation, to demand that the foundation appoint family members chosen by the Family Advisory Council. These family members would more appropriately represent the positions of the families than the currently sitting family members chosen not by the families themselves, but by the governor and the mayor. The leaders requested that I be appointed, along with Anthony Gardner and Patricia Reilly. Gretchen Dykstra told me that sometimes you can accomplish more by fighting battles from the outside. She thought that was more appropriately my role. She knew that none of us would ever be appointed to the board. When Gretchen Dykstra subsequently resigned as president of the WTC Memorial Foundation, a reporter asked her about the board's relationship to the families. With Paula Grant Berry, Christy Ferer and Tom Johnson as examples, Ms. Dykstra responded, "I think there was an element of elitism toward the families that was quite palpable ... and also a naiveté on the part of the families."[89]

Because of the speed with which Cantor was rebuilding, Howard decided to split Cantor Fitzgerald into two companies so that each could grow without sharing resources. In addition to keeping Cantor Fitzgerald, he formed BGC Partners, named for his friend and mentor Bernard

Gerald Cantor. BGC Partners would focus on the company's wholesale business, which included eSpeed. When large clients or money managers want to buy or sell an investment, they call Wall Street. When Wall Street's largest firms (Goldman Sachs, JP Morgan, Bank of America, Deutsche Bank) want to buy or sell, they use BGC Partners. In 2005, BGC Partners hired 1,000 brokers and its revenue doubled to more than $400 million.

2006

9 1 1

John Whitehead, chairman of the WTC Memorial Foundation, and Howard's fellow Haverford College alumnus, appointed Howard to the board in January 2006. Despite not having any of the family leaders that we requested, I now felt more confident that our voice would be heard. I took Gretchen Dykstra's words to heart. Howard would work with diplomacy, and I would continue to champion the rights of our families from the trenches.

*   *   *

The service was terrible. A new Greek restaurant opened in the Hamptons and Lewis, Nick Photiatis and I went to check it out. Nick placed our order in Greek. We waited and we waited. The two couples at the table next to us were having the same problem. We started talking. When one table received appetizers and the other didn't, we offered to share. The pretty blond at the next table who looked to be a little younger than I, introduced herself as Patti Frank and asked what I do. I hate this conversation. I'm not good at small talk. My life is heavy and dark. It's hard to not go there no matter what the conversation was before if I answer. "I run a charity." "Really? Which charity?" Here we go. "The Cantor Fitzgerald Relief Fund." "Ohhhh. Well it's about time that company does something good for those families." She then proceeded to lambast "the guy that runs the company." I silently took in the tirade. Lewis and Nick were looking on, thinking, "Oh, this is gonna be good."

I couldn't believe that four and a half years later, when you couldn't find a Cantor family to badmouth us if you tried, I was still hearing this. I bit her head off with the facts. I methodically laid out everything that Cantor Fitzgerald and the Cantor Fitzgerald Relief Fund had done. I concluded by telling her that we had given more than $100 million to our families in cash, not including the money we paid for their 10 years of health care. To an innocent bystander it probably sounded like, "Rah Rah Rah Ragga Rah Rah.... Rah Rah Rah!" I was both angry and alarmed that this was a conversation I even needed to have. Patti had the good grace to tell me that she was glad and that she just didn't know. She told me that someone she knew who lost someone at Cantor was actually in the restaurant. I told her to "ask him what he thinks of the company. I'm sure he knows who I am." When they saw each other, and she said who she was with, he came over and thanked me for all we have done for his family. After this blip, we found we had a lot in common. We shared a very pleasant evening, despite the food, and we exchanged numbers. Subsequently, Patti emailed me asking for a lawyer for her boyfriend. Because of her last name, I mistook her for a relative of Phyllis Frank. I immediately jumped right on it and accomplished all that she was asking for. When I realized my mistake, I started to laugh. Patti had now benefited from how the Cantor Fitzgerald Relief Fund treats its families.

There is absolutely no reason that I should confuse Gloria Ingrassia and Evie Reisman. They look nothing alike. Gloria is a statuesque brunette. Evie has coiffed blond hair, and, while beautiful, is older than Gloria. Yet they both have that stately elegance that you cannot buy. It's an indefinable quality. So I confuse them. They do have other similarities. They both lost their sons at Cantor and they have both been thrown into advocacy roles, in which they never expected to find themselves. Gloria and her husband Anthony attended every rally for Families for a Proper Burial and staunchly and consistently fight for the removal of remains from Fresh Kills. They always wore either a t-shirt with their son Chris's picture on it, or carried a placard with his missing flyer. Evie isn't one you would expect to see picketing, but she couldn't accept the idea of having a memorial wholly underground, a feeling shared by many of my families. She used the power of her pen. In a letter to the governor, she said the following:

> *As the parents of Frank Reisman, who was one of the thousands of Americans murdered on September 11, 2001 while he was at work as an employee of Cantor Fitzgerald, on the 104th floor of the World Trade Center, we protest most forcefully against the abominable plan to locate the Memorial in a dangerously and depressingly confined underground location totally unsuited to the gravity of the event being memorialized. The plan cruelly adds to the pain our family has suffered from that horrendous day and has, since then, only been compounded by such unfeeling, disrespectful and gratuitous insults as allowing the remains of our dearly loved son to be mingled with trash in a garbage dump having the ironic name of Fresh Kills. Please, Please, Please do not permit this unseemly and inappropriate construction to go forward...* [90]

Their sentiments are shared by Liz and Allan Horwitz, who wrote,

> *No memorial should be buried underground, especially this one, honoring people who truly worked on top of the world.* [91]

The current plan was to have both the memorial and the museum underground.

Bill Doyle and I were furious. We were on the phone on March 25, 2006, discussing the fact that the New York City Law Department sent tapes and transcripts of the 911 calls of 28 victims to their families in the mail, without any warning or notice of what the package contained. The recipients were devastated. I don't know how many times we told the powers that be that the families must not be surprised with upsetting information. They must be warned. On Monday, I called the Law Department and tried to see whether any of the packages hadn't been sent out yet, and whether they could be retrieved. I didn't yet know that one of them was coming to me. When I received a package, I knew what it contained. I didn't open it for quite some time. I couldn't listen to my brother's cries for help that never comes. On the 27th, the news of the 911 calls hit the *New York Post*. From the moment the press became aware of the release of the tapes, my phone didn't stop ringing. It was always reporters looking for the names of families who had received the tapes and transcripts.

It was because of a Cantor widow's outrage at receiving just a tape that transcripts were included with the tapes. The press corps wanted someone to share their tape with the public. These were not the words of operators whose job it was to field calls. These are the words of the men and women trapped in the building. This is not information that the press will receive from Bill or from me.

I called the New York City Law Department and reemphasized how vital it was that the names of these 28 families remain confidential. It was bad enough they received the package without warning. They did not need a media frenzy on top of that. I ultimately read the transcript. My brother calmly called 911 four separate times. And though I love listening to Gary's voice, I cannot listen to this tape. I put it away in case some day Howard's children want to hear it. On March 31st, a non-Cantor family released a tape. I refused to watch the news. I just couldn't.

Two years later, in 2007, I became Jane Doe. The redacting of the names of the 9/11 families who received the 911 tapes and transcripts was being appealed in court by the *New York Times*. I still would not allow these names to be released. I went to Howard and he sent me to attorney Mike Lampert. He prepared a brief and entered me in the lawsuit as Jane Doe. We fought for the privacy of our families. Ultimately, we were successful. The 28 families who received their dying loved ones' calls for help now had the right to divulge their identity or not, as they saw fit. It was an important win.

On April 4th, five months after we requested it, Lee Ielpi, a family leader and retired firefighter, Diane Horning and I met with the LMDC to discuss the human remains that were found on the roof of the Deutsche Bank building. Firefighter experts had been removed from the search of the building and we were there to ask for their return to the job. We didn't trust a search that wasn't done without firefighter oversight. We wanted the LMDC to issue proper protocols and to adhere to them. We didn't want any more remains turning up because a building or area hadn't been thoroughly searched. This had gone on long enough.

The next day I became part of yet another process. The "106 process" was the environmental review of the site. The preservationists were all on the committee. Anthony Gardner was trying to get the LMDC to preserve the footprints down to bedrock as an historic matter and he hoped that he would be able to accomplish this through the 106 process. I had no expertise whatsoever, and knew that there was a very real possibility that I wouldn't understand half of what they were fighting or talking about, but I was there as a consulting party to lend support. It was during this process that I learned they were removing the survivor staircase and actually taking it apart before reassembling in and later placing it in the museum. Here was also when they discussed preserving the slurry wall.

Howard managed to get the World Trade Center Memorial Foundation Board's Executive Committee to agree to meet with us on April 18th. We wanted to make rational and well thought-out presentations to help them understand what it was that we actually wanted, and how we could come together and support each other. As with the manufactured issues between the uniformed services and civilians, a lot of the information floating around was inaccurate and didn't support our actual positions. Anthony Gardner would give a presentation on the preservation of the bathtub area down to bedrock. He would make the Executive Committee understand that this didn't mean that we wanted an underground memorial. Underground would in fact be great as part of a museum experience, so that the actual box beam column remnants that are the outline of the towers could be seen. He would give the green light from the families to change the design. We wouldn't tell them that this was all Anthony's idea. We would give them all the components and let the idea be theirs.

I would give a presentation about the names, which would be part of the deal. I would tell them about the meetings and how the vast majority of us are in agreement about what we want. We have compromised even further and modified our names proposal. I would ask the Executive Committee, whose opinion should be stronger than ours, on how our loved ones names are listed. We will object to the proposed "symbolic tomb," which doesn't hold the remains of our loved ones and is ridiculous. Why should people come to a memorial and pay their respects to an empty box when there are 20,000 as yet unidentified remains?

Other family leaders will present the fact that we were reasonable when it came to the temporary restoration of the PATH station, which has now been made permanent without our knowledge or consent. We will give the arguments why a bus depot shouldn't be in the footprints underground and why the street grid across the site should be pedestrian. Anthony has found a way to modify the design in a way that will save the foundation hundreds of millions of dollars.

We hoped that if we presented the World Trade Center Memorial Foundation with a complete win/win package for us and them, we could show them how we can be a strong asset in their fundraising campaign rather than their adversaries.

The April 18th meeting went extremely well. We could see as individual committee members started to understand the positive ramifications of what we were saying. They could do away with the underground portion of the memorial and move the names above ground. The design change would immediately have the full backing of the families, and help save the foundation tens of millions of dollars in construction costs. The names would not be random. They would be arranged in accordance with the proposal we had modified and articulated, which is to say that they would be listed and identified with their affiliations in the proper tower, followed by their ages. The corporate affiliations would be on the bottom parapet where the panel designation is. The firemen would get ranks and be listed and identified with their engine companies. We showed them our mock-ups. It didn't look that different. We promised to help the Memorial Foundation fundraise. After some back and forth negotiation and discussion, we came up with a plan both the Executive Committee and the family leaders could agree to.

Everyone was on the same page. We thought that the battling was over. We could finally all move forward together with a united purpose, because the Executive Committee and the families were now all in agreement on this compromise.

But when our agreement was subsequently presented to the World Trade Center Memorial Foundation Board with the Executive Committee's backing, the discussion was all positive until Patty Harris, deputy commissioner appointed by Mayor Bloomberg, said that adopting the resolution was a declaration of "nuclear war" against Mayor Bloomberg. In the face of her comments, and having no desire to start a war with the mayor, the board tabled the resolution.

HOPE

On May 3rd, I was scheduled to move into a new office. Marianna went back to her job in accounts receivable and became "on loan" to me whenever I needed her. When her boss told me she had to move downtown with her department, I took a stand. What good would it do me to have an assistant who wasn't located anywhere near me? Either she had to stay uptown, or I had to move downtown as well. So, my office moved downtown right outside the South Street Seaport in the old Euro Brokers office space, at 199 Water Street.

Cantor Fitzgerald purchased Euro Brokers on May 21, 2005. Now in addition to running the Cantor Fitzgerald Relief Fund, I also run the Euro Brokers Relief Fund. Because the vast majority of my time those days seemed to be spent at the LMDC offices at One Liberty, it was okay for me to be downtown. It still wasn't easy for me to walk by the World Trade Center site. I found myself wondering if it would ever get easier. This was the same day that Zacarias Moussaoui got life in prison instead of the death penalty. The testimony our families had previously given prosecutors was used in the sentencing phase. The recitations of loss and terror communicated by the 9/11 families was chilling. On that day I also met with Alice Greenwald, director of the 9/11 Memorial Museum, to discuss her plans for the museum.

In addition to raising money for the 9/11 families, our Cantor Fitzgerald White Party Clambakes in Memory of Gary Lutnick raised money for wounded members of our military. On May 22, 2006, Howard, Kent Karosen and I visited Bethesda Naval Hospital. At Howard's instruction Kent purchased CD and DVD players along with new movies and CDs.

We went from bed to bed, visiting young men whose limbs were being held together by high-tech looking erector sets. Anyone who thinks the war in Iraq and September 11th were independent events is sadly mistaken. Wounded serviceman after wounded serviceman told us how he enlisted after seeing the attacks of 9/11. They looked so young and vulnerable lying in those hospital beds. They were mostly 18 to 22 years old, and one after another they told us how they wanted to go back. They wanted to continue to fight to keep us free. I'd never seen anything like this and its impact on me was profound. One young husband wouldn't eat his hospital food because his wife had run out of money and he wanted her to eat it. Howard took money out of his pocket and gave it to every person we visited, along with the electronics we had brought. Howard knew these men were bored in the hospital, so the entertainment we were giving out was very welcome. We remained committed to helping these men and women going forward. I decide the money we raised at the clambakes would be used as "gap money." We cover situations that existing benefits from the military or elsewhere do not. We have paid for things like a hotel room for a father when his son, who had been injuried by a roadside bomb, underwent specialized brain surgery in another city. Helping the military families is squarely in line with what we do every day with our own families. In recent years, my sister-in-law Allison started a biannual fundraiser also to ben- efit wounded members of the military and their families. Hearing their stories is heartbreaking.

Obviously, the wars in Iraq and Afghanistan were prevalent in people's minds. The declaration of war, whether we belonged in Iraq, our position in the world as a result, our conduct while at war, and the antiwar demonstrations were heavily reported. None of those things made any lasting impact on me because of the all-encompassing 9/11 cocoon in which I lived my life. Seeing these injured men and women opened my eyes in a very real way. My focus still didn't shift to wanting to become involved in world politics in an advocacy role. It just added another group of people to whom we would render care.

THE PROPOSAL

On May 4th, when Mayor Bloomberg announced that the memorial budget had been set at $500 million, cost estimates for the planned memorial were stated at almost $1 billion. Everyone agreed that it has gotten out of hand. This announcement set the stage for the changes to the memorial design that we had proposed at the April 18th meeting. Governor Pataki and Mayor Bloomberg appointed builder and developer Frank Sciame to review the overages and come up with a proposal to cut costs in half.

On May 31st, members of the Family Advisory Council met with Frank Sciame in his firm's offices. As he heard what was important to us in a memorial, he commented that a proposed cost-cutting idea was to not run the waterfalls in the winter. In fact, it was Michael Arad's stated preference to do away with the waterfalls completely and leave the entire memorial underground.[92] Mr. Horwitz raised his hand and said, "If you are changing the design, and the major element is waterfalls, and you are shutting off the waterfalls in the winter, then why aren't you scrapping the design and starting over? I mean, it's no longer what the jury selected."

Debra Burlingame called me in a panic that the museum was being sacrificed. Mayor Bloomberg was using the Sciame evaluation process as an opportunity to move or remove a September 11th Museum. Bloomberg suggested either moving the museum into the lobby of the Freedom Tower, which was a whole other political hotbed of its own, or doing away with a museum completely. At the time, we had no idea how close this was to becoming reality. The decision to jettison the idea was not out of respect for the story. It was because Mr. Sciame's committee discovered that "it would have spawned sticky real estate issues, such as a possible recapitalization of the tower project and potential loss of rentable space."[93] Howard told us to stay the course, because in his view he still thought we would get the victims' names listed above ground, the footprints cleared off and a museum that would be below ground.

Howard spoke with Governor Pataki about how important the listing of the names to the families was. He explained that if the names were listed the way the families wanted, they would become a powerful fundraising tool for the memorial. He pledged that if the families came on board they would raise at least $25 million for the stalled fundraising effort. He guaranteed any shortfall. The governor was delighted. Howard reiterated that who, more than the families, should have a say in how the names of their loved ones are listed?

When the Sciame report was announced on June 20th it basically recommended everything Anthony Gardner envisioned when we met with the Executive Committee back in April. It moved the names above ground. It did away with the level 30 feet below, and though he made it smaller, Frank Sciame left the museum underground on the tower footprints. When the LMDC announced a week-long public comment period, Anthony's WTC United Families Group encapsulated our outstanding issues and most of us submitted the same comments. We supported the Sciame plan with the following modifications:

– The names should be listed in accordance with the family names proposal and not in random order.

– The tomb must house the actual remains instead of the proposed "symbolic mortuary vessel" which is in the current plan. The housed remains should be located between the two tower footprints and not in the North Tower.

– Remove the infrastructure from the footprint remnants to allow visitors to transverse them at bedrock. This will give the visitor the correct historic scale of the towers. The abstract voids above are 30 percent smaller than the actual footprints.

    – The family room must be above ground.

    – The safety and security of the memorial and museum must be integral to the design.

    – The historic artifacts such as the tridents and Koenig's Sphere need to be returned to the site.

    – The visitor center should be renamed the World Trade Center Memorial and Museum Visitor Center in order to provide the museum with an aboveground component.[94]

The major accomplishment, according to Governor Pataki, was that the project would now stay on schedule to open on September 11, 2009.[95]

David Dunlap from the *New York Times* came to my office. We sat and talked for three hours. David had been writing about the 9/11 family issues for a long time now and was well versed. I didn't always agree with the positions he took, but he was usually fair. I spelled out the position of the families regarding the names. I showed him how we had simplified our proposal from the original submitted in October 2004. I spelled out the proposal we presented to the Executive Committee. I showed him that two-thirds of the families had individually signed their names to the family names proposal, and that we had the support of the uniformed services unions. This was an issue we had been fighting for many years and was not one we felt we could compromise on. We didn't oppose the Sciame report, but it didn't resolve the names issue. I told him that the families would not support this memorial if the names of their loved ones weren't listed appropriately and that families wanted to be in support and help fundraise. His article came out June 27th. Marsha Kramer interviewed me for CBS and that aired June 29th. Frank Sciame had previously said it wasn't in his province to resolve the names issue because it wasn't a budgetary factor, but that he would like to see it resolved.[96] It was exactly because it wasn't a budgetary factor that the families should have been successful.

On August 4th, I sent a letter and the revised names proposal on behalf of the families to Kevin Rampe, the president of the LMDC. More than 1,700 individual 9/11 families, civilian and uniformed service alike, had signed their names agreeing to our names proposal. It was no longer the family leaders speaking for the families. The vast majority of families had spoken for themselves. With the Sciame redesign came the removal of many of our issues—the amount of pedestrian traffic below ground, how visitors would get down into the lower level, safety and the number of ramps should no longer be a concern. The families' name plan was simple. With identified affiliations, loved ones' names would be easier to find. Names would be humanized. People would know that children died here and that people with the same name were different human beings. The grouping of companies and floors would show that the number of deaths increased exponentially above the planes' impact, but would not interrupt the "ribbon of names, as envisioned by the architect." Surely our loved ones would now be allowed to be identified with the group they worked and died with? They must know by now how important it is to treat all the victims equally.

LEGACY?

On September 6th, Hofstra University invited me, along with other family leaders, to participate in a symposium. After giving an interview on the names issue to NPR, I headed out to Long Island. I sat and listened to presentations and became alarmed when I realized that what September 11th meant to some of these students was that they were subjected to more and inconvenient security screening at the airports. To them, 9/11 wasn't a monumental, life-altering seminal event. It was a hassle. They had no idea that, years later, after the underwear bomber unsuccessfully attempted to blow up his flight on Christmas Day 2009, the hassle they faced would include full body scanners. He is currently awaiting trial and admitted to having ties to Yemen and al Qaeda.[97]

I left the symposium completely dejected, only to discover that someone had taken my umbrella, and when I got into my car in the pouring rain, it wouldn't start. Lewis, who was at his home in Long Island, came to get me with jumper cables. I was so tired. And it was my late father's birthday, which always brought me down.

Anthony Gardner's WTC United Families Group has been working on a civic responsibility curriculum program. He paired with educators from Queens College and fashioned a program appropriate for high school. His goal is to bring the stories from 9/11 to the schools woven into a teaching program. He has filmed interviews with the relevant politicians, family advocates and leaders, family members, survivors and residents. Howard and I both gave interviews for his program. My interview was the first time I was in the new World Trade Center 7 building overlooking the site. When Anthony asked me whether he could have his launching press conference at Cantor's offices I readily agreed. If children can learn from the tragedy of 9/11 and walk away with the message that they can bring about change, be it through philanthropy, advocacy or commitment, then that's a wonderful thing.

His program, which became the not-for-profit September 11th Education Trust, has now been incorporated in the curriculums of more than 2,000 schools. Only one of them is a New York City public school.

I had six events between September 8th and September 11th that I was scheduled to attend in honor of the five-year anniversary. First, I went up to Inwood Hill Park to visit the New York City Memorial Field of Honor that we helped John Michelotti put together. It was spectacular—2,979 flags, each with a person's name below it, flying in this field, grouped together by affiliation and listed in alphabetical order. I ran my fingers along the Gary flag. Sometimes I felt as if 9/11 were such a long time ago. Most of time I felt like it was yesterday. When I looked at this simple, eloquent, moving memorial I couldn't help but wonder why the memorial downtown was made so unnecessarily complicated.

September 9th, I attended a rally for WTC Families for a Proper Burial down at the WTC site. Posters and t-shirts were everywhere. "Mayor Bloomberg—It's Rest in Peace, NOT in Garbage." Diane explained that everyone was wearing purple and black because those are the colors used to drape public buildings when we are in mourning. She quoted a statement that is preserved on the wall at the Oklahoma City memorial.

We seek justice. The courts require it. The victims cry for it and God demands it.

Attorney and advocate Norman Siegal spoke about how on August 15, 2005, WTC Families filed a lawsuit to be granted standing to sue for the remains in Fresh Kills. Diane reminded tourists who have joined the rally that the dead are not here at Ground Zero. Their corporal bodies are in a garbage dump.

When the rally ended and we started walking toward the next event, I noticed the pictures that graced the fence of the WTC. I turned to

Lewis and said, "Look at this, they will put up pictures of extraneous things, but they won't put up pictures of the 9/11 victims."

At 1 pm, I left to go participate in a 9/11 quilt dedication at the Voices of September 11th forum at the Marriott. The enormous and beautifully constructed quilt has the names of our loved ones listed and a quilted picture of the towers. It took my breath away. But an ancillary sheet of paper told you which section of the quilt names are in, because they aren't in any discernable order. Makeshift row numbers were hastily attached to the quilt. No one could easily find their loved ones' name or likeness. It was frustrating and the listing of names became meaningless. I turned and looked at the other family leaders. This was the physical manifestation of exactly what we were all trying to avoid at the permanent memorial.

On September 10th, I went to the Tribute Center museum. This is the museum that is steps from the site Lee Ielpi's organization created to ensure that there was a place where accurate 9/11 information could be obtained. For the fifth anniversary, there were special times reserved for the families, and Lee asked me to come. The museum, which I never went to before, is very well done, but I am not the right audience. I know the story. It was too graphic and real for me. When I started the exhibit I was immediately confronted with a life that I remember and no longer have. I watched the images of the gatherings around Koenig's Sphere and heard the concerts as if I were right there, looking at these tall, imposing, monster-sized buildings that were like no other. Then there were the planes and the carnage. Then there was death, followed by the recovery effort. But they did listen to the families when it came to how the names should be listed. There was a huge wall of photographs. Gary's picture jumped out at me.

Then I went back over to the Voices of September 11th annual forum, where I am on a panel discussion. I followed that by racing to Central Park to start setting up for our memorial service. My core volunteers were all there. I exhausted every avenue, trying to get things donated to put on the chairs. Finally, a friend of mine and his artist friend designed and manufactured a t-shirt for us. On the front was our logo and the words "Cantor Fitzgerald Relief Fund Family" under two sunflowers. On the back, across two large sunflowers, are the words, "We Will Always Remember Because We Stand United." We then listed the Cantor companies past and present: Cantor Fitzgerald, TradeSpark, eSpeed, BGC and Euro Brokers. We put a t-shirt on every chair.

On the 11th, Lewis and I headed to Bayonne, New Jersey, where the Teardrop Memorial was being unveiled. The actual ceremony was scheduled for later in the day, but it conflicted with the Cantor Memorial. I was allowed to come earlier. The artist, Zurab Tsereteli, was there to meet me. He designed and constructed a moving memorial that can be seen from across the river in Lower Manhattan. It is shaped like a teardrop and has been donated by the artist and the city of Moscow. There are nine pathways leading up to the base of the sculpture, which has eleven sides, on which the 9/11 dead are listed in alphabetical order. It is touching. I thanked the artist. Through an interpreter he told us that he had made miniature sculptures for each of our families, with their names underneath. I assured him that we would distribute them for him. Lewis and I departed and headed back over to Central Park. Lewis's mother had gotten us chocolate flags, which couldn't be put out the night before. My right side started hurting me under my bra line. I told Lewis that before the Cantor Memorial started I needed to go home and change.

After five years, there were very few people at the Cantor Memorial in Central Park I hadn't seen at least once before. The truly kind families told me their names as they came up to me. I'm more aural than visual, so with this many faces sometimes I can't keep them all straight. Our volunteers sat at registration. Donna Dudek was once again running around helping Kent. This was the first memorial at which I spoke. It was the friendliest of audiences. I told them that I didn't possess the adjectives to make them truly understand who Gary was, and that a cliché was no less accurate because it applies to many of our 9/11 victims. Really, what I wanted to do was to thank them, because they helped me survive the last five years. I ended by holding up a heart that was placed on the chairs. I lifted my broken heart necklace. I told them that my heart was broken, but then I lifted the heart from the seat, and told them that they were helping to make my heart whole. Howard always says, "It takes a broken heart to heal a broken heart." By the time the ceremony was over, my side was really hurting me. I was exhausted and emotionally spent. I didn't go to the reception. I went home and broke down into tears.

The next day, Lewis and I drove out to the Hamptons and I went to the doctor. Much to my chagrin, I was diagnosed with shingles. If my brain thought I was superwoman, my body just disagreed. The doctor prescribed medication, rest and. above all, the avoidance of stress. How was I going to do that? If I hadn't been in so much pain, I would have laughed. I was quarantined from anyone that hadn't had chicken pox, which thankfully Lewis did. Howard and his kids were in the Hamptons. I wasn't allowed to see them and I was being forced to go 9/11 cold turkey. On October 1st, after being deemed noncontagious, I went into New York City for the Jewish holiday with my brother and his family. I couldn't fast because of the shingles and I was still in pain, but I needed to go say the prayer for our dead.

It had been over five years since September 11, 2001 and people expected that we should have "moved on" and healed. If we weren't able to heal, at least we should be able to hide our scars internally. Positive milestones abound—birthdays, weddings, births, promotions, new apartments, new hobbies, new and renewed friendships. There were many days we partook of good food, friends and company. We and the people around us accepted that there were buttons that, when pushed, would always emotionally cripple us for a little while. When we are required to fill out a medical form that asks how many children we have, or how many siblings and we don't know how to answer, that is a button. Do I have two or do I have one? Or, small talk, polite inquiries from strangers or people we haven't seen in a long time that invariable lead us to a story that we don't want to tell. "So, how have you been?" "Catch me up." "What have you been up to?" "Do you have children?" "What do they do?" Or we have gone to a movie, and there is a 9/11 trailer we didn't expect to see instead of an animated film, the buildings are coming down, or we've gone to a restaurant and someone at the next table is regaling their friends with their "where I was on 9/11 story" and we are forced to stoically overhear. This is how we can always tell who carries lifelong scars from the tragedy and who does not.

The 9/11 families and survivors who were there don't talk about it unless pushed or among their own. The ones who survived with their loved ones and their ability to sleep intact, do. Hearing the stories of someone's whereabouts and how they survived unscathed doesn't usually help a 9/11 survivor. It only emphasizes their difference.

Upon my return, I found out that Mayor Bloomberg was being pushed through as the chairman of the WTC Memorial Foundation. The family leaders arranged a press conference for the following day, October 5th. We stated all the reasons why Mayor Bloomberg was not the right candidate for this job. Anthony Gardner pointed out that while he was being touted as the fundraising savior, Bloomberg had been an honorary member of the board the entire time and hadn't raised money for the memorial in either that capacity or as the mayor. To the contrary, he had done more to block fundraising. When every issue was resolved, except the names, which Bloomberg blocked, and the Sciame report was agreed to and adopted, Bloomberg still did not raise funds for the memorial. He created the controversy that had such a negative impact on fundraising, and was now installing himself to save the day. If he used his position as mayor to impose his will, what chance did anyone have of the board standing up to him if he was also the chairman? Another family leader pointed out the egregious conflict of interest between being the mayor and the chairman of the board. He went on to tell us that this felt more like a coronation. Several families picketed outside the American Express building with signs that said "Vote No for Bloomberg" and "Ground Zero is not for $ale."

The board, which Michael Bloomberg and Governor Pataki appointed, voted him in as chairman. All the agreements we had with the Executive Committee were now null and void. Michael Bloomberg didn't want our names arrangement, and he'd just ensured that we wouldn't get it. The man who had said, "I am a believer in the future not the past,"[98] had now been put in charge of the memory of September 11th.

When Howard renewed the offer he previously made to Governor Pataki to newly appointed Chairman Bloomberg—that the families would raise $25 million for the memorial and he would guarantee that amount of money if we could agree on how the names would be listed—Mayor/Chairman Bloomberg reacted negatively and went on the attack. Rather than recognizing what a powerful force the families could be, he used the press to say, "Nobody's going to dictate with cash what's the right thing to do."[99] By taking over the chairmanship of the Foundation, that was exactly what Michael Bloomberg had just done. Howard responded that Mayor Bloomberg should "remember. We're talking how their loved ones' names are listed—nothing else. Who in the world cares more about the names than the loved ones of the people who died?"[100] We continued to gain no ground.

﹀   ﹀   ﹀

Every time we started to think that we had developed a handle on this living life without the one you love thing, and we and everyone around us accepted our "buttons" with whatever responses came with them, we would get slammed in a way we didn't anticipate. When a Con Edison worker revealed to the press that he had found body parts in a manhole at the end of October 2006, five years evaporated before our eyes. The murder of our loved ones was front and center once again. Ever since the remains were found in the Deutsche Bank building, we had been battling the LMDC and the city to have appropriate protocols and to bring in the experts from JPAC, the Joint POW/MIA Accounting Command. JPAC is the organization charged with finding the remains of our military overseas. Their motto is "Until they are home."[101] Our pleas went unanswered. Sally Regenhard's organization Skyscraper Safety Campaign, and Diane Horning's WTC Families for a Proper Burial put together a large rally held on November 2nd. When I saw the Esposito family, I gave them a big hug. Craig Esposito was a good-looking kid in his early 20s. He said to me, "Hey, Edie, look at this." He unzipped his jacket and raised his shirt. He had tattooed an almost life-size picture of his father's face on his torso. I smiled and shook my head. Only Craig. But there was a stark contrast between this memorializing tattoo and the fight to find and identify the people we love.

Despite overwhelming support from both the families and NY politicians, Mayor Bloomberg ignored us. Instead, he put the Department of Design and Construction (DDC) in charge of the review, the same agency that paved over the haul road running through the WTC site in March 2002 without doing a thorough examination, and launched a new recovery mission.[102] The "cleanup" was again going to Fresh Kills. We weren't getting fewer remains in the garbage dump, we were getting more. JPAC, which stood ready to assist in the recovery, could not come in without an invitation from the mayor. The city refused assistance from anyone and also controlled the testing of what was found. Between the 911 emergency calls, the remains being found, the movies being made, the battles about the development of the WTC site, and the other acts of terrorism that reprised 9/11 in the press, there was no safe haven from the spotlight that shined on the death of our loved ones.

We had to find a way to make the people in charge understand. I wracked my brain trying to think what else we could do. How could bringing the experts from JPAC to find the remains of our dead be objectionable? One night I was watching the news and a body of an elderly woman was found in a dumpster. People were outraged. When the story went on to reveal that she was dumped there by a family member who didn't have the funds to bury her, we were aghast. The perpetrator was arrested. No one should be left in a dumpster as a burial location. The 9/11 families who saw that newscast were genuinely confused.

Howard requested a meeting with Mayor Bloomberg because Howard had an idea to help move the names issue forward. They met in a diner on the Upper East Side. "What are we gonna do about this names thing, because I'm not giving in." Bloomberg was staying with the party line. Howard suggested that the Cantor names be identified and listed altogether in the North Tower where they worked and died, and that while it would not be random to us, we would make it appear random to the world. Cantor would arrange how their names would be listed, as long as they were not in alphabetical order. At that breakfast, Bloomberg agreed that he would move all of our people into the North Tower, and that we would have the right to list them altogether, as we saw fit. He told Howard that he would not agree to list anyone's age, floors or affiliations.

Steve Cassidy, president of the United Firefighters Association, had been squarely in our camp—until he wasn't.[103] After negotiating with Mayor Bloomberg, Steve Cassidy and the mayor came to an agreement. The mayor, contrary to the deal he had struck with Howard, would identify the uniformed service workers by their affiliations and would list and identify their units (battalion, ladder company, engine company, chaplain). In fact, he would accord the uniformed services personnel everything they had been fighting for except their ranks. Cassidy told Jim McCaffrey from Advocates For a Fallen 9-11 Heroes Memorial that this was the best deal he could get from the mayor. Ever since our first meeting in February 2004, the families of civilians and uniformed services workers agreed to work side by side, making what each group needed synonymous with every other. Cassidy sold out the civilians and settled for less than the whole for the uniformed service families without consulting them. The weighty political power of the unions, which had been our strongest weapon in the years-long names battle, was now gone. Steve Cassidy, with whom I had spoken and strategized on a regular basis, refused to take or return my phone calls, and the mayor refused to grant a comparable deal to the civilians.

When Dave Kravette, Howard's oldest friend and 9/11 survivor, called to congratulate me on winning the names issue,[104] I was still upset. I couldn't believe how this was being spun in the press. The baby step we were granted was Howard's conversation with the mayor. Our loved ones' names would now be allowed to be listed together in the appropriate tower as long as there was still the appearance of randomness. There would be no affiliations for civilians or designation of where

Cantor Fitzgerald's 658 victims begin or end. There would be no ages. There would be no parity between the way civilians and uniformed services personnel are identified. The listing of names around the pools would not tell the public anything about who the civilians were or what happened at this event. Floors would not be listed either, so the memorial would not show the visitor how the number of victims lessened as the floor numbers decreased. There would be no humanization of the civilian victims, no information to help foster an emotional connection by a visitor.

Without ages, there will be no distinction between a father and a son with the same name. No one will ever see that the Hansons lost a 2½-year-old child on the plane, or realize that the average age was 36. Planes will be identified. So will 1993 bombing victims and Pentagon employees. But when the mayor denied uniformed service workers their ranks, he also stripped the identification of military ranks. This outraged the Pentagon families. A three-star general died in the attack on the Pentagon, his service to his nation denied at this memorial. Civilians, meanwhile, are denied any identity and any identifying characteristic, and families will still have a difficult time locating their loved ones' names. It isn't a win at all. I asked, "Why do civilians not deserve the same respect and remembrance?" The North and South Towers now have entirely different identification systems, and the equality among all victims, which was a cornerstone of the Memorial Program and jury competition, is ignored completely.

On December 19th, with a final quarterly payment of $8,106, Howard sent our families the following letter:

Five years ago I vowed to rebuild Cantor Fitzgerald and to provide our families with steadfast emotional support and meaningful financial assistance. Together with our employees and our families, we pledged that Cantor Fitzgerald would remain as one company, one family, and one community. I further pl edged to you, on behalf of myself and the firm's partners, that we would work tirelessly to build the firm anew and fulfill our promise of contributing 25% of our profits to help the families of our friends, colleagues and loved ones who were lost on September 11th.

It is with great pride that I enclose our concluding payment of that five-year commitment on behalf of the Cantor Fitzgerald, eSpeed, TradeSpark and BGC team. As we pledged, the firm will continue to cover health insurance for those families who are eligible for another five years.

In the process of recovery and renewal, the firm's partners and employees are proud of the success Cantor Fitzgerald has achieved, enabling us to provide over $180 million to the families of our employees who were lost on 9/11. We hope that our profit-sharing pledge and the funds that have been provided underscore to you how immeasurably the loss of your loved one affected us and how deeply all of us at Cantor Fitzgerald care about you and your family.

I would like to assure you of our continuing commitment. As you know, the Cantor Fitzgerald Relief Fund stands ready to help any of our families who may need assistance. And, as a member of the board of trustees of the World Trade Center Memorial Foundation, I remain a strong advocate for memorializing the names of our employees together as part of Cantor Fitzgerald, and making sure they receive the recognition they deserve.

On behalf of the entire Cantor Fitzgerald family, I would like to tell you once again how deeply honored we were to have worked with your loved one, and how thankful we are that you are a member of the Cantor Fitzgerald family.

His commitment of 25 percent of the firm's profits for five years plus what the firm was paying out in health care would net the Cantor families more than $180 million, not including the additional $45 million Cantor paid in its October bonus payment. Because of the losses that Cantor suffered on 9/11 there was no bonus to speak of. Rather, it was another way Cantor took care of the families.

2007

WHO THEY WERE

When the press asked Howard to comment on the mayor's new names proposal, which had been approved by the Memorial Board the mayor now chaired, and on which Howard sat, he said,

> *Listing the names of the victims of the attack together in the appropriate tower is definitely a positive step. However, treating the civilians who were lost differently from uniformed workers by ignoring employees' affiliations just doesn't make sense to the victims' families, and it will be less meaningful to future generations of visitors to the Memorial.*[105]

Angela's husband, Glenn, has a marketing company called the Zagoren Collective. He agreed to help me. He designed a logo for us and, along with some of his willing clients, designed and shot a one-minute television advertisement for us. We didn't have any money, so everything was donated. Just like Debra did with "Take Back the Memorial," I now incorporated Savethe911Memorial.com as a new website and organization. We were going to try to get our position heard outside New York City's political circles, and see whether we could make it go viral on the Internet. Somehow we had to get a comparison of our mock-ups, which looked only marginally different from the mayor's plan to show how easily we could make a list of names "human," and have some equality between the mayor's employees and everyone else. We used the information contained on the missing person flyers to craft our message.

Everyone who talks to the families or comes to the World Trade Center site asks the same questions over and over again. "How old was he?" "Where did she work?" "What floor was she on?" We have never been able to fully understand why the mayor dug in his heels. Why must the victims' names be in "no discernable order?" I have two victims named Sean Patrick Lynch. Why should he care if ages are next to each victim so they can be told apart?

Before Michael Bloomberg took control of the WTC Memorial Foundation, the Executive Committee of this same board agreed to list the names the way the families wanted. Once he was in charge, agreement was nullified. It was almost as if, once we won the IFC battle and jettisoned a museum that he supported, he vowed never to let the 9/11 families win another battle.

This memorial belongs to America, arguably even the world. Our hope was that ordinary people who were touched by 9/11 would see an iniquity they probably knew little about and would care. It was a long shot, but I had to try. Debra Burlingame told me at the time that Americans had larger issues to deal with. The economy has been doing horribly and because of the subprime mortgage issue, people were fighting to keep their homes. The war in Iraq had taken its toll. Debra said that all America would see was that a big expensive memorial was being built to honor the dead and the families were complaining again. As she is talking all I can think is, "Oh my G-d, it's the station wagon."

This was the story. My mother was an artist. She made large pieces, both paintings and sculptures. Our car was too small for her to transport her artwork (this is the 1970s—pre-SUV). One year my father came home with a station wagon for her birthday. My mother plastered a smile on her face, said, "thank you," but was seething underneath. A station wagon was an enormous financial purchase, one that should have been discussed and made as a couple. Add to that, the station wagon my father selected for my mother was too short. Her artwork didn't fit in it. This extravagantly expensive purchase was useless to her. But, how can you be mad at someone who just bought you a station wagon?

The National September 11th Memorial at the World Trade Center site is like the station wagon. How can you be mad at someone who just gave you a half a billion dollar memorial? The irony is that we would have been fine with a smaller, less expensive memorial if it honored our loved ones in a manner we were comfortable with. Just as many of us would be fine with saving the massive expenditure of funds to open on the 10-year anniversary, before the ancillary but necessary services like restrooms and bus depots and security checkpoints are complete. We asked that our loved ones' names have a little context, and be easy to find. But how can you be mad at someone who gave you a station wagon?

I scheduled a press conference in the Marriott Hotel. We showed the side-by-side mock-ups to the members of the press. We aired our commercial. It was haunting. Against a background of a single violin, the young vibrant faces on the missing person flyers, some in wedding photos, flashed by. The information conveyed—age, company identification, floor was visible for all to see. "They were our first 9/11 memorials... They told the stories, they put a face on history. Now Michael Bloomberg wants a memorial in name only—a memorial that says nothing about who the victims were. Just a cold random list of names... A memorial in name only... is no memorial at all." We paid for a time slot on NY1. We posted the video on YouTube. We asked people to send it around. I didn't have the money to advertise. I had done all that I could. The mayor refused to budge. When Michael Bloomberg saw my brother at a meeting he jeeringly said, "How's your siiiister?" How could a person feel glee over trouncing the hopes of the families of dead people? Especially when what they were asking for would cost no extra money and should have been in their purview to decide? I will never be able to wrap my head around this. Instead I wrap my arms around my families in consolation. We have all tried our hardest.

When a child asks a parent whether he or she can do something, or have something, sometimes the parent says no. When the child asks why, the response is, "Because I said so." Like children, we never received an explanation why ages next to the names was so objectionable. But unlike parents, who usually have a good reason for saying no, there is no good logic behind this decision. If you looked at the names Frederick Hoffman and Michelle Hoffman next to each other and you saw their ages, you would know that Frederick was the father and Michelle the daughter. Why is letting the memorial communicate a story a bad thing? In the name of a layout that was supposed to provide "meaningful adjacencies," the public has been denied all of them, with the only explanation being, "Michael Bloomberg said so." And what exactly do Michael Arad's "meaningful adjacencies" mean? As an attempt to make his "randomness" more palatable, he has coopted and bastardized Howard's idea. He is allowing families to name two people who their loved one can be listed next to. There won't be anything on the memorial that lets you know who those choices are, why they were made, or the framework they are in. Beyond honoring that limited request, Michael Arad is planning on putting those names anywhere he deems visually appealing. Meaningful adjacencies aren't really very meaningful to the visitor who is looking at a random listing of names, nor are they meaningful without context.

Cartoon by Cox and Forkum. Copyright 2007. Reprinted with permission.

2008

A RECORD

The Memorial Museum had been hosting a conversation series to discuss issues with the family leaders that they wanted to keep us informed of, or get our opinion on. I didn't believe we had much say, but I went to the meetings anyway. Howard is the chairman of the Memorial Museum Program Committee, so I felt that the best chance of getting what was important to us heard was through a conversation with my brother and not a conversation series. The mayor appointed Paula Grant Berry co-chairman (Howard was already chairman of the Program Committee before the mayor took over), in an apparent attempt for City Hall to maintain control. To this point, I still couldn't see any place in the Memorial Museum where the general public would see who the 658 men and women who died at Cantor Fitzgerald were. I advocated that on a wall with photographs of all of the victims, they have a panel of buttons that allow different groups of pictures to be highlighted, such as Cantor, Marsh, firefighters, AA Flight 11.

At a meeting to discuss how to present sensitive material including graphic photographs, I saw some of the images for the first time. The footage was difficult to watch. Nothing prepared me for Beverly Eckert's StoryCorps interview. I had been working with StoryCorps and the Memorial Museum to make sure that every Cantor family did an interview that will be available on a computer terminal in the museum if you type in a particular person's name. It wasn't so much what Beverly says, because the conversation is reminiscent of so many I heard through the years, although listening to her recitation of her husband Sean's last morning and their conversation from the towers certainly wasn't easy. It was the raw emotion in her voice. It was the clear sense of loss and absence she communicated.[106] Even though on the phone, she had heard the horrible crack and avalanche of the building's collapse, as terrible as that day was, she didn't want to go to sleep because, "as long as I was awake, it was still a day that I'd shared with Sean."[107] I could brace myself against the images. I couldn't guard myself from that. How we present this information to children is of great concern to us all.

I had a meeting to discuss getting more Cantor family participation in StoryCorps and the Living Memorial project. There are too many programs and they have inundated and confused our families as to what is what. The StoryCorps interviews are the oral history that will be in the museum and in the Library of Congress. I have had StoryCorps use Cantor's offices for their interviews and I got them quiet and private rooms during the parents and siblings luncheon where they conducted interviews (which take about an hour apiece). The Living Memorial Project is something else. This is a project started by Monica Iken and subsequently received funding from the LMDC. Mary Fetchet from Voices of September 11th then took over and added a social work component. Families are basically asked to submit artifacts that the project will scan and make into a memory page. A visitor will also be able to call up this information from a computer terminal located in the South Tower if they put in that victim's name. The family can add, subtract or change their pages as often as they like. They can designate things to not be open to the public until they are gone.

Between the two programs, the families are trying both to communicate to the public what the memorial does not and to preserve a historical record so that generations to come can understand the truth of the human tragedy. Individual human beings died. We as a society were robbed of their lives. We want you to know what you don't know. We want you to understand and connect to what you have lost. I have no idea whether, after going through an entire museum, visitors will sit down at a computer and type in the name of someone they don't know to learn something about them. I hope they will. The only thing I can do is to ensure that the Cantor families are represented and give the public that opportunity.

After the meeting, for the first time since 9/11, I saw the battered Koenig's Sphere that used to so majestically grace the World Trade Center plaza. It was an upsetting experience. It could not be shown with less splendor. Here was the sculpture and symbol of a world that is now crushed but still resiliently stands. It was ignored by visitors, most of whom had no idea where or what it was, and it was covered in bird poop. It sat in its isolated location in Battery Park City, not on the World Trade Center site where it belongs, because Madeline Wils had successfully banished all reminders of 9/11 on behalf of the residents.

There is no question that the residents of Lower Manhattan have had serious issues to contend with in the 10 years since 9/11. When Christine Todd Whitman of the EPA said it was fine for people to return to their homes and offices, only for the public to belatedly discover that the air quality was not acceptable, it was horrifying. Being displaced from homes, enduring months of cleanup and seeing your neighborhood decimated before your eyes wasn't easy. The economic rebound of Lower Manhattan became of paramount importance to residents. But the view of some that the needs of residents and the needs of victims' family members were incompatible resulted, in my estimation, in throwing the baby out with the bathwater. The families didn't demand that the memorial site be turned into a cemetery. One of the first suggestions, brought forth by then Mayor Giuliani was that the site be a park. The desire to stave off this impending cemetery resulted in a residents' movement to make sure that no reminders of 9/11 be returned to the neighborhood. The one trident that will be housed in the Memorial Museum above ground was a hard-fought battle over many years, and can be seen only from a very limited vantage point. To date, Koenig's Sphere is being denied its rightful place on the site. Anthony Gardner suggested that the sphere be returned and dedicated to the rescue workers who have lost their lives to WTC illnesses post 9/11. That request was also denied.

The memorial will be low and surrounded by groves of trees. Residents won't be able to see the memorial from their homes. And even if they could, what they will see is the largest man-made waterfalls in the country. Even Chris Ward, the executive director of the Port Authority, referred to them as "the fountains" in a meeting we had with him about trying to return Koenig's Sphere to the site. We previously had a meeting with Stephan Pryor, then president of the LMDC (after Kevin Rampe), and he promised us that the sphere would be returned. The family leaders have been trying to make this happen since 2002.

But again, wage a battle, win a battle, ignore the win as if it never occurred. When I told Howard about Koenig's Sphere he said, "It has to come back. What is the museum going to do? Show visitors a picture of it in the museum when the real thing sits in Lower Manhattan? That's just dumb." I hope he is right. There have been lots of issues that I think are just dumb, that we haven't been able to successfully resolve.

❧ ❧ ❧

On February 25, 2008, I went to Washington, DC with Debra Burlingame and met with the military tribunal prosecutors at Fort Myer regarding the trials of the 9/11 co-conspirators. Colonel Morris and his team patiently and methodically described to a large group of family members how the trials would proceed. They fielded attacks from the Jersey Girls, who wanted to see Guantanamo closed and questioned whether the detainees can get a fair trial from the military. When one of them asked Colonel Morris, the head prosecutor, how they knew that they had the "correct Sheikh Mohammed," I thought that Debra was going to leap across the table. They explained that family members would be allowed to enter a lottery to go to Guantanamo and view the hearings from a galley when the 9/11 defendants were tried. After the meeting, Debra and I headed over to Arlington Cemetery to visit her brother's grave. We saw a group of young soldiers in uniform visiting the grave of one of their fallen Coast Guard brethren. We went up to them, explained who we were and thanked them for their service. We were two sisters, mourning the loss of our brothers in the company of soldiers mourning the loss of one of their own.

I sent the information about the lottery out to all of my families. I entered myself but I didn't win. Judy and Gary Reiss, whose son died at Cantor on 9/11, did. Gary is a big, warm-hearted teddy bear of a man. Judy, after the first several weeks when she was unable to leave her house because of the loss of her son Josh, ultimately became a strong voice of advocacy. In the wake of 9/11, Gary Reiss called Howard at home and said, "What can I do to help?" Howard gave his information to me, and I called Gary. We immediately established a connection and became friends. We understood each other's loss. The first time I met them was at a large town hall meeting in the city. I saw them again at the first memorial service. I asked them if they wanted to speak at the service on the first anniversary. They declined. They weren't ready. Judy told me that she has seen people look at her and turn and hurriedly walk into another aisle in the local supermarket because they don't know what to say. The same thing happened to us, when a rabbi at the 92nd Street Y (who is no longer there) saw Howard after a service, and consciously turned away from him and started walking down the street, before he caught himself, realized how unbefitting this behavior was for a rabbi, and came back to shake his hand. The alternative was that people stopped and stared.

I know the Reiss family well. I had spoken to them when they got the call on their wedding anniversary that one of Josh's bones had been found. I was told when they got the second call that the upper part of his body had been found, on a Friday at 5 pm when they couldn't call their rabbi. When their daughter had her bat mitzvah in January 2003, Lewis and I were invited and attended. When, as one of the 13 candles that family and friends were called up to light, a memorial candle was lit for Josh, it broke our hearts. To make matters worse, the temple was across the street from Rider College in New Jersey, which is where my brother Gary went to college.

And now Judy Reiss told me about their trip to Cuba. "Americans don't know how good these bastards have it. No one but the president of the United States has better health care than they do." She explained that they went to Cuba with three other victims' family members. They were the only Cantor family at the first hearing that families were invited to attend. One of the other couples is a 9/11 widow and widower who met at a meeting, fell in love, married and now have two children. Judy told me that when Colonel Morris met with them in the galley of the magnificent state-of-the-art courtroom that had been constructed for these trials, she was amazed at how much he knew about her son. I had previously heard about this $80 million courtroom that allows for time delay before information goes to the press galley, so that the judge can rule on security sensitive materials.

She told me that what these young people who are representing our country have to endure is unbelievable. "They throw excrement at them." "What do you mean, Judy?" I ask her incredulously. "I mean that they take pee and feces and they hurl it at them." "You saw this?" "Yes, we saw it." "Edie, have you ever been to a trial and seen a defendant decide it's time to go pray, so they can pray in the middle of a trial?" I thought about that one, and can't remember a time. "They stop the proceedings, let them go back and shower or whatever they have to do, change into their whites and pray. One of the defendants, who only has one leg because we saved him and gave him a prosthetic, knew we were there, so he took off his leg and slammed it down on the table. Their lawyers filed 250 defense motions, each one more ridiculous than the next. These guys admitted they did it and all these years later we are still dealing with this? It's ridiculous. But the island, it's beautiful."

On the morning of September 11th, I headed to Cantor's offices downtown. It was our annual Charity Day, which has grown into a day when celebrities, musicians and athletes come into the offices and get on the phones with the clients. This makes it fun for the employees who are donating their day's salary and for the clients who are doing more business knowing that 100 percent of Cantor's revenues are going to charity. Cantor and its public affiliate BGC Partners have raised between $9 million and $12 million each Charity Day. Cantor also supports all of the charities that are important to the participating celebrities as part of the day. Normally, I didn't go down to the office because I needed a more somber September 11th, but I wanted to be with Howard. He was doing a spot on Boomer Esiason's telethon, which was being telecast from our offices. I ended up being on the telethon as well. The energy in the room was infectious. The celebrities, who are coached by the actual brokers what to say, really got into it. Photos were snapped like crazy. Autographs were signed. Millions of dollars were raised for charity.

I left the office and headed over to Rockefeller University, where we were having this year's memorial service. We were scheduled to have it inside in their theatre in case it rained. I spent a lot of time assigning seats. The last-minute RSVPs significantly exceeded the number of seats in the theatre. Kent did an eleventh-hour hustle and we moved the entire event outdoors instead. Thankfully, in true victim angel fashion, the weather was beautiful. The bucolic landscaping was a perfect backdrop for our unadorned chairs (I could no longer get anything donated), which took up the entire lawn. Howard, Allison, Lewis and I left shortly after the reception began because we were invited by David Paine and Jay Winuk of My Good Deed to attend the Presidential Forum at Columbia University. Candidates John McCain and Barack Obama were setting aside their differences and meeting on the same stage. The event was not political and focused instead on civic responsibility. After the event, we were starving. It had been a long day. We went to Nero, the Japanese restaurant that Gary took us to when we enjoyed our last meal together on September 10, 2001.

Six weeks later, Barack Obama was elected the 44th president of the United States and our first African American president. He stated to a jubilant Chicago crowd, "If there is anyone out there who doubts that America is a place where anything is possible, who still wonders if the dream of our founders is alive in our time, who still questions the power of our democracy, tonight is your answer."[108] New York Senator Hillary Clinton became secretary of state.

Mayor Bloomberg had been considering a run for the presidency. After he abandoned those plans, he reversed his long-standing position on term limits, and convinced the city council to allow him to run for a third mayoral term.[109] Mayor Giuliani talked about extending his term by two to three months in the wake of 9/11, but in the face of two public referendums in 1993 and again in 1996 enforcing term limits, he declined to do so.[110] The following year, on November 3, 2009, Mayor Bloomberg won a third term by a very small margin. In his third term, Mayor Bloomberg switched back to his original position in favor of a two-term limit, now that the referendum was once again on the ballot and didn't apply to either him or the members of the city council who had effectively extended their own terms as well. The referendum passed on November 2, 2010.[111]

Cantor Fitzgerald continued to grow the company and to hire new employees. In the wake of the credit crisis, Howard steered Cantor clear of the debacle. Cantor expanded into investment banking, real estate lending and prime brokerage—establishing itself as a full service Wall Street firm again, but now focusing on serving the "middle market," or firms that the giant investment banks don't serve fully.

BGC Partners merged with eSpeed in April 2008. With revenues at $1 billion, it quickly became a force in the inter dealer brokerage business, where Giant Bank A (Goldman Sachs) sells and Giant Bank B (JP Morgan) buys huge volumes.

2009

TERROR TRIALS

On November 5, 2009, at the most populated U.S. military installation in the world, a U.S. Army major serving as a psychiatrist screamed "Allahu Akbar" before opening fire, killing 13 people and wounding 32 others. One of the victims was pregnant. His trial before a military tribunal is set for March 5, 2012. He faces the death penalty.[112]

When Debra Burlingame called and told me that she needed me to speak at a rally she was putting together across from the court houses in Foley Square against the Khalid Sheikh Mohammed trial being held in Lower Manhattan, I agreed. She said she needed civilian support. Once again, while for Debra and many of her colleagues this was a political issue stemming from whether this trial should be held in a federal court or a military tribunal, for me, that wasn't why I agreed to speak. I hadn't asked my families their collective opinion on where KSM, the 9/11 mastermind, should be tried nine years later, and therefore didn't have the right to speak on the subject. I took no stand on whether Eric Holder is or isn't a good guy. What I did know, however, was that blocking Lower Manhattan and making my families engage in this trial on the news daily was not a healing idea.

The rally was held on December 5th. It was a cold, rainy and dreary day. Despite that, there were hundreds of people crowding Foley Square. I found myself in a trailer with Brian Dennehy. I told him that we had recently taken a large group of the Cantor families to see him in *Desire Under the Elms*. He expressed his condolences. He was there to read an

eloquent letter written by the father of Daniel Pearl, the murdered jour-
nalist. The speeches were long, thought-provoking and intense. When
it was my turn, I figured the crowd had enough content on that dreary
day. I gave them a rally cry. Someone in the front row had a mega-
phone and was calling for the removal of Eric Holder in impolite terms.
I hoped that the message—that this wasn't the appropriate location for
this trial—wasn't going to be lost because of one person's bad behavior.

Originally, Mayor Bloomberg supported having the trial in Lower
Manhattan. When it was brought to his attention that it would cost the
city over $200 million, he changed his tune. No official decision would
be made as to the forum in which to try Khalid Sheikh Mohammed for
quite some time, we were successful in ensuring that it would not be
Lower Manhattan.

2010

THE LAYOUT

In an ironic twist of fate, I was charged with laying out the names of the 715 Cantor Fitzgerald and its contractor victims in the North Tower and 61 of the Euro Brokers victims in the South Tower. Michael Arad had come up with a scheme by which families could request two names to surround their loved one. He was calling it "Meaningful Adjacencies." Howard's deal with the mayor allowed us, rather than Arad, to arrange our names, as long as they still appeared to be in no discernable order. This concession cost my brother a pledge to the Memorial Museum of $10 million. Howard told our families at the last memorial service that we knew who their loved ones worked with, were friends with and probably died with. It wouldn't be one or two people. They would be surrounded, and not in a sea of strangers.

Laying out these names in a meaningful way, while trying to incorporate the Memorial Museum's adjacency requests, was an impossible task. My contact on the Memorial Foundation side, Allison Bailey, told me that the memorial would have panels with five lines of four names in a brick pattern. There would be 18 panels to a side. That meant 360 names on a side, with corner panels also with 20 names. Laying out the names was like an impossible Sudoku game. Instead of numbers, however, these were people I knew, or loved, or didn't know but now knew their families. I couldn't know that a layout wouldn't work until I got to the end of the wall. After days of trying to arrange the names by laying index cards on the floor in the required grid pattern, then moving names written on Post-its around, I called my brother. He told me he would get a computer programmer to help me. But I knew there was no way a computer could capture all of this and, at the very least, it would need a baseline. I kept working. Howard assigned me Dr. Jacob Loveless. Jake immediately grasped the complexities and said that with the variables we presented, this fell into the highest degree of difficulty for computers. He agreed that I would have to do the layout by hand.

The weight I felt on my shoulders was crushing. I was immediately pulled back into the months following September 11th when my world revolved around lists of the dead. I couldn't help but feel I was back where I started, with every highlighted line through a name an attempt at honoring a memory and helping those they left behind.

To really make this work, I needed information. Marianna and I pulled together a pre-9/11 departmental list. I talked to the surviving Cantor employees. I may as well have been asking them to relive every funeral. I transported them back in time with me. I asked which departments were on which floors. I found out who the bosses were. I learned which departments related to which others. We broke down every department by desk and by subsection. For example, equities lost 114 people but each desk within the department was like a mini-family. This layout needed to capture that. We talked to our families. We methodically recorded every relationship. Each adjacency got added to the Memorial Foundation's adjacency list as another requirement that must be met.

I called Darlene Dwyer, who ran Windows of Hope, which cared for the restaurant workers. I asked her to call Allison Bailey and tell them that she wanted her victims' names linked up to my arrangement for our food service provider, Forte Foods. In this way, at least the entire top of One World Trade Center (floors 101 through 107), would be listed together, even if the public was unaware.

I spent weeks in my pajamas on the floor with my index cards and Post-its arranging and rearranging the names of our dead. I told Jake that what I really needed was to enter a layout on the computer and then have the ability to move every name down a space if I wanted to add someone. He tried but came back and said that he could switch one person with another, but he couldn't do that "chook, chook, chook" domino thing that I wanted to be able to do in order to move hundreds of names down one space. That meant one mistake, one missed person, one unmet adjacency, one unfinished department on a wall, and that meant going back to square one.

I got up in the morning. I spread out my index cards and Post-it names. I arranged a panel and then wrote the names from that panel on a legal pad. I got to the end of the wall after laying out 360 names and found that I had one extra name. Two departments converged and I have two unrelated victims whose last name is Bowden. In my layout, the two Bowdens became one. I went to bed that night and I had a nightmare about one of the Bowdens being surrounded by the wrong people for eternity.

The next morning, I scrapped the entire layout and started all over again. Each time I put a name in a layout, I ran a highlighter through the multiple lists. I didn't want to use a name twice or leave anyone out. I did this so many times that I had lines that were half one color and half another, or shapes, because I'd used up all my highlighter colors.

Over the post-9/11 years, as life returned to a new normal, my weight started inching back up to where it had once been. Now the pounds dropped off again. I didn't go anywhere. I didn't do anything. I stayed for days and weeks at a time, on my floor creating layouts. One day our new puppy, feeling neglected, ran onto the Post-its and pushed a name off an index card. I looked at Lewis and said, "Well, I guess X didn't want to be in that spot."

I finally made it all fit. And then Allison Bailey changed the layout. It wasn't 20 names on a corner, it was now 9. I had to start over again. When I finished, she changed it again. It wasn't three corners, it was now two corners. It wasn't 20 names on a panel. It really depended on the length of the name. It could be 21. "How in G-d's name am I supposed to be able to do this?" Jake said, "Allison, this is a computer program. It's a computer that is going to cut the names. Tell me the spacing between each name, even a range, and we can lay out the names." "I can't. Michael Arad and his team are doing the spacing visually." It was a nightmare.

When I moved as far along as I could alone, I moved back into the city and started camping out with Jake at multiple computer terminals. I commandeered his conference room for all my index card and Post-it layouts. The employees who worked around us couldn't believe what they were seeing.

Jake managed to take the Memorial Foundation's software and improve on it. He color-coded our employees by department and we placed arrows between the adjacencies so we could see how this was working, and who we had to move. We did layout after layout until we felt we had it right. We submitted our layout to Allison. When she returned it, we saw that it had been revised and now ignored everything we had accomplished. I took their version to Howard. He saw that they had taken the COO of Cantor Fitzgerald and moved him out of the middle of the firm, to the contractor section because he was requested by someone from another firm. When he saw where the COO was placed, he asked where the up-and-coming executive the COO had been mentoring was located. The two names were nowhere near each other. Howard responded, "Not happening," and arranged a meeting with Joe Daniels, the president of the Memorial Foundation, Allison Bailey and me.

AN UNBROKEN BOND

When Howard and I met with Joe Daniels and Allison Bailey in his office, he was calm. I was at the height of my frustration, but I stayed quiet.

Howard told Joe that he had a deal with the mayor and that Cantor could and would list our names the way that we wanted to. He showed them the situation with the COO and how their layout didn't work for us.

Allison insisted that we must honor the adjacency requests that were submitted to the Memorial Museum. Howard said, "Look, Edie will get you a letter from every family for whom we cannot accommodate each and every adjacency, agreeing to our layout." Joe and Allison looked at each other, and Joe agreed. They wanted to make sure they were covered. Then Howard said, "One last thing. I want the two Cantor walls to be over here." Howard shifted the location of the Cantor names.

The memorial had them listed facing West Street, the area with the least amount of traffic, and the most difficult for the Cantor families to reach. Allison said that they were located where they were because there was a "cross building" adjacency request, so she tried to put them on the two corners nearest to each other. Howard says, "Well, where is Euro Brokers in your layout? Because they have a cross relationship with Cantor Fitzgerald." Allison and Joe agreed to shift the location of the Cantor names.

I called every family who had an adjacency request that could not be exactly met. Not a single one objected. They all sent Allison the required letter. I finished the Cantor layout. I had already submitted the Euro Brokers layout which I asked a former Euro Brokers and now Cantor employee to create. Then I had the prior head of the Euro Brokers Relief Fund review it. By this point, Jake and his team had written programs so that the computer had pretty much caught up to me. Jake printed out the color-coded layout with arrows representing adjacencies for me. We took over the executive boardroom and laid out the two walls the full length of the conference room. I brought in survivors and senior executives to go through the layout and make sure there weren't any mistakes, missed relationships or locations that they thought should be changed. They pointed out several problems and I managed to fix them.

Ari Schonbrun came in to review the layout. "Woooow," he said, the sound communicating his sadness at the extent of the loss. I started to tell him how incredibly difficult this was. For months I threatened to write a book called *All Roads Lead to Gertsberg*. Marina Gertsberg worked in accounting and had so many requests to be with her through the museum that there was physically no way to honor them all. It was the perfect example of how Michael Arad's design didn't work. We arranged and rearranged the "Gertsberg tree" countless times. Jake and I talked about how popular she must have been. Ari looked at us and said, "Do you know anything about Marina Gertsberg?" I acknowledged that I didn't know much. Ari said that she was a smart, beautiful young woman with piercing blue eyes. She had worked for the firm for only a week. "A week?" Jake and I looked at each other. We spent way more than a week laying out the Gertsberg tree.

We created a layout that, though it would never be perfect, was as good as I was able to get it. The memorial had given us a deadline. I was racing a clock. I gave Howard our layout to review a final time. Jake sent the layout to Allison Bailey with the caveat that it was still awaiting Mr. Lutnick's sign-off. I thought, "I'm near done."

Several weeks later, Allison brought back our layout after it had been "reviewed" by Michael Arad and his team. He had moved 500 of our 715 names. I was beside myself. Howard told me he would take care of it. We were not changing 500 names. He said Jake and I would have to sit down with Allison and work it out. I called her. She said she would talk to Arad and explain all of the variables at work in the Cantor layout and that he couldn't just move names around. She understood that to us, these were not just names, they were lives lost. The thing that made me angry beyond words was yet to come.

The memorial walls are in panels that connect to each other to make up an entire wall, almost like tiles with grout between them. Jake and I laid out each of our people so that no name would cross a seam. Because this is the final resting place of the 9/11 victims I don't think that, for example, Joseph should be on one panel and Smith should be on another. It's bad enough that Mayor Bloomberg won't let us put Cantor Fitzgerald on the bottom alongside N38, but I don't think that any family member should be told that their loved one is on panel N51 and N52. We already received them back in pieces, if at all. We had laid out a quarter of the victims' names without crossing any seams. The same could be done for everyone. Allison told me that because Arad had crossed seams for all the other victims, Cantor wouldn't match the design for the remainder of the memorial layout if we didn't cross seams as well. I asked why they didn't fix the rest of the layout. Allison said that they had spent way too much time on it, and they had already sent the South Tower names out to the contractors. I went to Howard in tears. This was just unacceptable. Splitting these names was the ultimate sign of disrespect.

Howard told me that this wasn't a battle I could win, and that I would have to let it go. It wasn't part of his deal with the mayor, even though at the time this wasn't something he could have anticipated. I can't dictate the design. I told Allison, "If one mother stands before the name of her child and cries, not because her child is dead, but because his name has been split in half, then the memorial has failed. There is a reason that headstones aren't split into pieces." Jake and I were forced to redo the layout yet again and run names across seams. I was saddened beyond words. I refused to change the 500 names. I refused to choose which family's loved ones' names would be desecrated.

Allison suggested that Jake and I meet with Arad and his colleague Amanda at his offices. I asked Allison to attend because she understood what went into our layout. Arad told me, "laying out the names is the most important thing you have ever done in your life." I thought to myself, "He did not just say that." When he told me that he wanted to move the names of victims we had so carefully placed because he didn't "visually like the way four Js look in a row," I excused myself from the room. If I responded, this meeting would be over. Allison came after me saying she would talk with Michael. There was nothing meaningful about the way this was being done. This was purely about the architect's aesthetic.

The Cantor panels were enlarged and placed around the walls of their conference room. Michael would show us what he considered to be problems. We would then tell him which names could be moved and which couldn't. Amanda brought in her computer so that we could make changes right there. Jake and I looked up at panels that looked perfectly fine to us. Michael ran a red magic marker on a diagonal across three lines pointing out the vertical space. He said, "I don't like this line. Can we switch this name with this name?"

Jake and I looked at each other incredulously. Sometimes we could humor Michael because the people would stay in the same department and keep the relationships we originally intended. Sometimes they wouldn't. My concern was having gone through so many different processes to get here, by moving things around to now accommodate Michael's spacing concerns, we would overlook a relationship. We met for days, going through the layout name by name. "You see how George William Morell is next to William George Minardi? I don't like that. I want to move one of them." When after trying various other placements he realized he couldn't change the placement, he placed William George Minardi's name across a seam. "You see how there are four Ms in a row? I want to break up the Ms." Didn't he realize that his name—Michael— was the most common male name in the Unites States? In trying to break up all the "Ms" he was putting together a group of names beginning with "R." He never even noticed. He started to separate a married couple because they have the same last name. He asked me the middle name of one of my victims because he might like the spacing better if the middle name instead of middle initial was there. I told him that the family chose to only have a middle initial, and I would not call and ask them to change it. He tried to take the senior executives off the corner.

The ultimate irony was that we were forced to honor the dictate that this appear in "no discernable order" or "random" to the world. No visitor is going to know the meaning behind any of this when they look at these walls. My hope is that the sets of siblings on our corners will cue the viewer to at least one Cantor Fitzgerald wall if not two. I called Howard and told him that we should pay someone to develop an app that lets you know all of the Cantor relationships, and provided our families and visitors with a map. He said he would talk to the Memorial Museum about doing that for every victim.

When I went to bed that night I couldn't sleep. I thought of a relationship that all of those incremental moves might have broken. I went back, reviewed the final layout again and gave it to Howard for approval. He approved our layout before the Arad changes, so I thought that if he had any changes, they would be slight.

It was late on a Sunday night. We were both at our houses in the Hamptons. Howard went through the layout and had a change of heart. He wanted to move around entire departments. He circled people that he felt should be somewhere else. I told him that I didn't know how I was going to be able to do that. He said he wanted it done. I was devastated. If Howard wasn't satisfied with this layout, if the arrangement didn't give him a sense of peace, if he looked at this and thought that people were in the wrong place, then I failed, on a catastrophic level. I went home and back to work. Out came the index cards and the Post-its. I stayed up all night. I counted names. I counted letters. I tried to move departments wholesale without breaking connections. I couldn't. I tried to move small groups of people. Basically, I started all over again. At 5 am, I came up with an alternative arrangement. It wasn't perfect but it was as close as I could get. Later in the morning, I got in touch with Allison Bailey and told her that Howard's changes were extensive. She said Joe Daniels would speak to Howard. I was still in the Hamptons. I had to get this new layout to Jake to get into the computer because it had once again all been done by hand. I didn't know what else I could do. I drove into the city.

Lewis and I were in the car on the way back out to the Hamptons when my phone rang. It was Howard. I asked him, "What happened?" "Edie, I went through the original layout with Stuart." Stuart Fraser ran government security bonds. "He reminded me about the relationships between the guys you have next to each other. They are where they should be. The layout is perfect, Edie." The layout of names of the Cantor Fitzgerald Relief Fund victims, as they will appear at the National September 11th Memorial, was finished.

There was a land grab for my office. I was not emotionally attached to the space because this was my eighth office in my fifth location (not counting my house) in as many years. Some astute Cantor Fitzgerald executive observed, "How often does Edie Lutnick actually sit in this office?" With my adopting the BlackBerry as an appendage, and a computer system that allowed me to work from home, it was true that I was in the office much less frequently. It started as "loaning" my office to a woman from human resources who would use it when I wasn't there, with the understanding that she would vacate when I needed it. Shortly thereafter, all pretenses were dropped and I got a sheepish call that they were going to move me out of my office. Cantor was expanding exponentially and space was at a premium. Post-9/11 Cantor had 302 employees. Now it has about 1,600 in the tristate area. Anyone who thinks I get special dispensation when it comes to space because I'm the boss's sister would be sadly mistaken.

A friend once told me that you spend so much time in your office that it should reflect who you are as a person, every bit as much as the decor in your home does. A visual trip around my office as we packed it all away was all I needed to capture, almost in its entirety, what my life had become. Under the clear plastic blotter on my desk were pictures. Gary at work; Howard and Gary, arms wrapped around each other; Gary, me, Howard, Allison and their kids at the naming of their third child, Casey; Lewis and Gary playing chess; Gary holding his cat surrounded by sunflowers before he took me to the U.S. Open in September 2001; Mary Jo Olson's mass card; a poem sent to me by a family member.

On top of my desk are angels sent to me by strangers who cared, and a small container of dried pink flowers from Shari so my office would always have color. Next to my computer is a yellow glass "rock" that was on my memorial chair. It says "Integrity." On the wall is my American Flag quilt with the picture and note from the quilter saying, "May this quilt bring you much comfort for now and always! Having the opportunity to help in this small way was a comfort and a blessing for me." I always wished I had her address so I could have stayed in touch with her. The framed picture of Gary from the Boomer Esiason event and a wooden sign that someone gave me with Gary's name and title, senior partner, grace the catty-corner wall. The next wall has the Flag of Honor canvas, created by John Michelotti and containing the names of all the 9/11 victims in the stripes, alongside a poster, listing the names vertically in a red, white and blue World Trade Center. And there is the Emigrant Savings Award, the Caring Hand, the Billy Esposito Foundation Award and the Mental Health Association Award, along with the proclamation from New York City Public Advocate Betsy Gotbaum that May 5th is "Edie Lutnick Day" in New York.

My bookshelves are filled with books and trinkets—an angel book donated to all the families, books written by the families, songs composed in their memory, a memory box, a memory bear. Framed pictures abound: Howard's four children, Kyle, Brandon, Casey and Ryan; Gary and I laughing as he lifts me in his arms; the post-9/11 "miracle" baby of Joyce and Ari Schonbrun; the new "Billie" in the Esposito family. Closer inspection reveals cards and letters from families, the miniature teardrop memorial with Gary's name, the wrappers from chocolate bars that were made with Cantor's logo and placed on the seats at one memorial, the New York mug, the heart rock with the word *peace* on it, also from the chairs of our memorial service, as well as an American flag made by children out of red, white and blue beads on safety pins, ribbons and pins. On the credenza sits a blue bear like the ones in the Chelsea Piers mosh pit and a big brown bear from the Michigan delivery.

On the wall by my desk is a cartoon. Our lost loved one Beth Logler's fiancé Doug is friends with a syndicated cartoon artist. He has drawn two children sitting on the roof of a house looking at the stars, which one observes are especially bright tonight. Instead of stars, it is the names of our loved ones, memorialized as they should be, as stars, as angels.[113]

Cartoon by Rick Detorie. "One Big Happy." Copyright 2002. Reprinted with permission.

In my locked desk drawer is the dog-eared master list. It has long since been replaced by a computer program, but I still use it as the definitive list for all things Cantor Fitzgerald Relief Fund. Underneath are the old checkbooks, filled with check after check in my handwriting, the newer checks written by Marianna and signed by me, and those blank— yet to be written—to address a need still unmet. My office screamed September 11th, but it was also filled with compassion, warmth and symbols of remembrance.

CONTROVERSY AND PEACE

In August 2010, when the issue of whether a mosque should be built 600 feet from the World Trade Center site came to my attention I was caught off guard. I don't know why I should have been. Battles that should never be conversations had consumed a significant portion of almost 10 years of my life. The WTC Memorial, "Reflecting Absence," is in theory all about the absence of verticality. The museum pavilion, the tallest aspect of the Memorial Museum which is entirely underground, is only a few stories high. In comparison, this mosque/Islamic cultural center would be 13 stories high with the symbol of Islam at the top. I just didn't think this could have any traction.

No one would really support putting an Islamic center 600 feet from the worst terrorist attack on American soil, perpetrated by Islamic extremists. This doesn't have anything to do with religion or protecting freedoms. This has to do with sensitivity, and that's what, in theory, religions are all about. But I had once again underestimated Mayor Bloomberg. He threw his weight and the weight of his office behind putting a mosque and Islamic cultural center in the old Burlington Coat Factory building two blocks from the World Trade Center site.

Many calls from outraged families started coming into my office. As the controversy grew and battle lines were drawn, I became more perplexed. Unless this is an attempt to rewrite history, or to focus attention onto "good Muslims" instead of having people pay homage to those who died at the hands of "bad Muslims," I don't know why the proponents insist on having it so close to the World Trade Center site.

When New York Governor Patterson offers the people proposing the mosque an alternative location and they refuse to take it, I am reminded of when the IFC was offered a similar deal and chose to cease to exist instead. It isn't about the message. It's about the location. The proposed location of this mosque is incredibly upsetting to my families. Just because you have the right to do something doesn't mean you should.

A debate rages, not just among the families, but among Americans across the country. President Obama takes a stand. Although I have chosen not to take a position in the press (others have that squarely in hand), the issue comes to me anyway in a circuitous manner. The debate has engendered such strong feelings that protests are being planned. A pro-Muslim rally is being planned for September 10th. In response, an anti-mosque rally is scheduled for September 11th.

My Good Deed, an organization committed to turning 9/11 into a National Day of Service and Remembrance, and an organization on whose board I sit, is taking a position. Their stand is that September 11th should be kept free of debate of any kind and remain focused on the lives that were lost that day. It is a position I can support and I agree to sign a letter saying that on behalf of my families.

The problem is that the founders of My Good Deed are making public appearances, and their opposition to the location of the mosque is not being made clear. The appearances they choose to make are viewed by some as politically motivated. Debra Burlingame's group, Families for a Safe and Strong America, pulls their support, and aligns with the proposed September 11th rally, which is being touted as anti-Muslim and extremist in the press and not just against this mosque location.

By advocating the protection of the emotional well-being of my families, I have been branded many things through the years. I was called anticulture when I didn't think it appropriate to have an exhibit of a bomb in a suitcase on the fourth anniversary of September 11th. I was antitolerance when I wanted the sanctity of the World Trade Center site preserved for the story of 9/11. I was anti-art when I wanted the ages listed next to the names of the victims in order to humanize them. I was antijustice when I didn't want my families, or any New Yorkers for that matter, subjected to the closing down of Lower Manhattan in order to try Khalid Sheikh Mohammed, the 9/11 terrorist mastermind.

Now again, because I want people coming to pay their respects to the 9/11 dead to concentrate on September 11th, I am branded anti-Muslim. I can tell you with certainty that I am none of these things. I prefer to think of myself as pro-common sense.

❤   ❤   ❤

On September 11ᵗʰ, I banished the word *mosque* from my vocabulary for the day. I went to the 92ⁿᵈ Street Y to get ready for our memorial service. I asked Jeff Parness of New York Says Thank You Foundation to bring the flag. The American flag that overlooked the World Trade Center site and was tattered and damaged, is being stitched back together again with other American flags of import. When the flag is completed it will be donated to the Memorial Museum. I have asked Jeff and he has agreed to bring the flag and let the Cantor Fitzgerald families add their stitches to the reconstruction. The flag is flown through our memorial service and is taken down and stitched during the reception by our families. The different flags sewn together to make a whole remind me of Koenig's Sphere and of the Thinker, Rodin's famous sculpture that used to be in Cantor's offices was damaged in the attacks and survived in its battered state only to be stolen from the site. All three are very powerful symbols of resilience. Howard and I both add our stitches. Some of our families who flew in for our service were so moved by the event that they offer to put together and help fund stitching ceremonies in Hawaii and the Carolinas where they live.

There was something very different about the memorial service from the services we had every year prior. The format was the same, but the feeling was different. Whereas before the singers sang "I Will Remember You," now a Broadway voice belted out "Bridge Over Troubled Waters." Before, one picture was on the screen when we read the names. Now, Howard had changed the design and there were three pictures that faded into each other at the same time. The pictures stayed on the screen longer and the layout allowed relatives to be up on the screen together.

There was something helpful about not seeing their faces staring out at us all alone. We still cried, we still missed them, we still grieved, but we weren't so bedraggled-looking in our grief. Pictures of new grandchildren, graduations, and weddings emerged before and after the service. New husbands accompanied wives, and new babies screamed when they awakened and were carried out of the auditorium by their mothers.

Gila Barzvi, mother of Cantor victim Guy Barzvi, had makeup on and her hair was styled. She smiled when she saw other families she hadn't seen in a while. I remember when the thought of a smile radiating from her beautiful face would be impossible to fathom. And when Anthony Galante, whose pregnant wife Deanna died on September 11th, introduced me to his new wife and baby, I wrapped my arms around him in gratitude that he had found a new and different future. I found myself wishing the same for his cousin, who stood with us, and had also lost his wife at Cantor that day.

There was a reunion feeling to the reception that immediately followed the service. Nine years of memories had been made since the person we loved perished. We shared their stories, but we also shared the stories of our lives which, whether we consciously recognize it, have imbedded themselves into our recitations. The fathers, whose children's names make up the Gertsberg tree, all stood together. When I saw Marina Gertsberg's father, I told him the story. These Cantor fathers have all become friends. I have ensured that their children will all be listed together at the memorial downtown.

Even I cry less often, although the lyrics of certain songs get me every time. I can't listen to Lonestar's "I'm Already There" without sobbing.

I also leave Gary's Bon Jovi CD in my car. When the top is down on the convertible, the wind blowing my mountain of hair back, I blare Bon Jovi's, "It's My Life"—*It's now or never. I don't want to live forever. I just want to live while I'm alive.* He certainly did that. And I cry with abandon in the privacy of my own car. We all love just as deeply as we did nine years ago. We just have to find a box within ourselves to house our memories, so that we can make new ones.

NERVES OF STEEL

I had to go back to Hangar 17. This time I had Lewis and Howard's executive assistant Matthew Gilbert with me. The Port Authority had been giving away the WTC steel. My wish that this would be turned into a museum wasn't realized, and the Port Authority wanted its hangar back. I had a meeting a while back with a UK foundation whose representative told me about the magnificent piece of steel he chose and was receiving from the Port Authority. If he was getting steel, why weren't we?

I immediately called Norma Madigan, external affairs manager and assistant to Chris Ward, executive director of the Port Authority, and asked her what was going on. She told me they put a notice in the paper. I'd never seen it, but that wasn't surprising. She said steel was being given to not-for-profits that requested it, with the goal of the Port Authority being to give away all of the steel by the end of the year. She explained the process and offered to help facilitate it. I immediately brought the issue to Howard's attention. I suggested Bernar Venet, a famous sculptor, a supporter of the Relief Fund and a friend of Howard's, as a potential artist to create a Cantor Memorial. Howard agreed and started speaking with the artist.

Now we were meeting Venet and his wife Diane at the hangar. Maybe it was because I had been there before, or because they had given away a significant portion of the steel already (I'd seen a girder strapped to the back of a truck being wheeled down the main street of Palm Beach, Florida on the news), or just the passage of time, but it didn't have the same impact as it did the first time. I saw what was missing instead of what was there. Bernar, on the other hand, was so moved by the steel pieces that he immediately scrapped his original thoughts and started redesigning on the spot.

It seemed that every piece of steel in which we had an interest was already tagged to go to a museum, firehouse, or the National World Trade Center Museum. This steel was going all over the world. It was tagged to go to Italy and to China. I couldn't help but think about how Mayor Bloomberg sold our steel to China at the beginning and they recycled it, the same steel that was now being tagged with such reverence.

We walked through hundreds of pieces of steel. We took pictures and tried to decide among what was left. I wished we could have preserved it all and taken every piece. I wondered how the power contained in this room could ever be conveyed by individual pieces. We were there for hours. We told the curator that we would take everything that was available. In addition, we made a list of the pieces we were specifically requesting.

Going to see the screening of *Project Rebirth* was a bit like old home week. Time has moved forward and so too have the family leaders. I don't see them nearly as often anymore. Many of them were in the room. I came with Darlene Dwyer. Monica Iken, Lee Ielpi, Bill Keegan from 9/11 Heart, with whom I had been working on issues surrounding recovery and rebuilding in Haiti, among others were there. *Project Rebirth* is a film that Stuart Fraser from Cantor gave money to, as did the LMDC and others.

The film follows five victims: two firefighters who lost brothers, a fiancé, a burn victim and Nick Chirls who was 16 when his mother Catherine died at Cantor Fitzgerald. The film juxtaposes interviews with these five people with the gradual rebuilding of the site. This was a screening for the 9/11 community that had been so supportive.

The highlight for me was footage they had of Nick giving his eulogy of his mother. As he called her a loving wife and sister nothing happened. But when he said "mother," a baby sparrow landed on his head. The memorial service was indoors. The sparrow allowed Nick to take it off his head and hold it in his hands. In a darkened theatre as I watched this I thought, "Wow, I'm not the only one with a bird." Nick worked for a while at Cantor. How did I not know this?

What was unusual about the film is that they never tell you that Nick's mother worked at Cantor Fitzgerald or that Nick did as well. *Project Rebirth*, which received most of its funding from the LMDC, seemed to be following the mayor's decree that no affiliations be allowed. The corporations that were harmed on September 11th, many of which no longer exist, were systematically being written out of the history of the day.

The recovery workers at the World Trade Center site who became sick and some who have died were getting some financial relief. The Zadroga health care bill was finally passed. At half the amount that was originally requested, it still allocated over $4 billion to compensate those with what are now being called WTC illnesses.[114] The recovery workers have had their own long and impossible battle with Mayor Bloomberg, and it's good to see them finally receiving funding. In 2004, the New York congressional delegates, led by Chuck Schumer, got $1 billion of FEMA funds allocated to New York City to compensate recovery workers. The city set up the Captive Insurance Fund. Rather than paying the claims of recovery workers, some of whom were dying, the mayor decided that the money should be used to protect the city from lawsuits as a result of the World Trade Center cleanup.

In 2007, after three years of fighting and multiple deaths without any recompense from the money, recovery workers brought a class action suit against Captive Insurance, the City of New York and Mayor Bloomberg. Chuck Schumer, in response, issued the following statement:

> *My intent along with that of my colleagues in Congress was to use this federal money to pay appropriate claims, not to fight claims.*[115]

After an additional three years of fighting, and more than $200 million spent by the City of New York fighting the claims of recovery workers, a settlement was reached just before the scheduled date for the city to present its argument that it "should have immunity from all lawsuits because it was responding to a terror attack."[116] The passage of the Zadroga Bill, in honor of the death of Police Department recovery worker James Zadroga, was in addition to the settlement. Mayor Bloomberg was seen on the news standing proudly in Washington at the bill's passage. Unfortunately, on July 27, 2011, WTC cancers, a prevalent condition among recovery workers, were denied inclusion in the Zadroga bill. The decision was based on there being insufficient evidence.[117] The exclusion caused outrage in the 9/11 community.

I always make sure that I see or speak to David Egan (father of Lisa and Samantha Egan—the big man who intimidated Ken Feinberg) over the holidays. The emotional pain that devastated this man and robbed him of his ability to be productive now causes him physical pain. When I started the conversation, he was despondent. He said that he starts tasks and can't finish them. Prior to 9/11 he was a prolific writer. Now, he doesn't write much. Even trying to keep a handle on everyday tasks and papers became too much for him. When David and I started talking about 9/11 issues, though, he perked up and you could hear some of the old feistiness in his voice. I told him that I had finished arranging the names layout.

David had once said that Mayor Bloomberg "has no common sense. Is he going to flip a coin and find a plot as far away from his father as he can? He doesn't have a clue about the human issues." I responded by wondering whether Mayor Bloomberg and Governor Pataki were going to forego their titles and scatter their names through the Memorial Museum so that people could queue at a kiosk or consult an app to find them, like we will to find our loved ones.

But David Egan has grown. He doesn't hate Michael Bloomberg anymore. He hates the things that he has done. I told David that he shouldn't buy me chocolate this year. I said that I want to come and see him. He told me he wasn't up for a visit. I asked him whether he minded if I called and checked up on him every few weeks. I just needed to hear his voice, to know that he was continuing to cope.

2011

THOSE WHO FOUGHT

After the holidays, I walked into Gary's (my) apartment and found a fruit basket waiting for me from Ethel Small. I spoke to Ethel a lot at the beginning. She is Wendy Small's mother. When Wendy died on September 11th, Ethel took on the task of raising Wendy's six-year-old son Tyrell. We had to figure out the best way to get financial support for him arranged given that he was a minor being raised by his grandmother and not his father. I hadn't heard from Ethel in years.

Every year Howard and Allison send holiday cards to our families. The card contains the pictures of their four children. When Ethel received the card at her home on John's Island, South Carolina, she decided to get back in touch. Wendy's son is now 16, and Ethel told me with the help of faith and therapy, he is doing well, that they both are. Recently, he even visited his father. When she asked how Howard's children were, I told her that it was funny. Kyle was now 14 and Ryan was now five. Kyle, who was so grown-up, was Ryan's age on 9/11. If we are lucky, time keeps going.

It was January 6, 2011 and I had just gotten off the phone with Jane Pollicino. Her husband Stephen worked for Cantor and we were catching up. I asked Jane when it was that I first met her. With so many family members, especially the ones I met at the beginning, it's difficult to recall. Jane told me that she first saw me at Howard's town hall meetings, but that we had a real conversation at the 2002 memorial service. We talked about how she was there at the names and proper burial rallies. She recalled when we went to court to support WTC Families for a

Proper Burial when they fought for the right to have the human remains removed from a garbage dump and the attorney for the city called our loved ones "undifferentiated dirt."

Then she told me things that I didn't know. She said that her support group for children and family led to four Cantor wives with similarly aged children becoming close friends. She recounted how the four wives, none of whom knew each other before September 11th, now travel together, and continue to do the "homework" the grief counselor gave them when they feel it is necessary. Then, several years ago, when their children became teenagers, they went to a new group for mothers wrestling with their teenagers. They picked up a fifth Cantor widow and added her to their group of friends. These are friends that understand each other in a way that others, even old friends, cannot.

Then Jane said, "Remember when you called me to ask if it was okay to pair me with a particular family for the 'adopt a family' Christmas program?" "Yes, I made you get a PO box." "Oh, that's right. I forgot about that. Do you know that we are still in touch with the family? They live in Indiana and send us presents every year. When my son got married, they even sent a present for Jenn [his new wife]," causing her to exclaim, "Now I'm adopted, too." I am delighted and dumbfounded.

In all these years, it never occurred to me that these programs could last so long or have such an impact. Jane went on to tell me that with everything that happened through 9/11, these Christmas gifts and the commitment and kindness of these strangers "who now feel like family" are the "positive life lesson" that she and her children take away from this. She said at the beginning that she didn't know what to make of my brother. But now when people ask her about "that guy from Cantor" she tells them, "He rebuilt the company. He made promises and he kept them, and I still have health insurance almost 10 years later. Do you know how huge that is?"

Michael Burke is a twin. When he and his brother showed up at rallies it was near impossible to tell them apart. When I saw them together it always reminded me of the twins who lost their sibling halves. But even though Mike Burke has his twin and his sister, they still weren't lucky. Their brother Captain William Burke Jr., Engine Company 21, is a recognized hero and a September 11th casualty. Like Debra Burlingame, Mike is a prolific and effective writer. He has been trying to get a presence for 9/11 artifacts above ground for years. He, along with a vast majority of 9/11 families, don't understand why the World Trade Center site needs to be denuded of any physical reminder of the destruction that occurred that day. With Anthony Gardner of the Coalition of 9/11 Families and the WTC United Families Group, he has advocated long and hard for the return of Koenig's Sphere, the tridents and the crushed vehicles to be placed among the trees. This wasn't a peaceful death or event for these victims. Something should remind the public of what actually occurred there, and two massive manmade waterfalls and an anonymous ribbon of names isn't it. The battle for the return of Koenig's Sphere is moving to the forefront again. We have been fighting for its return since 2002, and Mike Burke, after removing himself from the battles, returned once again to take the lead. I understood Mike's step back because it happened to me. When you get to the point where you realize that your frustration is creating anger, you recognize that you no longer have the ability to be effective as an advocate.

The mayor's strongest weapon is his lack of an emotional connection to the event, and the recognition of that connection is the biggest weakness of the families. Because we care, we are vulnerable. Because he doesn't, he is not. The mayor has opposed the return of Koenig's Sphere to the site every bit as much as he has opposed the listing of the names, the return of human remains and the removal of the IFC. He is doing it with the same strength and determination with which he supports the mosque. Michael Burke sent out an email January 27th through Bill Doyle's family list:

At this time the Port Authority is debating where to "return" the WTC sphere—to the center of the WTC plaza where it stood for 30 years and survived the attacks in place and was embraced by the people as an icon of the strength and endurance

of America—or to the corner of Liberty and West—where it
never was and its meaning is diminished and denied...

Without the sphere, the National September 11 Memorial at the WTC
will include nothing of September 11th, nothing of the WTC and nothing the nation embraced as commemorating 9/11.

Recently I toured the WTC site. That was when I learned that the
Port Authority and the City of New York engaged in a land swap so that
the entire memorial quadrant no longer belongs to the Port Authority.
The ability to return the sphere to the Memorial Quadrant rests entirely
in Mayor Bloomberg's hands. Also true, nowhere in the WTC memorial quadrant are the dates September 11, 2001 or February 26, 1993.
Neither are there plans to return the artifacts above ground.

When I signed a contract with the Port Authority for 22 pieces of
steel, I didn't realize right away that they hadn't given us any of the steel
that we requested. Because we told them we would take as much steel
as we could, they assigned us the pieces that "lacked character." This
process wasn't over, as I had thought it was. I returned to the hangar to
find out why China could pick steel but the company with the largest
loss of life on 9/11 and located in New York City couldn't.

It is our plan that some of the steel girders out at Hangar 17 will
one day be turned into a memorial to the Cantor Fitzgerald dead. It
is my hope that when people see a Cantor Fitzgerald memorial they
will remember those we loved and have lost. I hope that our memorial
will provide strength and comfort, in the same way that "Gary Lutnick,
WTC," does on my wrist or my broken heart does around my neck. It
is our vision that out of something broken will emerge something new,
profound and resilient. I feel that way about my families. We are broken.
We will never be the same. But we have persevered through unfathomable obstacles, and we are still here, with our shared humanity intact.

On January 31st, I went to a fabricator in Rockaway, New Jersey
to see the names of the Cantor Fitzgerald victims that we so painstakingly laid out, carved into bronze for the upcoming installation at the
WTC Memorial. As a round brush (that looked as if it should be on

the end of a vacuum cleaner hose) came down onto shining gold bronze and squirted out water with a loud "phsssst," I watched as the word "G A R Y" worked its way across the surface.

When this memorial opens on the 10-year anniversary, even with its failings, I hope my families will take comfort knowing that their loved ones' names are surrounded by people who cared about them, and that they were thoughtfully and lovingly placed. I hope that visitors will see that Cantor Fitzgerald starts on a North Tower corner with two sets of brothers—Andrew and Vincent Abate and Sean and Farrell Lynch—by the PATH train entrance. Our men and women's names then go south and fill the entire wall. On the next corner are the senior executives of the firm. That corner is by the entrance to the museum and has the brothers Joseph and Daniel Shea on it, as well as Howard's best friend Douglas Gardner, and Gary Lutnick. If you follow that connecting wall west past the entrance to where the museum will be housed, you will find Charles Zion. He is five panels from the end of the wall heading toward the south pool. Then and only then will you have seen the 658 men and women who died together on the 101st through the 105th floors, above the impact of the plane.

⁹⁄₁₁ NEVER CLOSES

At the Memorial Museum's request, I recorded 40 Cantor Fitzgerald victims' names to be used in the memorial part of the museum's exhibition space. Howard and Allison read 80 names last week. Marianna joined me to read the names of her sister-in-law and her friend.

Earlier in the day, the museum supplied me with a CD with the proper pronunciation of the 40 names I would be reading. As I went through, I was amazed at how many of them differed from what I believed to be correct. Even Marianna's last name was pronounced incorrectly. I called Marianna, and we contacted every family for whom I found a discrepancy. I couldn't get in touch with one family for a difficult to pronounce name. I called her surviving co-workers and people who worked with her sister (who is unreachable) for a definitive pronunciation. In every instance, our understanding of how to pronounce the names was correct. It made me very nervous about the other readings. I asked to review the recorded pronunciations for all the Cantor names.

When I arrived at the recording session, Todd Ouida's parents were there. Todd worked in foreign exchange options, and it was his sister Amy who was so instrumental in setting up the sibling support groups. We hugged. I said, "Oh, let me see your list of names." Mrs. Ouida replied, "I have the Risk Waters Conference." Her husband said, "I have Sandler O'Neill." I turned to the museum staff present and asked, "Why aren't they reading Cantor names?" "We don't know. Maybe all the Cantor names have been previously assigned." "Look, it's important that every Cantor name be read by either a Cantor family member or a Cantor survivor. It may not mean anything to the general public, but I want to be able to tell our families that when they hear a name that they recognize, even if they didn't read the name themselves, someone in the Cantor family did." They agreed to look into it and try to make sure that is the case. "These things are very important to us." Todd's father then added, "You have to understand. We are a family."

Eric Holder announced that Khalid Sheikh Mohammed and the four co-conspirators would be tried in military tribunals on the day that President Obama announced his candidacy for a second presidential term. Despite initial rejoicing that this issue was finally resolved, the wrangling continued and the trial's actual commencement remains in doubt. President Obama and Attorney General Holder reinforced their displeasure, blaming the forced decision on congressional failure to provide funds to try the defendants in federal court. Both vowed to continue fighting to change these circumstances. Win. Lose. Win. Refight.

Sally Regenhard from Skyscraper Safety Campaign is leading the charge to have the human remains of the 9/11 dead removed from the Memorial Museum. The battle rages in the press and across America now that, at this late date, the *New York Times* has inexplicably entered the fray. The issues that were hidden away and never resolved have a way of resurfacing. I am aware of what Sally's group is against—remains below ground—but I cannot get an answer as to what they are "for." They are requesting consultation with all the families, but experience shows that that will engender differing points of view, and then what? If they win the battle, will Mayor Bloomberg use the opportunity to keep the human remains from the site by either leaving them in the Office of the Chief Medical Examiner on First Avenue or bringing them to Fresh Kills? For nine years, Mike Burke has been advocating for the return of 9/11 artifacts above ground on the site with extremely limited success. I have no reasonable expectation that the WTC Memorial Foundation Board, led by Michael Bloomberg, or the residents who have vociferously fought against anything approximating a cemetery, will ever countenance a tomb above ground. Diane Horning's WTC Families for a Proper Burial was denied review of their case and argument for the removal of the remains from Fresh Kills by the Supreme Court of the United States. In addition to denying WTC cancers as coverable injuries, the Zadroga health care bill is now requiring dying rescue workers go through the FBI terrorist database before being considered for relief.

Bloomberg launched Bloomberg Islamic Finance Platform (ISLM), a solution for shariah-compliant products and services, as well as the Malaysian Ringgit (MYR) sukut index. Ex Deputy-Mayor Dan Doctoroff (and current president of Bloomberg L.P.) said, "Bloomberg is delighted to increase its commitment to serve this dynamic market."[118] The announcement created an ah-ha moment for many families who couldn't understand the rationale behind Bloomberg's staunch support of the mosque and cultural center 600 feet from the 9/11 memorial. The project, which is proceeding, is now called Park 51.

On a positive note, I spoke to Norma Madigan about Cantor not receiving a single piece of steel that we actually selected from Hangar 17. As a result of her efforts, we received two pieces of steel, one of which had originally been marked for China. We look forward to the day that it will one day be turned into a memorial honoring our loved ones.

OSAMA BIN LADEN IS DEAD

I am in bed, almost asleep. My phones start ringing. "Who the hell is calling me so late in the evening?" I can't ignore it. My heart starts pounding. It is my friend Shari. She tells me to turn on the television. I cannot believe what I am seeing. Smoke is pouring out of the office building where my two brothers and I worked. People covered in soot and ash are being evacuated. I am immediately transported back into September 11th. "Oh dear G-d, what has happened?" I am afraid to look down at the ticker, which once listed the names of the dead with the words "Cantor Fitzgerald" after every fourth name. I force myself. "Osama bin Laden is reported dead. We await the president of the United States, who will address to the nation."

I sit in my pajamas with my legs folded underneath me, my hand gently clutching my throat. I stare speechless. I am numb. I feel nothing. I listen and stare without actually seeing or absorbing. My phone is perpetually ringing. Texts and emails are pouring in. I am being congratulated. For what? Darlene Dwyer calls. She asks how I am feeling. I respond, "I'm numb. I'm afraid. What does this mean? Will there be retaliation?" She says, "I know. My skin is crawling." I sigh. "And I'm sad, Darlene. I'm so sad. I feel the loss of Gary all over again." The news is showing people dancing and singing in the streets at the White House and then down at the WTC site. The American flag is being flown. People are celebrating. I can't process the exultation. It doesn't make sense to me. It immediately reminds me of the countries who engaged in the same behavior when they learned the news of the successful September 11th attacks. The jubilation scares me. And how do you dance and sing at the site where 2,749 people were murdered? Gary is still dead. They are all still dead.

I email Allison. I need to know that Howard is home and safe. He is. I tell her that he needs to prepare for a press onslaught. It is Clarence

Jones who has thought of this, not me. I'm functioning on automatic pilot. His suggestion puts us slightly ahead of the curve. At 2:30 in the morning I talk to Howard. We decide that I need to come into the city to field media inquiries. I can't get there in time for the morning shows, but I need to come in. All the media outlets want Cantor's reaction.

I am up all night. By 8 am, I am back in the city I left the day before. I think, "It's okay. If anything happens, at least I will be with Howard." But he isn't there. He had previously committed to doing Boomer Esiason's charity telethon in Westbury, and the death of bin Laden isn't going to change that priority. I'm in New York City braving the day without him. This day brings additional emotions for me. Once I am able to put the loss of Gary back into a place in my heart, I can acknowledge how relieved I am that bin Laden will never be able to terrorize anyone again. As the news becomes more specific about the Navy Seal operation that accomplished this task, I am grateful to them and to the military who daily work so hard to keep us safe. I feel numb; I feel fear, pain from loss, relief (that Howard is alive), and gratitude to all who stood with us. These are 9/11 emotions, each and every one. We expected their resurgence for the 10-year anniversary, not in the first week in May.

I read the media that is out there. Once again, it is Mayor Bloomberg who makes me shake my head. "It is my hope that it will bring some closure and comfort to all those who lost loved ones." For the families, there is no closure when your loved one has been murdered. There is relief that bin Laden is dead and there is a sense of justice. There is guarded hope that this will somehow stem the wave of terrorism. There is the knowledge that this is yet another moment when the private grief of 9/11 families and public history converge. But closure? It is a word that immediately defines who deeply understands and who cannot. I go on television, radio and the Internet. My sentiments mirror those of the Cantor families.

At 10 pm, I walk into a video conference with Howard in the office. I apologize to the participants, run my hand down his face and finally get to kiss my brother. I am emotionally and physically exhausted in a way I haven't been in a very long time. My phone continues ringing and my texts are going wild. I think it will be more comments about bin Laden's death, but it isn't.

The news has reported that President Obama is coming to Ground Zero on Thursday to meet with the 9/11 families. My families start calling, texting and emailing. They want an invitation. Can I get them an invitation? I know as much about this as they do. I sit down to turn on the 11 pm news. Not for the first time, I wonder why nobody warned us. I make lists of people who want to go in the order that they called. Tuesday, Marianna starts getting bombarded in the office. We call all of our contacts to try to find out how this is working and who we need to speak with in order to include our families. What comes back isn't good. The president isn't really meeting with the 9/11 families. He is meeting with a small, carefully selected group of 9/11 families. Specifically, he is meeting with the family members on the WTC Memorial Foundation board and 9/11 family group leaders. From what I can gather they are using an old Family Advisory Council list to determine invitees; I am disappointed that he isn't having a large gathering with the 9/11 families. There are so many families that want to say thank you in person. I shouldn't have to represent that sentiment for them. They should be able to address him themselves. The meeting, which was originally to have 20 to 30 people, now has about 60. Through various lists, and our ability to add the first three callers, we have about 10 family members from Cantor Fitzgerald going.

My phones are still ringing nonstop. With the bin Laden news and the President Obama visit, the press is unrelenting. And then, I pick up my phone and hear a blast from the past. "Hi, Edie. This is David Dunlap from the *New York Times.*" David is writing a piece about the names. "David, why are you writing about the names in the middle of all the bin Laden, Obama stuff?" "I don't really write these kind of things anymore, but I spent so much time on the names I wanted to write this." He tells me that they are releasing the names layout app for the memorial tomorrow. I can't even believe it. I tell the plethora of reporters that call me the same thing. While I think the app, which we are working with the museum to improve, is better than having no information at all, it isn't an adequate replacement for the memorial telling the story. I remind them of the issues with the lack of equality, the absence of affiliations for the civilians and ages for all, and the names that will be divided across seams. I also tell them that we have done everything possible within the parameters we were forced to operate in to make this a comforting arrangement for our families.

I then call Allison Bailey Blais. How can they release this to the press and not warn the families? If they have released the app, that means someone can turn on the news and see their loved ones' picture, age and adjacencies without knowing it will be there. Have they learned nothing over the past nine years? She tells me that they sent a packet out to the families. "Really, Al? Because I haven't gotten mine yet and I'm the next of kin."

Thursday morning I am on the bus into the city when I get the first of many emails:

Dear Edie: The picture of Gary in the NYT insert for the map of names is beautiful and heartbreaking. What an horrific loss. I am sorry my friend. T

I ran around trying to protect my families, and the one who got slammed without notice was me.

I meet Howard at our offices at 199 Water Street. He, Allison and I are going to meet with the president at the WTC Memorial Foundation preview site on Vesey Street. President Obama is going to lay a wreath at the site. The daughter of Cantor loved one Glenn Wall wrote the president a letter and has been invited to participate in that ceremony. He will then come to us. For me, there is a surreal quality walking into this room populated with many of the family leaders that I haven't seen in years. Some of the organizations still exist. Many do not. There are small tables of eight. Each one has a seat marked "Reserved." After about an hour, President Obama comes in and says, "Hi everybody." He makes a short speech about remembering everyone we lost. He then goes around the room and spends a few minutes with each person. He never sits. Some people have specific agendas they want to address. Diane Horning raises Fresh Kills. Anthony Gardner and Lee Ielpi focus on 9/11 education programs. Debra Burlingame asks the president to challenge the decision to try those who engaged in the intelligence operations that allowed his administration to get bin Laden.

When President Obama gets to me, I tell him who I am and that I run the Cantor Fitzgerald Relief Fund. He says, "I know who you are," and he hugs me. I tell him that on behalf of my families, I want to thank him and the members of our military, and to express our gratitude that no one else will ever be terrorized by bin Laden's hand. He tells me that it is he who should be thanking me for all of my good works. He says, "You are a hero." Allison found three copies of *On Top of the World* in the preview site gift shop. I ask President Obama if he will sign them. As he is signing, he says to me, "Sell them. Raise money." He hugs me a third time. I thank him as he moves on to Debra Burlingame. Each conversation is private, and has an intimate feeling about it. The meeting is over as quickly as it began. The president departs and, as the doors open onto a beautiful day, we exit into a sea of media. Someone asks me if I think the president is co-opting 9/11 for political purposes. I respond, "There is no time when it is inappropriate for the president of the United States to visit the site where 2,749 people were murdered."

❧　❧　❧

As we stand outside, I tell Joe Daniels, the president of the 9/11 Memorial and Museum, that I have a suggestion for him. You can see him visibly cringe. He says, "Let me guess. You want me to create maps to give to the families so they can find their loved ones." He thinks he has me. "No, actually. I assumed that would be done. I think you should open the memorial to the next of kin for every family *before* you open it on the 10-year. If you don't do that, app or no app, family members are going to be distraught and frantic as they run around in circles looking for their loved ones' names in time for the names recitation." A Cantor sibling standing with us says, "Why would you just make it for the next of kin?" I look straight at Joe and respond, "Because I don't want Joe to tell me that it can't be done because it involves too many people." I walk away knowing that I had a choice. I could have been proven correct in front of the whole world, or I could protect our families.

As I get ready to go on Dylan Rattigan on MSNBC for the second time in a week, I turn to Lee Ielpi and I say, "Well, I guess this is practice for the 10-year anniversary." Inwardly, I'm wondering if I can get through this week, which still has my goddaughter Delia Tully Troy's communion and Mother's Day without Gary to come, without getting a shingles return.

I want to be able to tell you that there is a happy ending to this story, or that I can tie everything altogether in a neat package. Coping with death, however, like going through life, just isn't that simple. Every 9/11 victim's family member started out different from everyone else. Ten years later we are still a strong community born of tragedy, forged by support, enduring through love. These are our families. But each family member didn't give up their individuality when they became part of the Cantor community, just like their loved ones are so much more than one of the 2,980 names. Each family member deals with their grief differently and, as a result, they are in different places. Those places aren't engraved in stone. They are fluid. They change day by day. Week by week. Minute by minute.

I can follow a particular family member for you and you will feel a sense of relief that she is now remarried, in the bosom of a new family, maybe even with a new child. But catch that woman on a different day, maybe on the anniversary of her marriage to the victim, and you will find a different outcome. She will still cry. She will still feel bereft. She will still wonder, even though her new life is filled with love, how she was brought to this place. The mother who you see laughing with her friends at a birthday party, or the birth of a new grandchild, will always have a hole where her other child should have stood, and an unaddressable sadness. The Tribute Center, a museum that Lee Ielpi founded to teach about the events of 9/11 and memorialize our casualties until a permanent museum is established, gives tours led by 9/11 family and survivor docents. This is the first year that there are visitors to the site that have no firsthand recollection of September 11th. We as a nation vowed to "Always Remember." We fervently chanted, "We will never forget." Cantor Fitzgerald took those words to heart. It is because of the strength and dedication of the Cantor survivors that children can say, "This is where my daddy or mommy worked," as the firm and our families, with Howard's leadership, continue to thrive. Some of the children and brothers and sisters of our victims now work for the firm.

⌄ ⌄ ⌄

I cannot allow these ten years to have been about the terrible injustices wrought on the dead and the people they loved. They have to celebrate our allegiance, commitment, strength, courage, determination, survival and memory. No family that is part of the Cantor Fitzgerald Relief Fund had to handle the devastation alone. When they need or want us, Howard and I will always do our best to be there for our families. Having family is a gift that is not to be squandered. I came into 9/11 with a very small, but very close family. The day after 9/11 my family consisted of one brother. Now, my "family" could fill a banquet hall.

I hope that when I die, I will be fortunate enough to see my brother Gary again. I'm going to arrive and he'll say, "Hello, sister of mine." Then he will wrap me in his embrace. Because that is what we do, we hug. And then he is going to look at me and say, "Really, Eed? You thought I was a bird?"

GARY LUTNICK

36 years old. Successful. Smart. Handsome. Happy. Compassionate. Affectionate. Loving. Generous. Caring. Adorable. Great trader. Great smile. Loved his family, traveling, spontaneity, great food, trendy bars and restaurants, his friends, his car, his sunglasses collection. Gary loved life ... and life embraced Gary. Loved very much and missed every day by Edie & Lewis, Howard & Allison, and Kyle, Brandon and Casey.

Tribute to Gary Lutnick as part of Boomer Esiason's Cystic Fibrosis benefit, 2002

Epilogue

The 10-year anniversary of September 11th is not an ending. It is an opportunity for us to take stock in ourselves and to reflect on those we have lost, how we reacted and what we will do going forward. The hope for justice and remembrance for the 9/11 families continues to be a journey from enormous darkness to the gathering of strength, the determination and the commitment to progress onward. It's easy to give up in the face of a single obstacle and understandable in the face of many. Bureaucracy often slows progress, defies logic or rushes important decisions in the name of expediency. Facing the illogic of bureaucracy that often flies in the face of those it should be serving was and continues to be daunting. We never give up.

So where is everyone now and how have they fared 10 years later?

Mayor Bloomberg is finishing out his third term, which he managed to serve despite two public referendums reaffirming term limits. His term as the chairman of the WTC Memorial Foundation has no limits. The mayor's legacy is tied to the opening of the memorial because his other major projects—the Olympics, a new stadium, the airport land swap—did not come to fruition. Recently Mayor Bloomberg said that the memorial "leaves it up to the mind to tell the story. We aren't telling you what to think. We are challenging you to reflect."[119] No matter what one thinks of the memorial, it is less than it could have been had context been provided, and it is more than it would have been had the families not been involved. But what this memorial should do is have you remember the human beings who were murdered by terrorists on September 11, 2001.

I have no doubt that the families will be very emotional on the 10-year anniversary opening of the memorial. How can they look at the names of their loved ones at the place where they were murdered and not be moved? These moments will be captured and put forward as proof of the memorial's success. But that, like the revisionist history this book is attempting to correct, won't be an accurate assessment. Only time, and visits by those who did not experience 9/11 firsthand, will tell whether this memorial will be the emotionally arresting fulfillment of a nation's promise to "Never Forget."

Paula Grant Berry continues in her position as co-chair of the program committee of the WTC Memorial Museum. In 2009, Mayor Bloomberg appointed her director of harbors (the waterways of New York City), working for the New York City Economic Development Corporation at a salary of $125,000 a year.[120] Her background prior to her appointment was publishing.

Ken Feinberg, capitalizing on his reputation-building public relations job as the special master to the Victim Compensation Fund, was hired by BP to administer the $20 billion BP oil spill escrow account. His law firm received compensation of $850,000 per month through this past January. "Feinberg has faced repeated criticism about the slow pace of payment and the small size of checks to the victims, as well as complaints about lack of transparency and perceived influence from BP." In February 2011, Feinberg was ordered by the court to "clearly disclose that he is acting on behalf of BP" and is not independent, as he had been claiming as the reason fund recipients should trust his awards.[121]

The WTC Memorial Foundation and the Port Authority have assured that the above ground (thanks to the victim's families) WTC Memorial will open permanently on the 10-year anniversary, not on the temporary basis discussed with the Port Authority. The cost overruns at the whole 16-acre site, overages which will in large part be borne by the taxpayer, will top $2 billion.[122]

The site isn't finished, but it will be finished enough to allow a limited number of visitors to the memorial. The site will be surrounded by construction, and the survivors, most of whom witnessed the death of their friends and colleagues and suffered themselves, will be excluded from the WTC site on the 10-year anniversary. These exclusions include Lauren and Greg Manning, Ari Schonbrun, David Kravette and Stephen Merkel, all of whom will be embraced at Cantor's memorial service in the afternoon.

Currently, a fix of cold water piping is being run under the names and around the perimeter because someone realized that when you touched the bronze names in the heat of the summer, hands would be burned. Additionally, because the names are cut out as a stencil, the metal around the seams will not expand and make the seams "almost unnoticeable" as claimed. Many victims' names at the place where they died will forever be split in two as a design choice. Residents of Lower Manhattan are still discussing at their Community Board 1 meetings what to do about the buses that will now idle mercilessly on the newly connected street grid, until the underground bus depot (which thanks to the families is not on the South Tower footprint) is finished. Bathrooms for visitors were also not contemplated. The number of visitors starting September 12, 2011 is being carefully controlled to 1,500 a visit and tickets went so quickly that the Memorial Foundation ticket site crashed.

The app that I suggested to my brother became a reality for all victims. Although it needs additional information, such as why a name was chosen as an adjacency, it at least provides some information about a victim. It doesn't take away from the fact that the memorial should have communicated a story, but at least it tells the tech-savvy person something. The emotional impact of switching your gaze from a wall with a name to an iPhone and back to a wall remains to be seen.

The Memorial Museum is where many of us from the 9/11 community are pinning our hopes. While I have no doubt that this institution will also have its issues, in the eyes of our families this will become the de facto memorial. I take comfort in the fact that Howard and Debra Burlingame continue to have input into the process. Cantor gives space to the Living Memorial Project so that every 9/11 family has the opportunity to share their memories of their loved one with future generations and other families. We are also working with the Memorial Museum to make sure that every Relief Fund family records the name of their loved one for the public to hear when they enter the remembrance section of the museum, instead of them having to hear my voice, or Howard's or Allison's. Regardless, a Cantor voice will have read every name.

Jake Loveless and I are working on a book to distribute to all of our families at the WTC memorial service, which will help them to find their loved one, and through color-coded panels show them how they are listed within their departments and all of the internal relationships that existed. The map will also include an alphabetical listing with locations so that everyone can be found.

Michael Burke is still actively fighting for the return of the sphere. The battle has garnered press, including the *Huffington Post*, but to date the families still have not made much progress. The last suggestion was to put the sphere, which has to be moved from its Battery Park location, on the roof of a parking garage, or temporarily on the future site of WTC Building Two, because this is land controlled by the Port Authority. With the land swap giving the Memorial Quadrant to the WTC Memorial Foundation, hope is slim that the sphere will be placed there, thanks to Mayor Bloomberg. Mike Burke wrote a letter to the editor of the *Downtown Express* titled "Vanity is Appalling." In it, he tells how Michael Bloomberg will engage in a television production covered by the networks "to show that he got the memorial done by the 10th anniversary, because that is what is important here. And no one is supposed to notice that it does not even acknowledge the attacks, that with all the hoopla about 'absence' and 'memory' and 'rejuvenation of life,' 9/11 has been forgotten. Michael Arad will be there, admiring this monument to his experience on the night of 9/11, forgetting all about what happened that morning."[123]

Sally Regenhard and the Skyscraper Safety Campaign are still actively advocating on behalf of their membership. They continue their quest to have the unidentified human remains, which will be housed within the medical examiner's office at the Memorial Museum, removed. Sally, through her attorney Norman Siegel, demanded a meeting with Eric Holder to discuss the alleged hacking into the voicemails of 9/11 victims by Rupert Murdoch's News Corporation.

Diane Horning and WTC Families for a Proper Burial are still actively fighting to have the remains of 9/11 victims removed from the Staten Island landfill. Since the Supreme Court denied the organization the right to proceed with their suit based on a lack of standing, the city has dumped at least four feet of dirt on top of everything so that many of the items found and brought to the attention of the public are no longer visible. One section has materials that were dumped for nearly 40 days before any real sifting operations began. WTC Families requested the right to do some borings to see whether there were still human remains and bones present. The city fought the request and the court denied them the right to that kind of discovery—1,127 families still have no remains to bury.

Bill Doyle, from his retirement home in Florida, still communicates with the families regarding any new development or interview request. He is involved in the family class action suit against Saudi Arabia, as well as trying to get educational funds from Families of Freedom.

Lee Ielpi still works tirelessly to improve the Tribute Center Museum. Their tours of the WTC site are historically accurate and invaluable in teaching the story of 9/11. Lee's group has also started an education program for children, because we all believe the future of 9/11 is through education. The symbol of the Tribute Center is the origami crane, a sign of peace. The Relief Fund is partnering with Tribute to place cranes on the chairs at our 10-year memorial service.

Anthony Gardner now runs the New Jersey State Museum. His first order of business was to put together a 9/11 exhibit for the 10-year anniversary. Cantor Fitzgerald has loaned him pieces of a Rodin sculpture recovered from the WTC site. Anthony's September 11th Education Trust continues to make headway into the schools. Anthony designed the education segment that the Memorial Museum relies on. It was his and our dream that Anthony would one day work for the Memorial Museum, but politics so far have not allowed for that.

Debra Burlingame continues to fight against Islamic extremism, not only with respect to the mosque but also on a national level. Her writings and appearances have made her an identifiable face in the conservative movement. She continues to carefully monitor the prosecutions of Khalid Sheikh Mohammed and the other co-conspirators, who will now be tried in military tribunals in Gitmo, but as of this date, they still have not been tried. The lottery to allow 9/11 families to be in the gallery during hearings is being reinstated.

Juliet McIntyre, after working for the Relief Fund and then Cantor Fitzgerald, moved to California this month to pursue her dream of becoming an actress. She and her mother, Sharon (who is back to writing), have both committed to return for our memorial services every year.

Marianna continues to work for Cantor Fitzgerald in accounts receivable and to be my right arm. Her compassion toward our families cannot be overstated. She continues to be on loan to me whenever I need her, which is often.

My office is now a shared office on the 2nd floor of Cantor Fitzgerald's headquarters. I like it because I can walk into Howard's office and steal a quick pat of his face, and a glance at Gary's picture.

The steel pieces we received from Hangar 17 will one day be a memorial sculpture to our 658. In the meantime, we have divided up one piece of steel and will be giving a piece, in a box, to every Cantor family.

The Cantor Fitzgerald Relief Fund will continue long after the 10-year anniversary of 9/11. I'm committed to my families for as long as they need me. The direct financial commitment to the families ends this year, but our commitment to 9/11 causes, as well as to aiding in other disasters and tragedies continues in the distributions we make through Charity Day. The issues surrounding our families are always changing. My job in relation to our families will always be predictable in its unpredictability. At the moment, I am getting pictures of every family for the Memorial Museum, working on improving the information on their app, making a map of the memorial for their use, getting each family to record their names, and working with Kent Karosen to make our 10-year memorial service, which will be back in Central Park this year, as dignified and respectful as always. On the morning of September 11th, I will be at the WTC site with a clipboard, helping our families find their loved ones names. The following day, I will be at Cantor and BGC Partners raising millions of dollars for charity in our loved ones' names.

As a board member of My Good Deed, I am actively involved in turning 9/11 into a national day of remembrance. I had the privilege of speaking on a panel at my old high school to students about philanthropy and honoring the lives lost. Jericho High School will be writing notes of remembrance and support that I will place on the chairs at our memorial service.

Lewis Ameri has gone back to being an artist. After 17 years, he is still one of the three loves of my life.

Under Howard's leadership, Cantor Fitzgerald continues to thrive. The firm actively recruits new talent and opens new businesses. The philosophy post-9/11 had to be a focus on short-term gain in order to immediately take care of the families. Howard's pledge resulted in distributions topping $180 million, which makes me very proud. With the passage of time, Howard has once again been able to engage in long-term projects for the firm. The legacy of those we have lost is carefully woven into the fabric of Cantor Fitzgerald. On September 10, 2001, Cantor Fitzgerald had 960 employees in New York. Now it has about 1,600. The recovery of Cantor Fitzgerald is the legacy built in tribute to those we cared so deeply about.

Our families continue to be individuals in the context of a community. They change. They grow. They experience their losses both individually and publicly. The emotional time ahead will not be easy. With the initial $1,500 donation we gave our families to memorialize their loved ones, they have started more than 500 philanthropic endeavors. I think it is one of our finest achievements. Many of them, like A Caring Hand, which now has its bereavement center, are still going strong.

And what about you, the reader? When the tsunami hit in Japan, Cantor Fitzgerald donated all the revenue from its Japanese and Pan Asian offices for a week. The missing person flyers and searches in the rubble brought comparisons with 9/11. The reality is that the manner in which victims of tragedy are treated by those in charge still leaves a lot to be desired. Families are still fighting to pay the tuition of 9/11 children because the monies donated to charities on their behalf have not been distributed. There needs to be an overhaul and review of our philanthropic organizations. Watchdog agencies have emerged to try to arm the public with information, but a tax form showing the amount of administrative expenses taken doesn't tell the story. Politically, we need to take more control of the things that are going on around us. Involvement can certainly be on a national level, but it can also be something small. It's hard to make people care about something that doesn't directly affect them. But how we remember the dead, and how we treat those they left behind, ultimately becomes our legacy. Information and communication systems are woefully inadequate to prepare us for future disasters.

Still, having said all of this, I have hope. Because in the face of tragedy, finding a purpose larger than yourself can help. As I look toward my future, I don't know what I see. I do know that it will be a life with my 9/11 family.

Fifty percent of any of the author's proceeds will be donated to the Cantor Fitzgerald Relief Fund. The Relief Fund now raises money to assist victims of terrorism, natural disasters and emergencies. We have given money to the victims of 9/11, the 2004 tsunami, Hurricane Katrina, the earthquakes in Haiti and Japan, and injured members of our armed services, among countless other charities and organizations.

Acknowledgments

I always read the acknowledgments section of books. Not because I ever believe that I will see the name of anyone I know, but because I think doing so gives you a glimpse into the psyche of the author as they wrote the book. Thanks belong to many people, especially the family leaders who have toiled ceaselessly to help the families, the partners and employees of Cantor Fitzgerald past and present, and BGC Partners who supported us at every turn, the Cantor Fitzgerald Relief Fund volunteers it is my honor to have worked with, my friends and Lewis's family who are always there for me, and Gary's friends for always keeping him alive in your hearts. This book is as partial as a shutter click in the after-9/11 section of my life. It would be unwieldy if I included every story and every person. It is my sincere hope that, even if I have included you with this broad sweep of my thanks when you all deserve individual recognition, you know who you are and that I am eternally grateful.

In addition, I would like to thank the following people, who helped me through the process of writing this book: Margaret Atwood for teaching me structure while stuck next to me on a plane. I'm sure she had no idea what her knowledge would lead to. Nicole Davis for telling me about a writing class in the Bridgehampton Library, and Eileen Obser and the participants who kindly gave me confidence (never underestimate your local writing workshop!). Angela and Glenn Zagoren for doing everything they could think of to make this process easier for me, from Angela reading the earliest drafts, to Glenn designing my book cover and everything else I needed help with, which was a lot! The two Sheilas—Sheila Troy and Sheila White, Gay Snow, my cousin Edy McAndrews (yup, two Edies), Genevieve Baker, Barbara Lamb and Neil Gaiman for suffering through early drafts and giving much-needed advice. Laurie Fabiano and Seth Godin for teaching me that if conventional methods don't produce results, that doesn't mean your story has to stay hidden; and Shari Clayman-Kerr, Barrie Brett and Shiya Ribowsky for their friendship, critiques and incredible wisdom. Todd Grossman for helping me research when my limited Internet skills rendered me helpless, and Lisa

Raymond for the "AnUnbrokenBond" website. Donna Dudek, Emilia Roll, Petra Nemcova, John Forte, John Altorelli, John D'Agostino, Sharon Abramzon, Stephen Grant, Jay Mandel, Robert Levin, Helene Godin, Anne Kreamer, Shannen Rossmiller and Stuart Connelly for graciously sharing their expertise and advice. For refreshing my recollection, family members Jane Pollicino, Irene Boehm, David Egan, Phyllis Frank, Jennifer Gardner, Greg Manning, Danielle Gardner, Richard Pecorella, Hans Gerhardt and George Stergiopolous, and family leaders Bill Doyle, Mary Fetchet, Diane Horning and Lee Ielpi, with a special thank you to Debra Burlingame, Anthony Gardner and Darlene Dwyer, who were absolutely invaluable to me over the course of these 10 years as well as reading drafts and providing insight. The Cantor employees who were incredibly supportive, Matthew Gilbert, Robin McKenna, Brian Fleishhacker, Magdy El Mihdawy, Katie Bishopric, Ken Greenvald, Edgar Rojas, Rafael Ramirez, Michael Lampert, Michael Brinton, Stephen Merkel, Stuart Fraser, Paul Pion, Kent Karosen, Joe Noviello, Matt Claus, Danny LaVecchia, Patrick Troy, Ari Schonbrun, Robert Hubbell, Lana Raymin, Teddy Chamarro and Amanda Zapp, and the Cantor employee without whom I could not operate the Relief Fund, and whose compassion toward the families is unparalleled, Marianna Scibetta Taaffe.

My gratitude to my core volunteers: Juliet McIntyre, Sharon Lefkowitz, Carolyn Ciplet, Vincent Perez, Romina Levy, Mary Jo Olson (posthumously) and Marion Monsanto (posthumously), Avi Lopchinsky, Mary Beth McDonough, Carmen Suarez and Juan Godoy. And I couldn't forget my clambake and memorial volunteers who still show up every year, the twins—Jason and Jonas Reuda, Lilly Perez, Jake Lefkowitz, Ailbhe Mullen, Alice Zobian and thanks to Lewis's family—Stan Ameri and Jill, Victoria and Erika Gordon and to his mother Joan Ameri, for always being one of my and the Relief Fund's strongest supporters, and to Allison, Kyle, Brandon, Casey and Ryan Lutnick for being the loves of my brother Howard's life.

This book took a very fast trajectory. I wrote it. Then Shana Kelly and Robert McAndrews edited it with insight, skill and compassion.

Cantor executive Jake Loveless read the manuscript and as always wholly supportive, brought me to Clarence B. Jones. Clarence believed in the importance of telling this story with a passion and conviction that he backed up at every turn. His anger over the injustices done to Cantor and the families kept me focused on getting this story told. I am humbled that he wanted to write the foreword and blessed to now refer to him as friend. Clarence then brought my manuscript to his publisher, Airie Stuart. I knew after our first meeting that I didn't want to do this book without her. Airie taught me what a superb editor can do for a manuscript. It is Clarence's commitment and Airie's, Shana's and Robert's skill that turned my manuscript into a book that Joy Clough skillfully edited and Maris Bellack formatted with precision. The result is *An Unbroken Bond*. I don't know what I ever did to deserve the support of such wonderful people, but I am forever grateful and in awe.

Just as acknowledgment doesn't mean thanks, there needs to be a section that goes far beyond thanks, to inexpressible love and gratitude. This category is reserved for three men. To my brother, Howard Lutnick, for his vision, leadership and love. To my brother Gary, whose smiling face and sharp wit remain forever before my eyes. And to Lewis Ameri—I do not possess the skill to articulate how lucky I am to love and be loved by this extraordinary man. These three men are my heart. To our Cantor Fitzgerald Relief Fund families and their loved ones, who stand beside Gary, up above—it is my honor and privilege to be your voice, when you have your own and when you don't. I will always continue to admire and support you. And, last, to the reader, I hope that I have been able to communicate the strength and fortitude these families possess in the face of unimaginable obstacles. They are strong and resilient. They are smart and loving and compassionate. They have suffered a terrible loss and have survived with dignity and grace. They, along with me, will always be so grateful for the kindness you have shown us.

Notes

1 Cantor Fitzgerald, and Cantor companies eSpeed and TradeSpark, Forte Foods (food service providers), Euro Brokers, Citibank (visitors), Rand Thompson/Merlin (Temp employees), Kestrel Technologies, Global Crossing Holdings, Ltd., BMO and Cantor trade contractors, PM Contracting Company, Inc, Unique Infrastructure Group, National Acoustics, Midmanhattan Woodworking Corp, IPC Kleinecht-Union#3, Forest Electric, SMCK.

2 "Another WTC Victim Identified, Nearly 10 Years After Attack," *NBC New York*, last modified May 13, 2011, http://www.nbcnewyork.com/news/local/911-Remains-Identified-WTC-Attack-Ground-Zero-Sept-11-121732719.html.

3 "America: A Tribute to Heroes," Wikipedia, last modified Jul. 12, 2011, http://en.wikipedia.org/wiki/America_A_Tribute_to_Heroes.

4 Tom Seessel, "The Philanthropic Response to 9/11: A Report Prepared for the Ford Foundation" (Trenton, NJ: John S. Watson Institute for Public Policy, Thomas Edison State College, August 2002), http://www.fordfoundation.org/pdfs/library/philanthropic_response.pdf.

5 Jaime Holguin, "Red Faces at the Red Cross," CBS *Evening News*, last modified Feb. 11, 2009, www.cbsnews.com/stories/2002/07/30/eveningnews/main516886.shtml.

6 "The American Red Cross Response to the World Trade Disaster During the Past Year," (American Red Cross in Greater New York, Sept. 11, 2002), http:www.nyredcross.org/media/ar2002_insert.pdf.

7 Nichole M. Christian, "Friend Stole Tower Victim's Card, Police Charge," *New York Times* New York and Region, Oct. 20, 2001; John Marzulli, "Dead Pal's Credit Is Used for Spree," *Daily News Police Bureau Chief*, Oct. 19, 2001, http://www.nydailynews.com/archives/news/2001/10/11/2001.

8 News Release, New York County District Attorney, Nov. 13, 2002, http://manhattanda.client.tagonline.com/whatsnew/press/2002-11-13.shtml; Firehouse Forums, http://www.firehouse.com/forums/archive/index.php/t_43752.html.

9 After ten years I still hug them every time I see them. Both still work for Cantor. Anthony is retiring at the end of 2011.

10 "Osama bin Laden Timeline," *Atlanta Journal-Constitution*, last modified May 3, 2011, http:www.ajc.com/news/nation-world/osama-bin-laden-timeline-933044.html.

11 "Ann De Sollar on Larry King," Angelfire, www.angelfire.com/ia/GrapeApe/anndesollar.html.

12 "Brokaw's Asst Tests Positive for Anthrax," ABC News, Oct. 12, 2001, http://abcnews.go.com/Entertainment/story?id=101890&page=1.

13 The number of free seats given to uniformed services personnel varies from 5,000 to 7,000 depending on the publication, as does the length of the concert. "The Concert for New York," Jim Carrey online, Sept. 28, 2001, http:www.jimcarreyonline.com/recent/news.php?id=456; "The Greatest Moment in the History of The Who – October 20, 2001," Associated Content, Feb. 25, 2008, http://www.associatedcontent.com/article/567147/thegreatest-moment-inthe-history.html?cat=37, http//www.vh1.com/news/features/america-united.

14 Tom Seessel, "The Philanthropic Response to 9/11: A Report Prepared for the Ford Foundation" (Trenton, NJ: John S. Watson Institute for Public Policy, Thomas Edison State College, August 2002), http://www.fordfoundation.org/pdfs/library/philanthropic_response.pdf.

15 "September 11 Compensation Fund Regulations Announced," U.S. Department of Justice, Dec. 20, 2001, http://www.justice.gov/archive/victimcompensation/pressdec20.pdf.

16 Kenneth P. Nolan and Jeanne M. O'Grady, "A Year Later the September 11th Victim Compensation Fund," http://www.speiserkrause.com/publications/compensation_fund.pdf.

17 "Richard Reid," Wikipedia, last modified Aug. 3, 2011, http:en.wikipedia.org/wiki/Richard_Reid; Pam Belluck, "Threats and Responses: The Bomb Plot, Unrepentant Shoe Bomber is Given a Life Sentence." New York Times, Jan. 31, 2003.

18 Seessel, "The Philanthropic Response to 9/11."

19 "Osama bin Laden Timeline," Atlanta Journal-Constitution, last modified May 3, 2011, http://www.ajc.com/news/nation-world/osama-bin-laden-timeline-933044.html.

20 Michael Cooper (compiled by Anthony Ramirez), "Liaison Named for Victims' Families," New York Times, Feb. 11, 2002, http://www.nytimes.com/2002/02/11/nyregion/metro-briefing-new-york-manhattan-liaison-named-for-victims-families.html?scp=2&sq=christy%20ferer%20named%20special%20liaison&st=cse.

21 David Dunlap, "Blocks: An Unclear Role for an Oversight Agency at Ground Zero," New York Times, Nov. 10, 2005, http://query.nytimes.com/gst/fullpage.html?res=940CE1DE123 EF933A25752C1A9639C8B63.

22 Robin Finn, "Public Lives; Working Through the Pain to Honor a Brother's Life," New York Times NY Region, Feb. 26, 2002.

23 Christy Ferer, email message to All, including author, Apr. 2, 2002.

24 New York Audit Reports, U.S. Department of Housing and Urban Development, Feb. 7, 2011, http://www.hud.gov/offices/oig/reports/ny.cfm;http://www.planyc.org/taxonomy/term/693.

25 Deborah Sontag, "Broken Ground: The Hole in the City's Heart," *New York Times,* Sept. 11, 2006.

26 Christy Ferer, email message to author, Mar. 14, 2002.

27 Christy Ferer, email message to All including author, April 18, 2002. "I think this is a good time for everyone to personally begin the process of defining just what is sacred ground and how that impacts just what goes on below and above grade and how that affects which portion of the 16 acres."

28 Deborah Sontag, "Broken Ground: The Hole in the City's Heart," *New York Times,* Sept. 11, 2006.

29 Stephen P. Bank and Michael D. Kahn, *The Sibling Bond* (New York: Basic Books, 1982).

30 "She Is Still Missing to Us," MSNBC, last modified May 31, 2002, http://www.msnbc.msn.com/id/3067205.

31 Christy Ferer, email message to All, including author, May 17, 2002. "I feel your pain over this date decision.... I have been trying to work on the Mayor personally.... to no avail. Maybe the weather will delay the date!! In the meantime.... I hate to say this.... but perhaps we should pick our battles... there may me [sic] more important things down the line to fight for..."

32 Fallen Brothers Foundation, May 17, 2002, http://www.fallenbrothers.com/community/showthread.php?p=2725.

33 "Traffic Likely in World Trade Center Rebuild," *New York Post,* Jun. 12, 2002, http://www.gothamgazette.com/rebuilding_news/news_contentall.html.

34 Henry Richardson would go on to design the 9/11 Memorial for Danbury, Connecticut. His much larger *Tikkun* sculpture is in Israel.

35 "Fresh Kills Park Project," New York City Department of City Planning, http://www.nyc.gov/html/dcp/html/fkl/fkl_index.shtml.

36 "9/11 World Trade Center Steel Artifacts (History Channel)," Salvage Car Sale, http://www.salvagecarsale.net/911-world-trade-center-steel-artifacts-history-channel.

37 It is questionable whether the mayors even had the legal right to make the sale, as the WTC steel technically belongs to the Port Authority of New York and New Jersey.

38 "Baosteel will Recycle World Trade Center Debris," China Internet Information Center, Jan. 24, 2002, http://www.china.org.cn/english/2002/Jan/25776.htm; "WTC Steel Removal," 9-11 Research, last modified Apr. 26, 2009, http://911research.wtc7.net/wtc/groundzero/cleanup.html; "Destruction of Evidence," Remember Building 7.org, http://rememberbuilding7.org/destruction-of-evidence.

39 Jennifer Ahern Lammers, "An Analysis of Survey Response Information About Funds Raised and Services Provided by 9-11 Related Charities," (Better Business Bureau, July 2003), http://www.philanthropyhub.com/about/list-of-writings/9-11charities-report.pdf.

40 "Gary Lutnick: One-Third of a Trio," New York Times, Jul. 14, 2002, http://www.nytimes.com/2002/07/14/national/portraits/POG-14LUTNICK.html.

41 Lisa Colangelo and Greg Gittrich, "Rudy: 'Grand' Memorial, Clashes with Mayor's View on WTC Tribute," New York Daily News, Jun. 14, 2002, http://www.articles.nydailynews.com/2002/jun/14.

42 Michael Bloomberg, meeting with family leaders at City Hall, Apr. 15, 2003.

43 Michael Powell and Michelle Garcia, "Ground Zero Funds Often Drifted Uptown, Money Also Went to Luxury Apartments, Washington Post, May 22, 2004, A01.

44 Edith Lutnick, "Put the Memorial 'Where the People We Loved and Lost Lived,'" Gotham Gazette, http://www.gothamgazette.com/rebuilding_nyc/features/public_hearing_one/victims_families/lutnick.shtml.

45 John Rosenthal, "The Future of Ground Zero: Daniel Libeskind's Perverse Vision," Policy Review, Jun. 1, 2004.

46 Michael Cartier, email message to the author, Aug. 21, 2002.

47 Associated Press, "Pataki: No Construction on Footprint of Towers," St. Augustine, Jul. 1, 2002, http://www.staugustine.com/stories/070102/nat_kr000615.shtml.

48 Lower Manhattan Development Corporation, Press release, Jul. 2, 2002, http://www.renewnyc.com/displaynews.aspx?newsid=d52ab4d6-be15-4630-913b-14b3af54377f.

49 Paul Goldberger, Up from Zero: Politics, Architecture, and the Rebuilding of New York (New York: Random House, 2004), 215.

50 Deborah Sontag, "Broken Ground: The Hole in the City's Heart," New York Times, Sept. 11, 2006.

51 "Osama bin Laden Timeline," *Atlanta Journal-Constitution*, last modified May 3, 2011, http://www.ajc.com/news/nation-world/osama-bin-laden-timeline-933044.html.

52 Elizabeth Kolbert, "The Calculator," *New Yorker*, Nov. 25, 2002.

53 Timothy J. Burger and Maggie Haberman, "Fund-Master's Gibe Riles S.i.,"
New York Daily News, Nov. 20, 2002, http://articles.nydailynews.com/2002-11-20/
news/18209451_1_kenneth-feinberg-rep-vito-fossella-victims-relatives.

54 Tom Roger, email to the author as part of FAC, Nov. 5, 2002.

55 Stephen Push, email to author as part of FAC, Nov. 5, 2002.

56 Carol Ashley, email to author as part of FAC, Nov. 6, 2002.

57 Edward Wyatt, "Outspoken 9/11 Widow Joins
Memorial Panel, New York Times, Nov. 28, 2002,
http://www.nytimes.com/2002/11/28/nyregion/outspoken-9-11-widow-joins-memorial-panel.
Monica appointed after "family members complained publically that rebuilding officials were
ignoring people who have sometimes criticized the rebuilding effort."

58 Monica Iken, email message to the author, Dec. 5, 2002.

59 "Draft Memorial Mission Statement and Memorial Program,"
Lower Manhattan Development Corporation, Jan. 30, 2003,
http://www.learn.columbia.edu/courses/newyork/pdf/Draft_Memorial_Mission.pdf.

60 Ibid.

61 Phil Hirschkorn, "Families Sue September 11 Compensation Fund Administrator," CNN,
Jan. 28, 2003, http://articles.cnn.com/2003-01-28/justice/wtc.families.lawsuit_1_kenneth-
feinberg-victims-compensation-fund-suit?_s=PM:LAW. Amended complaint dated Feb. 21, 2003.

62 *Colaio, et al. v Feinberg Amended Class Action Complaint*, Civ. No 03 Civ. 0558 (AKH), 03
Civ. 1040 (AKH), 03 Civ 1129 (AKH), (Apr. 14, 2003), Hearing Transcript, 109.

63 In 2011, the 2nd circuit affirms WTC developers settled with the airlines and airline security firms for $1.2 billion. Mike Cherney, "2nd
Circuit Affirms $1.2B WTC Insurance Settlement," *Law360*, Apr. 8, 2011,
http://www.law360.com/articles/237833/2nd-circ-affirms-1-2b-wtc-insurance-settlement.

64 Maggie Haberman, Panel to Decide on a Separate 9/11 Memorial,
New York Daily News, May 31, 2003, http://articles.nydailynews.com/2003-05-31/
news/18233195_1_lmdc-memorial-wall-rescue-workers.

65 Pace University before the Memorial Jury, "Transcript"
(Roy Allen & Associates, Inc, Jun. 5, 2003), 22–24.

66 "City Releases 911 Calls from World Trade Center Attack," *USA Today*, Mar. 30, 2006,
http://usatoday.com/news/nation/2006-03-30-sept11-911-calls_x.htm.

67 "EPA's Response to the World Trade Center Collapse: Challenges, Successes, and Areas
for Improvement," Office of the Inspector General, Environmental Protection Agency,
Aug. 21, 2003, http://www.epa.gov/oig/reports/2003/WTC_report_20030821.pdf.

68 "Christine Todd Whitman," Wikipedia, last modified Jul. 17, 2011,
http://en.wikipedia.org/wiki/Christine_Todd_Whitman.

69 "Rudy Giuliani during the September 11 Attacks," Wikipedia, last modified May 19, 2011,
http:/en.wikipedia.org/wiki/Rudy_Giuliani_during_the_September_11_attacks;
Ben Smith, "Rudy's Black Cloud", *New York Daily News*, Sept. 18, 2006, 14; Anita Gates,
"Buildings Rise from Rubble while Health Crumbles," *New York Times*, Sept. 11, 2006;
Dust to Dust: The Health Effects of 9/11, prod. and dir. Heidi Dehncke-Fisher, 2006.

70 *Atlanta Journal-Constitution*, posted May 3, 2011.

71 Peter F. Cannavo, *The Working Landscape: Founding, Preservation, and the Politics
of Place* (Cambridge, MA: MIT Press, 2007), 145. Wils "almost single handedly kept the victim's
families from installing the WTC Sphere as a memorial in the Tribeca Park that was
their first choice."
    Greg Gittrich, "9/11 Kin in Battle of Wils," *New York Daily News*, Mar. 12, 2003,
www.nydailynews.com/topics/Madelyn+Wils. "Wils shot back that people downtown suffered
through the attack, and that human remains were found in people's homes. 'Would you suggest
that we mow down their apartments?' she asked."

72 "Reflecting Absence," Chosen for WTC Memorial, Jan. 6, 2004,
http://www.lowermanhattan.info/news/-reflecting-absence-53860.aspx.

73 Philip Nobel, *Sixteen Acres, Architecture and the Outrageous Struggle for the Future of Ground
Zero* (New York: Picador, 2005), 253–54.

74 David W. Dunlap, "Memorial Faces Setback Over Names," *New York Times*, Jun. 27, 2006,
http://www.nytimes.com/2006/06/27/nyregion/27names.html 9/11.

75 Monica Iken's living memorial project has begun receiving funding from the LMDC so she
also is now appointed to committees.

76 Except Tom and Ann Johnson, but they are willing to defer to the group.

77 Unless there is the possibility of not getting what they want.—then Lee Ielpi doesn't want to give them up, because "It's better than nothing."

78 "The First Six Months," The September 11ᵗʰ Fund, United Way-911-6month.pdf.

79 Michael Saul, "Games at Fresh Kills?" *New York Daily News*, Nov. 11, 2010, http://articles.nydailynews.com/2004-11-10/news/18271563_1_mayor-bloomberg-fresh-kills.

80 Monica Iken doesn't sign because she wants pictures, something the rest of us would love to have but do not believe we will be able to get. She undercuts our effort to present a united front by sending her own individual proposal a few days before our proposal is released. The LMDC and mayor then take the position that they have received "multiple" proposals (i.e., the families cannot agree and therefore they need to make the decision), and ignore that ours has the support of two-thirds of the families.

81 Kevin Rampe, letter to author, 2004.

82 Debra Burlingame, "The Great Ground Zero Heist," *Wall Street Journal*, Jun. 7, 2005, http://online.wsj.com/article_email/SB111810145819652326-IVjfINjlaJ4n5usa4KGaayIm4.html.

83 Press conference from Cox and Forkum, June 2005 archive, Jun. 20, 2005.

84 May 30, 2005, http://www.ifcwtc.org/donations.html (now defunct). The author possesses the actual page copies from the website at the time of the IFC battle.

85 Douglas Freiden, "Kin Slap Art Center's 9-11 Pieces," *New York Daily News*, Jun. 24, 2005, http://articles.nydailynews.com/2005-06-24/news/18290716_1_ground-zro-world-trade-center-site-hallowed-ground.

86 "'Site'-seeing tour, Bid for new '9/11' cultural homes," *New York Post*, Jul. 15, 2005.

87 "Assault on Free Expression at the WTC Site," The Free Expression Project, 2005, http://www.fepproject.org/commentaries/worldtradecenterchron.html.

88 Michael Arad's brick pattern has lines 1, 3, 5 left justified and lines 2, 4 indented.

89 Deborah Sontag, "Broken Ground: The Hole in the City's Heart," *New York Times*, Sept. 11, 2006.

90 Evie Reisman, email message forwarded to author, Mar. 10, 2006.

91 Alan Horwitz, email message to author, Mar. 6, 2006.

92 Tom Stabtle, "Rescue Mission: Sciame Takes a Major Detour to Make Sept. 11 Memorial Feasible," *New York Construction*, Nov. 2006, http://www.sciamedevelopment.com/NYC_1546.pdf.

93 Ibid.

94 http://wtcufg.org/default.asp?page%20Name=News%20and%20 Events&mode=Build&NewsID=218 (now defunct). Confirmed by interviews with Anthony Gardner.

95 Stabtle, "Rescue Mission."

96 David W. Dunlap and Charles V. Bagli, "Revised Design for 9/11 Memorial Saves Many Features and Lowers Cost," Jun. 21, 2006, http:www.nytimes.com/2006/06/21/nyregion/21memorial.html?pagewanted=all.

97 "Judge Won't Delay Accused Underwear Bomber Trial," Reuters, Jul. 7, 2011, http://www.reuters.com/article/2011/07/07/us-usa-security-airlines-idUSTRE7664WN20110707; "Umar Farouk Abdulmutallab," Wikipedia, last modified Aug. 5, 2011, http://en.wikipedia.org/wiki/Umar_Farouk_Abdulmutallab.

98 Deborah Sontag, "Broken Ground: The Hole in the City's Heart," *New York Times*, Sept. 11, 2006.

99 Paul Colford with Michael Saul, "Mike: WTC Name Fix Is a No Dough," *New York Daily News*, Oct. 21, 2006, http://www.nydailynews.com/archives/ news/2006/10/21/2006-10-21_mike__wtc_name_fix_is_a_no-d.html.

100 Ibid.

101 "Joint POW/MIA Accounting Command," Wikipedia, last modified Aug. 15, 2011, http:en.wikipedia.org/wiki/Joint_POW/MIA_Accounting_Command.

102 Greg B. Smith, "More 9/11 Pain Unearthed," *New York Daily News*, Oct. 22, 2006, http://www.nydailynews.com/archives/ news/2006/10/22/2006-10-22_more_9-11_pain_unearthed__ma.html.

103 David W. Dunlap, "Memorial Faces Setback Over Names," *New York Times*, Jun. 27, 2006, http://www.nytimes.com/2006/06/27/nyregion/27names.html 9/11; David W. Dunlap, "Plan Is Changed For Arranging Names on Trade Center Memorial," *New York Times*, Dec. 14, 2006, http://www.nytimes.com/2006/12/14/nyregion/14names.html.

104 David W. Dunlap, "Plan Is Changed For Arranging Names on Trade Center Memorial," *New York Times,* Dec. 14, 2006, http://www.nytimes.com/2006/12/14/nyregion/14names.html.

105   David W. Dunlap, "Still, the Question of Displaying the Names of 9/11," *New York Times*, Jan. 11, 2007, http://www.nytimes.com/2007/01/11/nyregion/11blocks.html.

106   Beverly Eckert was killed in the plane crash of Continental Flight 3407 on February 12, 2009. She was on her way to Buffalo to celebrate the birthday of her late husband Sean Rooney.

107   "After Sept. 11, 'He Wanted Me to Live a Full Life,'" NPR, StoryCorps, May 5, 2011, http://www.wbur.org/npr/135995930/he-wanted-me-to-live-a-full-life.

108   Alex Johnson, "Obama Elected 44th President," MSNBC, Nov. 5, 2008, http://www.msnbc.msn.com/id/27531033/ns/politics-decision_08/t/barack-obama-elected-th-president.

109   Sara Kugler Frazier, "Bloomberg Now Backs Two-Term Limit in His Third Term as Mayor," *Huffington Post*, Oct. 25, 2010, http://www.huffingtonpost.com/2010/10/25/bloomberg-term-limits-_n_773570.html

110   Jennifer Steinhauer with Michael Cooper, "The New York Primary: The Incumbent; Giuliani Explores a Term Extension of 2-3 Months," *New York Times*, Sept. 27, 2001, http://www.nytimes.com/2001/09/27/nyregion/new-york-primary-incumbent-giuliani-explores-term-extension-2-3-months.html.

111   Michael Kurtz, "Revisiting Michael Bloomberg's Term Limits Controversy," *Current Intelligence*, Nov. 12, 2010, http://www.currentintelligence.net/features/2010/11/12/revisiting-michael-bloombergs-term-limits-controversy.html.

112   "Fort Hood shooting," Wikipedia, last modified Aug. 1, 2011, http://en.wikipedia.org/wiki/Fort_hood_shooting; "Judge sets 2012 Trial Date in Ft. Hood Shooting Case," Reuters, MSNBC, July 20, 2011, http://www.msnbc.msn.com/id/43826990/ns/us_news-crime_and_courts/t/judge-sets-trial-date-fort-hood-shooting-case/.

113   Reprinted with permission of Rick DeTorie.

114   "Zadroga Act Goes Into Effect As 9/11 Health Clinics Open Up for Business," CBS New York, July 1, 2011, http://newyork.cbslocal.com/2011/07/01/911-health-bill-goes-into-effect-today/.

115   William C. Thompson, "9/11: Three Years Later," City of New York, Aug. 2004, www.comptroller.nyc.gov/bureaus/bud/04reports/9-11-3years-later-securing-federal-pledge.pdf

116   "Injured Ground Zero Workers slam WTC Captive Insurance Co and Mayor Bloomberg Over Misuse of FEMA Funds," PR Newswire, July 17, 2007.

117   NBC *11:00 News*, Jul. 27, 2011.

118 "Bloomberg Releases Comprehensive Islamic Finance Platform," Bloomberg, Feb. 3, 2011, http://www.bloomberg.com/news/2011-02-23/bloomberg-releases-comprehensive-islamic-finance-platform.html.

119 *Beyond 9/11: Portraits of Resilience*, Time/Life documentary, 2011.

120 http://seethroughny.org/PayrollsPensions/tabid/55/payrolls/statepayrolls/tabid/69/Default.aspx?BRANCHID=5, accessed Aug. 6, 2011.

121 Harry R. Webber and Brian Skoloff, "Kenneth Feinberg: Gulf Will Recover from BP Oil Spill in Three Years," *Huffington Post*, Feb. 2, 2011, http://www.huffingtonpost.com/2011/02/02/kenneth-feinberg-bp-oil-s_0_n_817501.html.

122 Josh Margolin, "PA Plays $2B Hide and Sneak at WTC," *New York Post,* Aug. 12, 2011, http://www.nypost.com/p/news/local/manhattan/pa_plays_hide_and_sneak_at_wtc_4kyVQ9LTVwRJ0HtDWECbIO

123 "The Forgotten Ones," Letters to the Editor, *Downtown Express*, vol. 20, no.41, Feb. 23–March 1, 2011, http://www.downtownexpress.com/de_409/letterstotheeditor.html.